CLIMB TO GLORY

CLIMB TO GLORY

The Adventures of Bill Hackett

June Hackett

and

Ric Conrad

K2 Books

Published by K2 Books
14718 SW Trout Creek LN
Beaverton, OR 97006

Copyright 2003 June Hackett and Ric Conrad

First Edition, 2003
Printed in U.S.A

Edited by Bruce Patterson
Book design, typesetting and layout by Anita Jones
Cover design by Ric Conrad and Richard Ferguson
Cover creation by Richard Ferguson
Cover photographs of Bill Hackett/Washburn and Hackett courtesy of the
        Washburn Collection
Cover photograph of K2 from William D. Hackett Papers (WDHP)
Charcoal portrait of William D. Hackett by Lon Haverly, 2001
Verithin pencil illustrations of McKinley and K2 by Dee Molenaar, 1997,
        1994, 1997, 1993, 1994, 1992
Interior chapter header illustrations/photographs conceived, created and
        arranged by Tai Brown
Interior photo insert arranged by Tai Brown

Library of Congress Cataloging-in-Publication Data

Hackett, June, 1924-
    Climb to glory : the adventures of Bill Hackett/June Hackett.
        p. cm.
Includes bibliographical references.
ISBN 0-9710724-2-6 (trade paper : alk. Paper)
Hackett, Bill, 1918-1999. 2. Mountaineers—United States—Biography. I. Title.

GV199.92.H323 H33 2001

                                2001037514

Forward inquiries about our quanitity discounts to the publisher

*A portion of the proceeds from the sale of this book will be donated to the
10th Mountain Division Scholarship Fund*

Hara Publishing
P.O. Box 19732
Seattle, Wahington

For Bill, Forever...
— June

"Climbing needs no justification, no more than does watching a sunrise, or listening to a great symphony, or falling in love. A man climbs because he needs to climb; because that is the way he is made."

—James Ramsey Ullman

The White Tower, 1945

TABLE OF CONTENTS

ACKNOWLEDGEMENTS

We are greatly indebted to the following mountaineers for their recollections of Bill and their past adventures and expeditions: Robert Anderson, the late Harold Bangs, David Bohn, the late John Carter, the late Dorothy Clark, Randall Kester, Dr. Charles Loveland, Robert McGown, Russell McJury, Dee Molenaar, Pat Morrow, Dick Powers, Dr. Bradford and Barbara Washburn, Alan Striker who accompanied Bill on his last ascents in Colorado, and Wendell H. Stout, son of Bill's Boy Scout troop when Bill made his first of eighty-eight ascents of Oregon's Mount Hood.

We thank the following members of the US Army who served with Bill during the Second World War: Robert S. Labby, Headquarters Company, 2nd Battalion, 87th Mountain Infantry; Hank Lewis, I Company, 86th Mountain Infantry; Russ McJury, I Company, 87th Mountain Infantry; Judge Thomas Stewart, Headquarters Company, 87th Mountain Infantry; and the late Harold E. Bangs, Associate Member of the 10th Mountain Division, 55 Stn. Hospital. Special mention must be made of the contributions of Dick Powers, D Company, 87th Mountain Infantry. He endured extensive interviews and edited the war chapters for this project. We would additionally like to thank Hugh Evans, A & C Companies, 85th Mountain Infantry, who, with his wife Ann, edited the entire manuscript and made significant contributions to the war chapters. We thank them most sincerely.

Special thanks must be expressed to the staff of the Mazamas, the Portland-based mountaineering organization established in 1894: Executive Director, Keith Mischke; Librarian, Bob Lockerby; and Club Secretary, John Godino, for their continual assistance and support of this project. We additionally thank the staff of the *Oregon Special Collections Department* at the University of Oregon for their generous assistance.

We additionally thank those individuals who took the time to read and edit portions of the manuscript: Tai Brown, Ann Evans, Hugh Evans, Eldon Fitzgerald, Carol Gillette, Dee Molenaar, Michael

Ohlinger, Bruce Patterson, Dick Powers, Chris Small, and Chuck Taylor. We certainly appreciate the guidance and assistance of Ursula Bacon, Sheryn Hara, Anita Jones and Richard Ferguson.

We would like to thank mountaineering artist and K2 veteran, Dee Molenaar for writing the introduction and for authorizing the use of his beautiful McKinley and K2 illustrations. He additionally reviewed and edited the entire manuscript. We thank Tai Brown for the authors' portrait that appears at the back of the book. He additionally designed the mountain silhouettes at the beginning of each chapter, created the computer graphics that accompanied Dee Molenaar's illustrations, and designed and created the photo insert. Richard Feguson designed the book cover and Anita Jones designed the text. We thank them most sincerely. We thank Vera Dafoe, historian for the Mazamas and close friend of June Hackett, for use of her poem that appears in the last chapter.

It was a special privilege to have counsel from John J. Duffy (86-HQ-2), current President of the 10th Mountain Division, and John Imbrie (Company C-85th). Imbrie is a noted Professor Emeritus of Brown University.

We would additionally like to thank Robert and Virginia Plainfield for introducing us to Thorn and Ursula Bacon.

—June Hackett & Ric Conrad

Portland, Oregon
January 31, 2002

Dee Molenaar, a former mountain guide and park ranger in Mount Rainier National Park, was a member of the 1946 Mount St. Elias Expedition, the 1953 Third American Karakoram Expedition to K2, and the 1965 Mount Kennedy Yukon Expedition. He is the author of *The Challenge of Rainier* (1971), and is a noted geologist, cartographer and mountaineering artist. His work has appeared in numerous publications, including; Robert Craig's *Storm & Sorrow in the High Pamirs* (1977), R.J. Secor's climbing guides to Aconcagua and Mexico's volcanoes, as well as Fred Beckey's *Cascade Alpine Guide* series (1973). An Honorary Member of the American Alpine Club, Molenaar is a highly respected member of the mountaineering community.

INTRODUCTION

In 1999, the sudden passing of Bill Hackett brought a need to examine more closely the life of a man whose remarkable achievements and controversial personality have been frequently debated in both military and mountaineering circles.

As a member of the Mazamas mountaineering club in Portland, Oregon, Bill learned his climbing skills as a teenager on the rock ridges and ice slopes of nearby Mount Hood. By the age of twenty-two he had made fifty ascents of the mountain by eleven different routes, including three first ascents and two second ascents. Bill's early climbing skills led to his joining the 10th Mountain Division during World War II. For his achievements in the Apennines of Italy he was awarded the Combat Infantry Badge, two Bronze Stars and a Silver Star for Gallantry in Action. After the war he decided to remain in the military, and was proud to have served his country in Europe during the height of the Cold War and later, in the Korean and Vietnam conflicts.

One of Hackett's distinguishing characteristics was adeptness at continuing his mountaineering adventures while being paid by the government for his travels. Bill routinely used military aircraft to reach the remote peaks of the world. Included among the first of such "GI travels,"was his participation in Bradford Washburn's 1947 expedition to Mount McKinley. Following this, Hackett became the first person to reach the summits of both McKinley and Logan, the first American to climb Aconcagua, the first American to climb Mt. Kenya, and the first person to reach the summits of five continents. By attaining the high points on five continents, Bill pioneered the Seven Summits Dream and he was pleased to live long enough to see Dick Bass and Pat Morrow achieve the goal.

Besides serving as a training officer in the US Army's Mountain and Cold Weather Training Command at Camp Hale, Colorado in the early 1950s, Captain Hackett served as Environmental Training General Staff Officer at Fort Monroe, Virginia. In Europe Bill held a variety of posts and was an intelligence officer in Korea and Vietnam. Following World War II, he served four years as a research and development field test officer for equipment and clothing. While in that position, he made many cold-weather ascents in Canada and Alaska, and his efforts helped improve various cold-weather clothing and equipment, such as streamlining the arctic uniform from twenty-three to fourteen pounds.

In 1960, Bill organized and led the German-American Karakoram Expedition to K2, which was turned back by storms at 24,000 feet. Bill found it interesting to be climbing beside a former German mountain trooper only fifteen years after the war. In 1963, with the rank of major, he took a disability retirement and returned to Portland, founding the Bill Hackett Company, a successful sporting goods manufacturers' representative organization.

Even after attaining both geographic poles, sailing through the Northwest Passage, and having climbed many of the world's greatest peaks, Bill was not ready to gracefully accept retirement from his life of action and mountain travel, forever certain that he hadn't accomplished enough during his lifetime. It was no surprise to those who knew him that he made reservations for a space flight during the budding "Civilians in Space" program, which effectively ended with the death of a civilian schoolteacher in *The Challenger* disaster.

In 1985, at the age of sixty-seven, Bill joined a Canadian-American expedition to Antarctica to climb Mt. Vinson. Miscellaneous travel included trips to both the North and South Poles, two journeys around the world and a voyage on a Russian icebreaker. Miscellaneous honors included the US Army's commendation medal for meritorious achievement in the field of expeditionary mountaineering.

But Bill was a loner in his military life, and his hard-driving, militaristic attitude did not fair well with many of his civilian climbing companions and he rarely sought to climb recreationally with them. He saw himself as an extremely confident man, but was unaware that others perceived him as being somewhat of a stubborn recluse. He saw himself as passionate where others felt he was obsessive. He could be strong, kind and trusting of friends, although he was rarely forgiving of past transgressions.

Bill's intense and introverted nature probably began during his traumatic childhood, after his mother abandoned him when he was only five years old; he spent much of his life trying to prove that he was worthy of recognition. He was nearly unable to accept failure; his defeat on K2 in 1960 weighed heavily on his mind and he rarely shared any information regarding the trip to even his close friends.

It was my pleasure to become better acquainted with Bill and his wife, June in recent years through their hosting gatherings of mountaineers at their home on the forest heights overlooking northwestern Portland. There, over the years, they had been entertaining such climbing luminaries as Brad and Barbara Washburn, Eric Shipton, Fred Beckey, Lowell Thomas, Jr., Joe Wilcox and numerous other veterans of Alaskan and Himalayan expeditions. And it was apparent that here was deep respect for Bill Hackett as a friend, who as an unrelentingly ambitious mountaineer was perhaps the most misunderstood climber of his generation.

Bill had little time to write his autobiography and his flamboyant life story would not have been told without the persistence of his wife, who engaged young Portland writer, Ric Conrad to do the job. With meticulous research into the climbing diaries of Bill and his compatriots, Conrad here skillfully answers many of the questions about Bill Hackett and his place in mountaineering history.

—Dee Molenaar
Burley, Washington
April 28, 2002

CHAPTER I

The Apprentice

"After a look at that ribbon of ice which soars from the glacier in one unbroken sweep to the top of Mount Hood, any fool could have stated with great authority, 'That's impossible! It can't be done!' But Russ was nineteen and I was seventeen, blithely unaware of the impossibility."[1]

—Bill Hackett

There are moments in a man's life that influence him so much that it changes him forever. For Bill Hackett, July 22, 1933, was just such a moment. On that particular sunny Saturday afternoon, he would experience sensations and emotions that would fuel his life's ambitions in the decades to follow. Bill's Boy Scout troop in Portland, Oregon had planned on making an ascent of Mount Hood. At 11,239 feet, the mountain was the highest in the state and one of the most challenging peaks in the Cascade Range.[2]

The Native Americans had named the great peak *Wy'east* and they avoided her slopes out of fear and respect. From the late 1850s through 1919, an ascent of Mount Hood was an experience reserved for either the Portland-based Mazamas mountaineering club or the very wealthy adventurer. Only those with adequate income could afford to take the time off such a journey required. In the 1920s however, massive road improvements opened the Mt. Hood Wilderness to the general public. The journey from Portland to the mountain's base that once took three days by stagecoach, now took three hours with the advent of the automobile. John A. Lee, a prominent member of the Mazamas took full advantage of this easier accessibility and began leading climbs up Mount Hood that were not authorized or sponsored by his climbing organization. These forays were labeled *Outlaw Ascents* and once started, the floodgate of individual pursuits on the great peak had been opened. By 1930, the 'Golden Age' of mountaineering on Mount Hood had started and Bill Hackett would become an integral part of its rich history.[3]

Scoutmaster Roy Stout had been a civil engineer in Portland and had taken part in these early outlaw ascents. He was so drawn to the peak and its beauty, that he organized an ascent for the boys under his care. The easiest route to the summit then, and now, was the Traditional South Side route. It would be four years before Timberline Lodge was built so the ascent would need to begin at the standard south side debarkation point—Government Camp. The boys would need to ascend over 6,000 feet of snow and talus slopes to the wind-swept crown of Oregon. The general consensus was that the boys would be unable to complete such an undertaking but the Mazamas had documented that even small children could ascend this particular route if properly disciplined and motivated. Stout believed his boys could make the journey and set his plan in motion.

Bill Hackett was only fifteen years old at the time but he was more than thrilled to take part in the ascent. He was one of seven scouts who had signed on board for the journey. Two other scouts that accompanied him that day were John Carter and Russ McJury. These boys would go on to make several ascents throughout the Cascades with Bill. They were awakened around 2:00 AM. They strapped on their caulked boots and were handed alpenstocks, four to five-foot high wooden staffs capped with metal hooks or spikes, tools that were standard climbing equipment from the late nineteenth century through the early 1930s. The European ice axe would not reach the hands of the average American climber until the mid-1930s. Garbed in simple woolen clothing and caps, the scouts began their ascent under the safety of darkness. Ice conditions were at their best during this time and the boys made surprisingly fast time over the Palmer Snow Field. They continued their ascent up to Triangle Moraine, stopping only periodically to ensure that the group stayed together.

A quick hike to the top of an ice ridge known as the Hogsback brought them to a position where they could fully appreciate the beauty of Mount Hood. There the boys stood, completely surrounded by the awe-inspiring geologic wonders that young Hackett would never tire of re-visiting. Below them to the east was the Devil's Kitchen, named for the foul-smelling sulphur that emanated from volcanic vents known as fumaroles. This area would not hold a winter coat of snow due to the continual heating underneath. Bill would recall that the area smelled like rotten eggs but he was fascinated with the rocks nevertheless. Behind the Boy Scouts was a sizeable andesite plug called Crater Rock. At the northern base of this rock was a large fumarole, a volcanic vent belching noxious gasses high into the air. Hackett and McJury watched these gas clouds rise higher and higher until they drifted over the summit itself. To the west was another region of volcanic activity known as the Hot Rocks. Though smaller than Devil's Kitchen, it was still impressive to both scientist and novice alike. The boys' vision scanned the inner crater walls clockwise from the southwest to the southeast. These walls were broken up into individual sections that were still virgin territory at the time— Hawkins Cliff, the Flying Buttress, the East Crater wall and the crumbling Steel Cliff.

Mr. Stout gave the word to depart and his boys began their ascent up the steep crater wall through an ice channel then known simply as The Chute. Only a year earlier, a youth by the name of Glenn Gullickson had fallen 800 feet to his death from this very point. Stout and his boys exercised extreme caution during this, the most technical portion of the route. When they reached the top of the chute, the true summit was just a leisurely walk to the east along the summit rim.

The sights and sensations Hackett experienced on the summit of Mount Hood rivaled those within its crater. In the distance to the south, he spied Mount Jefferson and some of the other Central Oregon peaks in the Cascade Range. To the north were Mount St. Helens, Mount Adams and mighty Mount Rainier. There were other sites for the curious on the summit itself. In those days a two-story wooden structure was situated on top of the peak. Constructed and owned by the US Forest Service, it was the base of operations for fire lookouts whose job was to spot new blazes from its panoramic viewpoint. Liege Coalman, who designed and built the structure in 1915, spotted 131 fires during his first season atop the volcano. Hackett, McJury and the other scouts walked completely around the cabin, marveling at the fact that all of these materials had been carried to the summit on the backs of climbers such as themselves. Stout had the boys rope-up and one by one they were anchored and allowed to crawl to the northern edge of the summit rim. As a curious Bill peered over the edge, the sight that greeted him took his breath away. Unlike the south side of Mount Hood, which held gentle slopes clear up to the final 1,000 feet, the north side was dramatically different. He was looking over 3,000 feet straight down the north face! Little did he know that in only three years, he and McJury would make history by making a first ascent up a steep and forbidding portion of this rock face.

—•—▪◦▪—•—

When Bill returned to Portland he looked back to the east towards Mount Hood. From that day forward, he never looked at the mountain in the same way. "I have been there," he thought to himself, "I have been to the top and it is mine!" He now wanted to say the same for the multitude of peaks he had seen from the summit of Wy'east.

From 1933 to mid-1936, Hackett's climbing resume only held but ten alpine ascents; four climbs of Mount Hood via the South Side route, California's Mount Shasta by the Horse Camp route, two ascents of the Middle Sister, one of the North Sister and only two ascents that could even be labeled technically challenging. While on a trip through Central Oregon, he made these latter two ascents on two consecutive days and received some much-needed rock climbing experience. On September 1, 1935, he made a solo ascent of Mount Washington's North Arête. This 7,794-foot basalt pinnacle that seemingly rose straight up from the surrounding terrain was rarely climbed during the Great Depression. It was too isolated and too difficult a peak for the masses and only the most competent of climbers even attempted it. Though Bill had joined the Mazamas mountaineering organization that year, he disregarded their advice to continue climbing more standard routes and chose instead an ambitious undertaking—The North Arête. Although today this route is considered one of the easiest paths to the summit, Hackett was attempting it solo, with limited experience and with no escape plan. Unlike the majority of his future mountaineering ventures, he performed little, if any, research on this particular peak, choosing instead to climb by the 'seat of his pants.' He would go on to reach the summit without incident and once there, spied a small mountain to the northeast that captured his attention. Bill decided to make an immediate descent and drive to the base of this secondary peak.[4]

The following day, Hackett made another ascent, this time the Southwest Arête of Three Fingered Jack, the peak that had so captivated him the previous afternoon. This time he climbed with a party of Mazamas, led by another Mount Hood personality—Everett Darr. A veteran alpinist with far more experience, Darr taught Hackett some advanced moves that he would be able to use on countless occasions in the future. Their goal at the moment was the 7,841-foot Three Fingered Jack, a mixture of basalt and pyroclastic debris notorious for its unstable rock. In addition, the final two pitches were considerably risky as they were extremely exposed. During this particular ascent, Bill learned more from Darr than just new climbing hand holds. He learned that climbers don't always scream when they fall. While they were making their ascent of a rock chimney, Darr took pity on the younger climber and took the lead. "A second later," Bill would recall, "I heard a grating sound. Darr came diving past me, still hanging on to the rock that had given way with him. I could feel the breeze from his body, and then I heard the sound as he hit on a pile of boulders. Fortunately, he wasn't critically hurt. He sprained his ankle and cracked a few ribs. Fearful that I might follow his rapid line of descent, it took a little coaxing before I could be persuaded to climb down to him."[5]

With only these ten alpine ascents to his credit, Bill approached Russ McJury in June of 1936, with a dangerous proposal. He wanted to make a first ascent of a difficult portion of Mount Hood's Eliot Glacier Cirque Wall, the 3,250-foot north wall that the boys had marveled over three years earlier. The face itself had been climbed before but by notable mountaineers such as Arthur and Orville Emmons, Colin Chisholm, and Mark Weygandt, a climbing guide who would go on to make 588 ascents of the mountain!

McJury and Hackett agreed upon their objective and set about procuring the necessary equipment for such an endeavor.

Up till the summer of 1936, Bill had used an alpenstock as he had on his first climb with Mr. Stout and the Boy Scouts. By now he knew such a tool was obsolete and desperately wanted a good quality ice axe. Such equipment had been used in the Alps for over three decades but it took a considerable amount of time for Cascade mountaineers to adopt its use. McJury fashioned his own axe while working in Franklin High School's metal shop. Hackett on the other hand, had other ideas:

> "I commissioned my friend and fellow mountaineer, Martin Vinyard, to craft this most important tool, because of his skills in working with metal. I designed my new ax a bit different from the European standards of the era. The slightly longer shaft and pick would give me greater security in belaying, better efficiency in cutting steps downhill, and safer and easier glissading. The adze, wider than usual, would make step cutting easier and more efficient."

In regards to crampons, the metal points affixed to the bottom of climbing boots, Hackett saved up his money to buy the best pair he could find. Oscar Eckenstein, who led the first expedition to K2 in 1902, had designed a pair of 10-point crampons that had served two generations of mountaineers. Bill coveted these crampons like no other piece of equipment he would ever own in the future. They were hand-forged in Austria and purchased with hard-earned money from the Beebe Company, one of the earliest importers of climbing gear in the Pacific Northwest.

Bill additionally felt that some last-minute rock climbing might help later on during the main objective. For this, he and John Carter turned their attention to the crumbing basalt rock found in the Columbia River Gorge. Bill's theory was that the loose, flaky rock found in the gorge would more closely resemble the conditions he and McJury would encounter high atop Mount Hood. They made successful ascents of Rooster Rock, Crown Point and the Pillars of Hercules. But they didn't stop there; they spent additional time training on some of the hard to reach columns and pillars in the region.

At 5:30 PM, Saturday evening, June 27, 1936, the proverbial whistle blew at the Gilbert's Store and Bill eagerly exchanged his warehouse apron for his rucksack. Darrel Tarter, who was driving his Plymouth to the north side of Mount Hood, picked up Hackett and McJury on his way. It was Tarter's intention to solo the Sunshine Route and since he was headed for the same debarkation point as the boys, he agreed to drive them to the mountain. The winter snows had melted just enough to allow them to pass and they barely made it to Cloud Cap Inn, an old cabin on the northeast slopes built in the late 1880s. While Tarter established camp for the night, McJury and Hackett shouldered their packs and thanked him for the ride.

The boys weren't tired and were anxious to get moving so they began their ascent up the moraines bordering Eliot Glacier. Eventually, they descended onto the glacier itself and roped up, making incredible time up to the base of the North Face Cleaver. Once there, they decided to catch a few hours of sleep before continuing on to cross the bergschrund near dawn. The first golden rays of the Sunday morning sun illuminated the upper slopes magnificently. When Bill first saw the wall he remarked, "After a look at that ribbon of ice which soars from the glacier in one unbroken sweep to the top of Mount Hood, any fool could have stated with great authority, 'That's impossible! It can't be done!' But Russ was nineteen and I was seventeen, blithely unaware of the impossibility."

The pair climbed steadily for eight hours, alternately taking the lead. The angle of the ice ranged from 45-60 degrees or more in sections. Today's twelve-point crampons have two teeth that point straight ahead for use in direct climbing but in 1936, the boys only had the ten-points and were forced to cut steps in the ice, an exhaustive and time-consuming chore that few of today's climbers can truly appreciate. Steep ice and rock outcroppings were tackled with care and precision. There was no thought of the clock or breaking any speed records. "We were fortunate to encounter rime ice," Bill would recall, "ordinarily a hazard in itself, but on this particular day it held the loose rock in place and actually made our route safer."

During the course of the day's work, they caught glimpses of Tarter crossing the Eliot Glacier far below, heading towards Horseshoe Rock and Cathedral Ridge. The boys couldn't spend too much time looking down while the immediate danger was still above them. Their pace was slow, and the sun had plenty of time to warm the upper portion of the virgin route. Sizeable rocks that had previously been frozen in place were becoming loose and began falling on the unsuspecting climbers.

Hackett writes:

"Russ and I alternated leads to a point about 200 feet below the summit of the mountain. There we veered horizontally west (right) to the top of the North Face Cleaver. That placed us directly below Cathedral Rock, which Gary Leech had claimed for a first ascent in 1934. Our position was still a number of rope lengths below our goal, and we proceeded with great caution on exceedingly steep and unstable rock and ice. The rock directly above us was alarmingly smooth, and Russ was standing on my shoulders searching desperately for handholds. At best, a shoulder stand (or *courte echelle* as climbers call it) is a shaky position to hold. Russ' nailed boots were biting into my shoulders, and I was teetering precariously under his feet, when suddenly I heard a whizzing sound. Something went 'bang!' a short distance over our heads. I nearly tumbled over backwards. There was another 'bang' and then both of us yelled at once. Someone on the summit above was throwing firecrackers over the north face!"

— ≡◆≡ —

"Cut it out!" Bill shouted. "We're in a tough spot here!" McJury looked overhead and spied two climbers poking their heads over the summit cornice.

"Heck!" one of the climbers called back, "We were just practicing for the Fourth. Anyhow, we never expected anyone to come up that way!"

When McJury and Hackett reached the summit they were immediately surprised. The US Forest Service cabin, which normally took some time to reach once the summit rim was attained, was directly in front of them, not more than three feet away! Members of the Wy'east Climbers club; Ralph Calkin and Joe Leuthold were waiting on the summit, having just completed a first ascent of a difficult portion of the inner crater wall. Bill was elated to meet with and share experiences with climbers that he greatly admired. Only after speaking with Leuthold did Hackett truly appreciate the fact that he had added a chapter of his own to the rich history of climbing on Mount Hood. He wanted more experience, more first ascents and more summits under his belt.

Bill Hackett greatly respected the Wy'east Climbers and Joe Leuthold in particular. The 'Climbers' were the most hard-living, talented and exclusive mountaineering association on Mount Hood. The Hood River Crag Rats (1926) and Portland Mazamas (1894) had specific requirements to join, but if these requirements were met, no one would be barred from membership. The Wy'east Climbers however, were another story. They were formed in 1930 by some of the most talented alpinists in the state: James Harlow, Alfred Monner, Don Burkhart and Ray Atkeson among others. To be accepted among their ranks initially required no prerequisites other than the approval of the members themselves.[6] Though such a situation seemed ideal, there were plenty of the state's climbers left off their roster list. Bill's name was among these.[7]

Though Bill never determined why he wasn't accepted into the Wy'east Climbers, their leaders were nevertheless his primary instructors in advanced rock climbing. Joe Leuthold and Everett Darr were two members who generously passed on to Bill the benefit of their extensive alpine experience. These men were among the first in Oregon to elevate rock climbing to an art form and in the process, dispel the belief that certain pinnacles in the Cascades were unclimbable.

Joe Leuthold was born in Switzerland in 1906, and came to the United States at the age of nine. His first of sixty-four ascents of Mount Hood took place in 1929, and from the beginning he demonstrated the great endurance, skill and patience that would endear him to the mountaineering community. He made several first ascents throughout the Cascade Range, the most notable being Wy'east Mountain, Riddle Peak, and Bonanza Peak. He would go on to make a first ascent of Mount Hood's Sandy Glacier Headwall (1937) with

Russ McJury. Leuthold married Laurita Abendroth in 1946, and their daughter, Toni made a name for herself in US Skiing competitions. Though Leuthold and Hackett rarely saw eye-to-eye with each other in regards to politics or religion, they shared a common interest in moving the art of rock climbing forward. They believed that such climbing was a worthy pursuit in and of itself and should not be seen as mere practice for higher ascents. Armed with this common agenda, Leuthold would teach Bill, among others, some of the advanced climbing skills that he would employ in the decades to come.[8]

Everett Darr was born in Memphis, Tennessee in 1907, and his family moved to Oregon shortly thereafter. He became fascinated with skiing in early 1927, and was introduced to mountaineering three years later. Though not a charter member of the Wy'east Climbers, he quickly joined their ranks and began making his own first ascents. In 1931, accompanied by Ralph Calkin, Darr made a first ascent of a variation of Mount Hood's Wy'east Route. Darr and Leuthold were one of the best climbing pairs around and together they led the party that made the first ascent of St. Peter's Dome in the Columbia River Gorge. Darr's primary contribution to Bill Hackett's climbing career was his avocation of an all-weather approach to mountaineering. Darr climbed when he wanted to climb and not merely when the weather allowed it. Bill soon adopted this philosophy and though it caused alarm among his friends and family, it provided him with invaluable experience in wilderness survival and navigation, and exposed him to climbing conditions rarely experienced by the fair-weather mountaineers.[9]

If Bill respected Leuthold and Darr, he nearly worshiped the Lone Wolf of Government Camp, Gary Leech. Where Leuthold had taught technique and Darr provided inspiration, Leech would instruct Bill in how to climb solo.

From the 1790s to the 1980s, the majority of the world's mountaineering associations frowned upon climbing alone. Hidden crevasses, avalanches, rock fall and a host of other natural dangers were present in the alpine environment and to face them with only a partner or a few companions was considered challenge enough. 'Reckless, unduly hazardous and completely foolish' were the words used to describe solo climbing. The bond between climbers on a rope was so strong that to even think of ascending any other way was considered sacrilegious. The climbers on Mount Hood were no exception. There were however, several climbers on the mountain during the Great Depression who openly advocated solo climbing: Irving Lincoln, Smoke Blanchard and Ole Lien to name the most prominent. Gary Leech, the self-proclaimed Lone Wolf, clearly led the pack.[10]

Gary Denzel Leech climbed Mount Hood over 116 times. He would nearly always sign the summit register with the entry, "Gary Leech, Gov't Camp, Outlaw." The term *outlaw* in those days referred to anyone who strayed off the established route or, in the words of Smoke Blanchard, "...committed the ultimate sin of climbing alone."[11] We don't know much about Leech but what we do know comes from three main sources: Blanchard's memoirs, Leech's unpublished journals, and the recollections of long-time Government Camp residents. Leech's record of first ascents on Mount Hood is indeed impressive: The Inner Crater Wall's Flying Buttress (1933), Castle Crags (1933), the South Wall of Illumination Rock (1936), and the rock's East Arête (1933) and North Face (1938).[12] The climb that impressed Bill the most was Gary's solo first ascent of the Cathedral Spire (1933), on the mountain's famous north face. He had made this historic ascent without an initial reconnoiter, without crampons, or even an ice axe. An alpenstock was his only piece of climbing hardware at the time.

Though it was Hackett who introduced Smoke Blanchard to mountaineering, it was Leech who took both the boys under his wing and taught them a great many things. He instructed them in the technique of surmounting rime ice, proper stemming in rock chimneys, and even dihedral work. He taught them that equipment could be made from garden tools, that weathermen were always wrong, and that researching a route ahead of time could help avoid pitfalls down the line. He taught them self-arrest techniques, gave advice on proper footwear, and how to properly probe for hidden crevasses. As an avid solo mountaineer, Leech was especially adept at locating these hidden dangers. Normally, a climbing partner or partners can assist in your extraction from a crevasse but when you climb alone, self-reliance is the rule of the day. Though Bill eagerly adopted nearly all of Leech's suggestions, he flatly rejected one of the Lone Wolf's trademark techniques. Leech would always sprint down Mount Hood's south side routes, something Bill could never understand nor adopt.

Even though Bill could be counted on to climb under nearly any conditions, he always remained cautious and clear thinking. To run downhill at fast speeds, over uneven terrain was, to Bill at least, a broken leg just waiting to happen.[13]

⊷⊶ ⊯⊹⊞ ⊷⊶

One of Bill's fondest recollections of his early days on Mount Hood was an ascent with Leech on what is today called the Leuthold Couloir. On Sunday, July 9, 1939, they made a fast ascent to Illumination Saddle, an area of snow in between Illumination Rock and the mountain proper. Encountering a quick drop off, they rappelled down onto the Reid Glacier. They then headed north and made a cautious traverse of the glacier, ending up at the base of an extensive hourglass-shaped couloir. This thin ribbon of ice and snow separates Castle Crags (Hawkins Cliff) from Yocum Ridge. Leech allowed Hackett to take the lead, an honor Bill quickly seized upon.

Hackett would record:

> "I started upward, marveling at the ice flutes hanging like giant feathers from the south side of Yocum Ridge. We dodged occasional stones, which released from cliffs above. I kicked steps steadily upward, gazing apprehensively at the hanging rock gardens alongside Castle Crags above us, all of which appeared imminently ready to melt out and crash down upon us. Our route topped out at the Queen's Chair, where we caught magnificent panorama of the north side. We then veered due south, climbing a ridge of snow to a point on the crest several hundred feet west of Mount Hood's summit."

⊷⊶ ⊯⊹⊞ ⊷⊶

When the climbers reached the summit cabin they embraced, congratulating themselves on their success. They sat down and enjoyed the surrounding view. For Leech this was but another successful adventure in a long string of mountaineering ascents. For Hackett however, it marked the first time he had ever climbed with someone he considered a living legend. He would of course go on to climb with internationally recognized mountaineers but Bill would never forget this memorable ascent in the summer of '39.

Hackett and Leech agreed on many mountaineering related strategies for climbing but Bill wasn't a purist when it came to solo climbing. He understood its necessity, as self-reliance is a must for any serious mountaineer, but he could never fully embrace the practice itself. To keep such skills honed however, he would embark on solo ventures at least twice each climbing season. Only a month after his ascent of Hood's North Face with McJury, Bill would solo the mountain when history was being made again. On July 19, 1936, the Mantle Club of Portland led 411 people to the summit via the Traditional South Side Route. Bill, who loathed such crowds, decided to try his hand at a solo ascent of the inner crater wall. He researched the route by meeting with Leuthold and the companions that had made the first ascent. He then hitched a ride to Government Camp and immediately embarked on his ascent. He paced himself through the trees but once past timberline, he opened up, setting an impressive pace. He stayed clear of the long line of humanity making its way up the Palmer Snow Field and instead, chose a longer route up Zigzag Glacier towards Crater Rock. Once there, he crossed paths with the Mantle Club and continued his solo push through the Devil's Kitchen and on up the inner crater wall. Following the route descriptions he had received from Leuthold, Bill reached the summit and made the first solo ascent of this challenging and visually stunning route.

In July of 1941, John Carter accompanied Hackett on a five-day journey that resulted in successful ascents of Mount Rainier, Baker and Shuksan. They piled into Carter's 1941 Ford Mercury and headed north for Mount Rainier. Sixty years after the event, Carter fondly recalled, "We were in a rock nest of sorts above Steamboat Prow, over 10,000 feet above the valley floor. Night had fallen and I can vividly remember that it was incredibly cold outside. We were melting snow for some tea water and it was so cold outside neither of us wanted to take our hands out of our warm sleeping bags. He and I went round and round, prodding the other to test the water with his fingers to see if it was warm enough. It's been quite a few years but I'll never forget that night. We went on to summit the following day and then drove north to Mount Baker." Hackett and Carter had summitted Rainier on July 28. Two days later they made a successful ascent of Baker via the Coleman Glacier Route. Undaunted, they made yet another ascent the following day, the Fisher Chimneys Route on Mount Shuksan. On their return journey to Portland, Hackett was behind the wheel of the Mercury, racing through the city of Tacoma at an excessive speed. No sooner had Carter called his attention to the speed than a police officer pulled them over and gave them a ticket. They had to follow the officer down to the police station where they were informed they would need to pay a thirty-five dollar fine before they could leave town. Not having any money, the pair was forced to leave Carter's spare tire as payment![14]

Carter offers the following comments on his old climbing companion:

> "Bill was considered an up-and-comer amongst the Mount Hood climbing group. He was a couple years younger than the rest of us and when you're that young, just two years can set yourself apart from your peers. He was kept out of the Wy'east Climbers and I know that bugged him quite a bit. Bill could be startling blunt sometimes and this could antagonize some people. He could be pretty cocky on occasion but he was always honest, never claimed to have climbed anything he hadn't climbed and was always prepared to back up his boasts with proof. He was also pretty popular with the ladies and I know that upset quite a few of the boys in Government Camp. I remember he was able to win the heart of Mary Johnson, who was so beautiful I couldn't even talk to her. He was truly something else."[15]

Carter recalled Bill's stamina and humor above timberline: "His endurance was legendary, but I was even more impressed with his technical climbing skills. I could always trust him to take the lead on a particularly nasty pitch. His sense of humor should also be remembered. One time we were climbing the west side (Leuthold Couloir) route on Mount Hood, which is pretty steep. Bill was in the lead far overhead. Seemed like every time he would move he would send a shower of rocks down on my head. I was wearing a stocking cap but it didn't seem to help. When we came to a point where we could rest, I told him he was causing rocks to fall on me. He just smiled and said, 'Just don't let a big one hit you.'

In his later years, Hackett loved to recount his adventures on and around Mount Hood. One day, he and a climbing companion got it in their heads to make a first ascent of the three-story rock chimney inside Timberline Lodge. Without a rope or equipment of any kind, they scrambled up the tower of rock. The guests were delighted when several employees tried to shoo them away with broomsticks. Another time, Bill and skiing legend Hjalmar Hvam took it upon themselves to ski down the wooden stairwells inside the lodge. Again, the employees were not impressed.[16]

"Camp Blossom Cabin was a secondary home," Bill would recall, "We worked six days a week during the Depression, so as soon as that whistle blew at 5:30 PM on Saturday, off we went to the mountain." Between 1933 and 1939, Bill had to get a ride from a friend or hitchhike to Government Camp. From there he would scout around town and see if any of his climbing buddies were game for an ascent. Alone or in the company of fellow climbers, he would make the 2,000-foot elevation gain to a two-story wooden cabin in a clearing near the edge of timberline. Timberline Cabin was the primary structure on the south side of the mountain until the construction of Timberline Lodge. Members of the Mazamas and Wy'east Climbers used the cabin in the early 1930s as a base of operations for south side ascents. In this small structure, Bill would catch a few hours of sleep before continuing his ascent.[17] When Timberline Lodge was under construction in 1936, Hackett started dating the daughter of the inn's night watchman. This guard, who approved of the match, allowed Bill to sleep in the building at night while the workers were away.[18] Bill would buy day-old bread at the bakery and tuck it inside his sleeping bag to eat while viewing the mountain through an unfinished window. The ascent itself would occur that evening or the following morning. Near 5:00 PM, Sunday evening, Bill and his friends began their descent to the Lodge or "Govy," as Government Camp was affectionately called. From there, the difficult chore of finding a ride back to Portland began. Bill was never late for work as a result of climbing. He would always look back upon that period of his life with fond and vibrant memories. But like every chapter in a man's life, one must end before another can begin.

⊷ ⸺✦⸺ ⊶

CHAPTER II

The Road to Italy

"The Army skier's best by far!
He'll drink you under the bar!
The roughest, the toughest, we're dirty and mean,
Hungry and lean, but our rifles are clean."[1]

—*"87th's Best By Far,"*
Songs of the 87th Mountain
Infantry

When the bombs fell on Pearl Harbor, Bill Hackett had just been promoted to assistant manager of the Gilbert Brothers sporting goods store. He was in charge of their new ski department, had a brand new car and additionally worked swing shift at the Kaiser Ship Yards on Swan Island. He had amassed an impressive climbing record and was beginning to make a name for himself in the tight-knit mountaineering community.[2] He was proud of the ascents he had made and looked forward to further adventures in the Cascades and Canadian Rockies. Only a month after the tragic events in Hawaii, he received notification that he had been drafted into the Armed Forces. Within days he reported for Army Basic Training at Fort Riley, Kansas. A man who had grown to love the ice-covered mountains, Bill now found himself surrounded by a stark, featureless landscape.[3] The young soldier's adventurous passions were soon rekindled when he heard through the Army's grapevine that mountaineers and skiers were being scooped up by the War Department to be trained for mountain warfare. Hackett knew immediately that this was the place for him. With a little research and a lot of determination, he completed the necessary paperwork and set about volunteering his services. The Army was requesting letters of recommendation from civilians, and here, John Carter was able to lend a hand. Carter wrote complimentary letters for Hackett and Russ McJury, both of who initially found themselves serving in the cavalry, of all places.[4] For weeks Bill anxiously awaited word from his superiors.

The military authorities could not ignore Hackett's climbing resume. When he entered the Army he had climbed Three Fingered Jack, Middle Sister, North Sister and mounts Shasta, Washington, St. Helens, Jefferson, Stuart, Rainier, Baker and Shuksan. More impressive were his sixty-one ascents of Mount Hood by ten different routes in a seven-year time frame.[5] He had climbed rock of varying quality and had extensive experience climbing different types of ice. He had experience climbing solo, in small groups and even larger parties. He was an accomplished skier and was a regular participant at the competitions held at Timberline Lodge.[6] He was a perfect candidate to serve in the 87th Mountain Infantry Regiment. When he received word of his new assignment, Bill couldn't have been happier. Soon he would be joining the ranks of fellow climbers Joe Leuthold, Russ McJury and Glen Asher. At the time of Bill's arrival, the regiment was little more than battalion strength but it would grow to become the 10th Mountain Division, comprising the 85th, 86th and 87th Mountain Infantry Regiments.

Men from all over the country were either assigned or voluntarily flocked to recruiting stations to join the 87th at Fort Lewis, Washington. These future soldiers, like Bill, were skiers, mountain climbers or those experienced in alpine survival. Bill was surprised to learn that others had been trappers, lumbermen, cowboys, forest rangers and even muleskinners.[7]

When he arrived at Fort Lewis in April of 1942, Hackett was immediately informed that he would be departing in eight weeks for the Canadian Rockies. He was being assigned to a seventy-five-man detachment, bound for the Columbia Ice Fields at Athabaska Pass. British Prime Minister Winston Churchill had initiated plans to retake Norway from the Nazis and he knew he would need sturdy vehicles that could safely transport mountain troops over snow, ice and glaciated surfaces. Bill became a member of the team that would spend four months testing vehicles originally designed by the Studebaker Corporation.[8]

Accompanied by fellow enlisted men, a handful of officers and civilian technicians, Bill departed by rail for Canada. For a young man who had spent most of his life in the Willamette Valley, the journey offered plenty of new sights and sounds, as well as new adventures that he dutifully recorded in the diaries he had maintained since 1939. The men traveled north to Vancouver, British Columbia, and from there, boarded a Canadian Pacific Railway train to Banff, Alberta. For the last leg of their journey, the men piled into the waiting trucks that would take them up the road to Lake Louise Junction.

In the ensuing four months, the amount of work these dedicated men performed was phenomenal. Base Camp was established at Sunwapta Pass beside the Athabaska Glacier. A road was constructed up the moraine to the end, or *snout* of the ice field. Hundreds of trees were chopped down and used to bridge gaping crevasses in the ice. Two-and-a-half ton rigs equipped with chains were used to haul supplies and equipment to an advanced base camp. An elliptical track measuring four miles was created in order to conduct the necessary tests twenty-four hours a day. In addition to the back breaking roadwork, Bill found himself driving a bulldozer, cooking meals, acting as a transport officer, and yes, even serving for a time as the latrine orderly.[9]

The men were using several types of prototype vehicles, but the most promising was a personnel carrier on tracks that met with high praise among the men. This vehicle, with modifications, would later be dubbed the *M29 Weasel* and served the troops well in Colorado. Bill recalled that a Mr. Cole, vice president of the Studebaker Corporation, was so pleased with their progress he bought a round of beers for the men assembled for an evening's entertainment.[10]

Hackett was fascinated with the region and would note that he saw "no end of beautiful peaks!" Even with his heavy workload, Bill still managed to make a variety of mountaineering ascents during the few off-hours he was afforded. Wearing his Army-issue Bergmann Boots with Tricouni Nails, he achieved over sixteen summits during his stay. His favorite ascents during this time were the South Face of Mt. Fairview, the East Face of Mt. Columbia, and mounts Castleguard, Kitchener and St. Piran.[11]

The team departed the Canadian Rockies in September and returned to Washington State. When Bill returned to his usual barracks he noticed that the regiment had grown considerably during his four-month absence. In December, the troops were ordered to report to Camp Hale, Colorado, just north of Leadville. Here, Bill found training grounds that would better simulate the unfamiliar conditions they would encounter in Europe.[12]

Camp Hale was situated west of the Continental Divide, roughly 9,480 feet above sea level and was constructed from scratch for the sole purpose of housing and training the men of the 87th Regiment. A mile-long ski tow with rope tows was erected at Cooper Hill. Inside each of the barracks there were ski-waxing rooms. Hackett found the training educational as well as entertaining. There were courses on skiing, snowshoeing, avoiding avalanche paths, and driving dog teams. Bill applied for and was granted a position as a ski instructor, a position he relished. The men learned how to build snow caves and emergency shelters. Units spent time at higher altitudes, performing maneuvers and testing experimental cold weather gear. Detachments bivouacked in the mountains surrounding camp, many times at altitudes in excess of 12,000 feet.[13]

When spring arrived, the men learned forest fire-fighting techniques, mule packing and rock climbing. Elderly Arctic and Antarctic explorers from past expeditions were brought in as civilian advisors. Renowned mountaineers from both sides of the Atlantic shared their advice and expertise. The men of the 87th entered extreme training evolutions they were not always prepared for. The casualty rate ran pretty high at times: with ankle and leg injuries during ski runs, back and head injuries from rock climbing and the occasional occurrences of frostbite and hypothermia during long marches in the surrounding mountains.

Though Bill was happy serving with his fellow soldiers, he nevertheless felt depressed.[14] Like many of his fellow soldiers, he wondered if all of their training and skills would ever be put to use in the European theater of war. The topic continually reared its head in the mess hall, the barracks and in the field. On D-Day, June 6, 1944, Bill heard of the Invasion of Normandy and wondered if this would mean imminent deployment. When word reached the troops that they were being ordered to Camp Swift, Texas, Bill was certain their time had come to see action overseas. His hopes were dashed when he and the other members of the 87th endured repeated twenty-five mile speed marches at night with no word of deployment.

Soon after his arrival in the Lone Star state, Hackett received word that his application to Officer Candidate School had been accepted. He was ordered to report to the Infantry School in Ft. Benning, Georgia. In late November, he graduated and proudly wore the bars of a commissioned Second Lieutenant, Infantry. Only four days after graduation, he went home to Portland on leave and made an important decision. He proposed to and married Miss Naydene Bishop on November 27, 1944.[15]

The couple had little time to celebrate. In a few short weeks, Bill's unit was at last ordered to ship out for the European theater of war. On the gray morning of January 3, 1945, Bill boarded the *USS West Point* in Newport News, Virginia, just one of thousands reporting for duty.[16]

— ⋅≡⋅ —

The General Quarters alarm was sounded at 7:30 AM aboard the *USS West Point* waking Bill from a deep slumber. It took a few moments for his memory to kick into gear. "I'm in the Army," he thought to himself, "heading for Europe!"

"Move Bill! Move!" someone cried nearby. Bill threw off the Army-issue wool blanket and cotton sheets and ran for the nearest exit. When he reached the main deck he saw a sea of humanity moving about. Over 8,000 troops were aboard and thousands upon thousands of men were scrambling to pre-designated locations. Though the official rule was men should proceed 'up and forward on the starboard side of the ship and down and aft on the port', this procedure was soon forgotten amidst the confusion. Bill turned and spied Allied air cover overhead. What could be wrong? Had we struck ground? Had there been a collision of some sorts? A man-overboard? Before he could even reach his designated position, Bill and the other soldiers had received word to step down from the alert. Though he was pleased that there had been no cause for alarm, Bill was certain that once he reached their destination...there would be.[17]

Later that afternoon, Bill was leaning against the ship's railing, watching the Rock of Gibraltar loom into view. It was a sunny afternoon, a rare occurrence at that time of year, according to the other members of the crew. At his first sight of Europe, Bill couldn't help but reflect upon the events that had brought him there and wonder what the future would hold for him once he landed.

Hackett had enjoyed his brief journey across the Atlantic but knew in his heart that he could never join the Navy and spend any great length of time at sea. He was, however, surprised at how fast he and his friends had adapted to life on the waves. True, there were bouts of seasickness and the usual complaints when crowded troops were forced to congregate in small areas, but overall, morale was high. There were two meals served per day, a late breakfast at 9:00 AM and an early dinner at 4:00 PM. Water for shaving and showering was turned on for only one hour in the morning and one hour in the evening, somehow accommodating the needs of over 8,000 men! Bill stood various watches for two to four hours at a time, exercised, and strolled the decks to pass the time. The ship's orchestra did what they could to entertain the troops, but the waiting was nearly unbearable for a man used to continual movement. Lights were out at 9:00 sharp each night and Bill eagerly greeted the darkness as it meant he was one day closer to Europe.[18]

On the sixth day out to sea, an incident occurred that Bill would recall years later. Just after dawn the sleeping men in the berthing compartments below the dispensary were rudely awakened when large ocean swells outside ripped the life rafts loose and sent them crashing through the port side of the ship. Three plates buckled and tons of icy seawater poured into the hold! Fortunately for the troops aboard, the compartment had been nearly vacant but men were soon wading in waist-deep water to retrieve their personal affects.[19] The damage was shored up but Bill couldn't help but think about the men aboard the *Arizona* and *Oklahoma* at Pearl Harbor. Bill was used to being outdoors where he always felt he could find an escape route should he ever encounter trouble. To be trapped inside a vessel, knowing that his options were limited was a fate he wouldn't wish upon his worse enemy.

In the late afternoon of January 13, the *West Point* passed by the towering Isle of Capri and docked in Naples, Italy. After a nine-day crossing of the North Atlantic, the men of the 10th Mountain Division stared over the ship's rails and marveled at the multitude of sunken ships in the harbor. In the distance they could see shattered homes, bombed out factories and crippled rail yards. The docks were teeming with sailors and onlookers. Bill anxiously looked for a view of Mt. Vesuvius, a sight he knew he could receive from the harbor. Unfortunately, a series of rain squalls had all but obscured the great peak.[20]

In July of 1943, Allied Forces landed in Sicily and the invasion of Italy soon followed. The bombing of the San Lorenzo and Littorio rail yards helped speed the fall of Benito Mussolini. Axis troops abandoned Rome and Allied amphibious forces landed south of Naples in early September.[21] Nearly a year and a half later, the 10th Mountain Division arrived in an Italy still reeling from the war. Both sides of the struggle had surged in different geographical areas in order to grab land, supplies and armaments. The recent winter had been hard on the Italians and Allied troops alike. It was in this cold, impoverished atmosphere that the division personnel began loading men and their equipment onto railroad boxcars headed north.[22]

Immediately following their debarkation from the ship, Bill boarded an Italian four-wheel rail car, which, he was soon told, would take him and his colleagues to Rome and beyond. Just after midnight the freight train moved north under an overcast sky. Hackett slept on the floorboards with twenty-six other men, each trying to find some space to stretch out in the cramped baggage car. They cooked Army C-rations over *controlled* fires in the center of the car. Each town and village they traveled through bore the scars of war. The once beautiful cities of Littoro, Cisterno and Anzio were now ghostly, war-torn remnants of their former selves.[23]

After a brief stop in Rome, the train continued north where the terrain, and its inhabitants for that matter, appeared to be in better condition. Their rail journey ended near Leghorn where the men were herded onto awaiting trucks. Without a moment's rest they were transported to a staging area north of Pisa, roughly forty miles from the front lines. Bill was impressed with the grandeur of the rugged mountains that loomed to the north, and began to look forward to learning the land's technical climbing routes. In the days to come the men would be moved from village to village until they ended up headquartered in a farmhouse four and-a-half miles from the front lines. Their training in mountain warfare was about to be put to the test.[24]

News of enemy forces arrayed against the allies in Italy came from intelligence briefings filtered down to the junior officers. Every hill between Bologna and a line twenty-four miles north of Florence remained in German hands. The Nazis commanded strategically crucial peaks along the crest of the Apennine Mountains west of Bologna and north of Florence to the Serchio plains in northwestern Italy. Some twenty-five divisions strong—more than a quarter of a million men—occupied the steep mountains, villages and valleys in the region. Armed with machine guns, mortars and the latest artillery, they were in a position to halt the progression of any advancing Allied force. The Americans were not alone in their quest for continual territorial gains. The British and even the Brazilians were attempting to push the lines forward and re-supply their troops.[25]

Hackett and the First Battalion bivouacked near Villa Colli. Captain George F. Earle, one of the early historians for the 10th Mountain Division, would describe the terrain and nighttime activities at this bivouac:

> "The bivouac area near Villa Colli was a good seven air-line miles to the rear of the 92nd Division, and the unit's position was strategic rather than tactical. From that vantage point, they could be rapidly shifted to either the coastal plain or to the Serchio Valley—avenues of approach where the Germans made alarming penetrations in the past. Directly to the front, however, was a series of jagged mountain peaks and ridges, and deep roadless valleys that had never seen any action, and were only scouted by occasional patrols of both sides...the system of setting up tactically, with guards, outposts, and gun emplacements further supported the belief that this was more than a training area. Consequently, the area developed into a hot-bed of flashing lights, green and blue flares, skulking figures on ridges, and assorted rifle, pistol, and machine gun shots. Patrols discovered houses with candles set by the window so that the shade might be drawn and raised for the enemy."[26]

With his unvarying personal habit of recording daily activities in his diary, Bill noted with characteristic brevity that men such as he—men who had never seen a day of combat service—performed the patrol work for the whole regiment! On February 12, 1945, Bill would record his first encounter with the enemy. He was leading a squad of men on a night patrol and his point man detected a four-man enemy patrol. Hackett and his men exchanged fire for nearly five full hours with three separate patrols! Bill called for flares to illuminate the field and ordered eighty-one mortars to be fired on the enemy position. He recorded the events in his diaries with the same tenor and space devoted to the weather, what time he awoke, or what he had consumed for lunch.[27]

On February 16, Bill was pleased to write to his parents that he had not only been transferred to Headquarters Company, but that he had had his *second* bath in two months! In the days that followed, he would move closer and closer towards the mountains that would prove to be the true battlefields for the men of the Tenth. Under the cover of darkness, they arrived in the town of Vidiciatico where Bill and other officers found lodging in an old hotel. That evening he was briefed by his superior officers, who stated that the "entire division would be committed for the taking of Mt. Belvedere." Bill was assigned to the mobile reserve.[28]

German Field Marshall Kesselring had boasted that the Allied troops could never penetrate his mountain stronghold, and for over five months, the Field Marshall had been right. German troops had repelled every attempt to advance that the American Fifth Army had made. Kesselring's *Winter Line* seemed impregnable. William Lowell Putnam, who entered the US Army as a private and worked his way up to First Lieutenant, would note in his *Green Cognac: The Education of a Mountain Fighter* (1991), that the Winter Line "was not a prepared and heavily fortified arrangement such as the one in eastern France named for the World War I sergeant, Andre Maginot. Instead it was essentially the crest of the high country of the Apennines dividing the Po River drainage from that to the south. It was to this area of difficult terrain that the Axis forces retreated when they failed to hold the line at the Arno River."[29]

To combat this *Winter Line*, General Hays, commanding officer of the 10th Mountain Division, convinced the commander of the

Fifth Army that the first objective should be the taking of 3,876-foot
Monte Belvedere and its surrounding territory. The mountain was
heavily patrolled by the enemy. Taking the peak would require serious sacrifices. The benefit however, would be a strategic tactical
advantage for the Allies. Riva Ridge, overlooking Monte Belvedere,
would provide the foothold the men of the Tenth would need in
order to gain the momentum and territorial advances that would follow. It was clear that in order to seize Belvedere, Riva Ridge would
have to be taken. Plans were drafted exploring one scenario after
another. In many ways, the answer was before them all along but several officers were hesitant to embrace the plan—a nighttime assault
on Riva Ridge! The men of the Tenth would have to climb quietly
under the cover of darkness in order to catch the Germans off guard.
The plan might just work if fair weather held and the element of surprise could be maintained.

It was one of the darkest days of Bill's life when his company
was passed over for the assignment of the assault on Riva Ridge. It
remained the greatest professional disappointment in his life up until
his defeat on K2 in 1960. Hackett had to contend himself with initial
support work but held out hope that events would change and he
would be able to make a more direct, significant contribution to the
coming offensive.

Hal Burton would record the men's self-confidence and
demeanor at the time:

> "The 10th at this moment, just before blooding in
> battle, was supremely self-confident, composed
> largely of men who felt themselves elite beyond any
> other American division. The conclusion was rea-
> sonably accurate: certainly there were infinitely
> more college graduates and college students, infi-
> nitely more men from moneyed families, and the
> only group of men in the Army who found common
> cause in a sport. It could even be said that the divi-
> sion was more elite than the Brigade of Guards, for
> there only the officers were, in the English sense,
> gentlemen, while in the 10th Mountain Division
> gentlemen, in the American sense, permeated every

level up to the echelon of West Pointers and career officers at the top of the pyramid."[30]

＊＊ ≡◆≡ ＊＊

By February 18, 1945, the entire division was on the move. The daring nighttime assault on Riva Ridge had begun—one of the most ambitious military operations ever attempted using untested troops. The 86th Regiment would make up the main assault force while the 85th and 87th would remain in mobile reserve. With each passing day, Bill Hackett's resolve to engage in the fight grew steadily. Though his company had no orders to penetrate the high grounds on Riva, he knew that sooner or later he and others would be called upon to dislodge the enemy from the region.

At first light on the morning of February 19, the company to which Hackett was temporarily attached, slipped into the bombed out village of Corona. The bodies of dead German officers littered the streets and Bill quickly noticed that there were American losses strewn through the streets as well. The early morning light cast long shadows and it was only upon closer inspection that Bill's men were able to determine that a serious hand-to-hand struggle had occurred here. Bill wondered how it had started and who had won. The bodies were mixed together and there were no clear battle lines. It was street fighting, house to house with no clear objective other than small territorial gains.

Later that afternoon, Hackett was still thinking about these soldiers when he rounded the corner of a house whose roof had suffered a direct mortar hit, dumping the ceiling on the floor inside. As he stepped away from the protection of the corner, there, not fifty feet in front of him, was a German grenadier wearing a white battle dress uniform. In an instant, the grenadier had raised his machine pistol to bear. Bill would later recall that even while he clumsily reached for his 45-caliber pistol, he knew it was too late. Then, right behind him, exploding in his ears was the sudden stuttering sound of a Browning Automatic Rifle (BAR). The German who faced him was lifted from where he stood by the force of the bullets striking his midriff and was blown back several feet, falling dead at the edge of a nearby olive grove.

＊＊ ≡◆≡ ＊＊

Deafened by the clatter of the BAR, Bill turned to see an American soldier lower his smoking weapon and grin at him from a face still bearing burnt cork camouflage for night patrol duty.

"Sorry I had to shoot so close to your ear, buddy," said the man, giving a casual salute while disappearing around the corner of the house. The buzz in Bill's ears lasted for the next few hours and it reminded him of the old Army saying, "When your number's up, all the praying in the world won't change it." He never saw the soldier with the BAR again but always remembered the sly grin on those chapped lips.

A few days later Bill was transferred to Company C of the First Battalion under the command of First Lieutenant Morlan Nelson.[31] The Company occupied a defensive position near the summit of Monte Belvedere and Bill was hoping to make a good first impression. The first evening he was with the group, his right foot struck a home-made lamp fashioned from a C-ration can filled with dirt soaked in gasoline. Across the muddy, straw-laden floor it tumbled, igniting the fuel, straw and dried-out wood underneath. The dugout quickly filled with black, choking smoke. The officers were unable to escape since doing so would expose themselves to enemy fire. Instead, the officers grabbed the appropriate gear and quickly extinguished the flames. After all the commotion settled down, Bill had to endure the good-natured ribbing of his new executive officer, Second Lieutenant Dick Powers. The two had first met back at Camp Hale and would become life-long friends.

Richard 'Dick' Powers, Bill would discover, was also from Portland, Oregon, although their paths had never crossed. Powers attributed this to the fact that he had joined the Army on September 16, 1940, over a year before the attack on Pearl Harbor. In November of 1941, Powers saw a notice on the company bulletin board that indicated the Army was forming a ski troop. Though he had little previous climbing experience, Powers had skied a bit in high school, so he signed up thinking the worst the Army could say was no. He was interviewed for membership and initially received the 'don't call us, we'll call you' communiqué. He waited patiently for the results.

On the morning of Sunday, December 7, 1941, Powers was polishing his motorcycle in front of his barracks at Ft. Lewis, Washington. A couple of enlisted men were playing a game of catch nearby while others were engaged in a friendly game of football. Suddenly, one of the men from inside the building ran out and cried, "Hey! The Japs just bombed Pearl Harbor!" Powers ignored the man, thinking he either had a hangover or was simply half-asleep. Another man stuck his head out the window and gave the same alarming announcement. Even then, Powers was skeptical. He had heard the rumors that the Japanese Imperial Fleet might try to incite a war but he felt certain it would be the Philippines or some other target. Only when another American serviceman in Powers' barracks set up a radio in the courtyard did he truly believe that the event had transpired.

"What do we do?" Powers asked their duty officer, the man in charge at the time. The officer instructed them to assemble their weapons. "Talk about paranoia!" Powers would later say, "Everyone thought that the next airplane that might fly overhead would have *meatballs* on the wings." Powers discovered that the doors to the supply room were locked and that the supply sergeant was out playing golf. Someone from the crowd yelled for Powers to get on his motorcycle and go retrieve the sergeant.

Powers jumped onto his motorcycle and sped north on a gravel-strewn, one-lane road. He was forced to skid to a halt in front of the North Gate of the Army base. There, a sentry pleaded with him for confirmation of the news of the attack. Powers briefly relayed what little information he possessed and asked to be allowed to pass. He then aimed his bike north and proceeded to ride as fast as he could in the direction of the city of Tacoma. Only after he was a considerable distance from the base did he stop. "The light came on in my skull" he would remember, "that's not the golf course where the sergeant would be playing! He'd be down south in Nisqually!" Powers spun the bike around, kicking up gravel in the process and accelerated back towards the base.

When he was fast approaching the only traffic light for miles around, he could clearly see that it was red. He rode right through it without hesitating. The golf course he was looking for was located just south and off to his right so he fishtailed onto another gravel road and rode to the edge of the greens. He stopped long enough to ask someone where Sergeant Riccard could be found. An individual who knew the sergeant said he could be found on 'such & such' hole and off Powers flew, straight over the fairway, tearing up the terrain as he went! Like Steve McQueen in the movie, *The Great Escape*, Powers drove his motorcycle over the pristine-cut grass, dodged sand traps and eventually slid to a halt next to a startled Sergeant Riccard.

"What in the Sam hell are you doing?" the sergeant cried.

"Get on this thing!" Powers replied, "The Japanese have bombed Pearl Harbor and you're the only one with the keys to the supply room!" Surprisingly, the sergeant didn't ask for further information. The pair turned around and sped off toward Ft. Lewis. As Powers approached the traffic light for a second time he shook his head.

"Damn thing's red again!" he yelled back to Riccard, unsure whether the sergeant could even hear him over the engine noise and rush of the wind. Again, Powers sped right through the light, hoping there would be no other traffic to slow their progress. Riccard, seeing the maneuver, gripped Powers tighter for fear of falling from the bike. Only half a mile further, they turned onto the road leading to the north entrance to the base. Powers continued on until he reached the supply room door itself. Once there, Riccard immediately bailed off the back seat of the motorcycle.

"Damn it, Powers!" he screamed, "We're at war now. I don't know what's going to happen during the next few years but whatever it is it ain't going to be *near* as bad as that motorcycle ride!" Dick Powers was the type of soldier Bill Hackett could relate to. They would fight together, laugh together, drink together, and remain friends for over half a century.[32]

⊷ ▰▸▰ ⊷

With the capture of Riva Ridge and Mt. Belvedere bolstering the Army's confidence in General Hays and his mountain troops, orders were dispatched from Fifth Army Headquarters for the spring offensive. Members of the 87th Mountain Regiment were to advance on April 14, attacking Hill 909, 913, and 903 among others. The attacks jumped off from Mount della Spe and other points near the town of Castel d' Aiano. The orders directed them to "seize, occupy and defend" initial objectives prior to daylight. They were to drive north toward Corona and then split their forces—taking a series of hills occupied by German forces. The American General Staff carefully reviewed their maps of the terrain they hoped to occupy in the weeks to come. Elevation figures were listed in meters above sea level, information that was critical for planning ground assaults. This numbering system also served a dual purpose as the number indicated the hill's elevation in meters, information that was critical for planning ground assaults.

Curtis Casewit would write that, "By mid-March, the situation had changed for the worse for German forces everywhere. The Russians were getting closer to Hitler's Berlin fortress. On the western front, the Allies had reached deep into Germany. Field Marshall Kesselring unexpectedly left to replace Field Marshal Karl von Rundstedt in the West.... The Tenth Mountain Division had now blasted through more than half of the Apennines.... The final spring offensive was planned for April 12, 1945. The British Eighth Army would push along the Adriatic coast. Beside them would be the American Fifth Army. But once more, the Tenth Mountain Division was chosen to fight in front of all the Allied units, a sort of dagger through the last Apennine chain."[33]

When Bill Hackett learned about the capture of Riva Ridge, he was obviously elated but disappointed that he was unable to participate in the main offensive. For the time being, he would have to contend himself with serving in the mobile reserves. He couldn't help but hope for a position of leadership in the taking of the next military objective—the push to reach the Po River Valley! Late March and early April of 1945, would be a period in Bill's life that he would look back on with mixed emotions. He met soldiers that would become life-long friends, he received training that helped him in both his military and climbing careers, and he also witnessed scenes of senseless destruction and watched helplessly as the men under his command fell one by one.

—————

CHAPTER III

Brothers in Arms

*"Only nine remained of the original forty-five men
in my platoon."*[1]

—Bill Hackett

April 1, 1945, was Easter Sunday and Bill knew the Spring Offensive was nearing. On that day, the division's role in the campaign was beginning to take shape. The men of the Tenth were to break through the northern Apennines, drive the Germans out and sweep across the Po River Valley. This valley held enough food and provisions to supply an enemy counter-attack, so it was imperative that the Allied objectives be taken quickly and efficiently. The men of the Tenth understood that the element of surprise, that had been so crucial in the taking of Riva Ridge, would now be absent. The Germans were beefing up their defensive positions in preparation for the coming campaign.

The Americans learned that they were facing three German regiments of the 334th Division. These troops had taken to posting notices in the mountain villages, warning the Italian hill people of the need to evacuate their homes, "Your district," the signs said, "may become a battle zone within the next few weeks. In order to save your life and your property, it is in your interest to evacuate this district up to the line *Semalano di Sopramonte, Righetti, Montetorte* and find safety north of this line. The area has to be evacuated by the fifth of April at 19:00. Whoever shall be found in this area after that date shall be shot as a spy without challenge."[2]

Despite the grim warning, hundreds of the evacuees sought safety and protection in the south behind American lines. On April 2, the area near *Castel d' Aiano* was completely overrun with herds of cattle, goats, and pigs, accompanied by their owners. They brought with them what little possessions they could, loaded on wagons or carts or even on their backs. For days, truckloads of livestock and civilians were shipped to the rear of the combat area.

While they waited for the Spring Offensive, the 87th Mountain Infantry prepared for the battle to come. The weather turned in their favor and the days were mild and warm. The fruit trees throughout the Apennines, many shredded by artillery fire, were in full blossom. The mountain trails, which had been constructed for ox carts had been destroyed in certain sections by US Army trucks bringing provisions to the front lines. Tanks, personnel carriers and heavy equipment stretched to the rear as far as the eye could see. For the average member of the Tenth, the long column of Allied machines was a welcome sight.[3]

There were personal tragedies that reminded the men of how precious life was in the war zone. When Lt. Powers described to Bill about an incident at Campo Tizzoro, it was a sobering reflection for both of them. Powers had been coaching soldiers in routine rifle prac- tice on April 3. Two men who manned phones in the target pits 150 yards away, Privates First Class William Huff and Prentis Davidson were suddenly electrocuted when a stray bullet severed a high-ten- sion wire. The live wire fell to the ground across the telephone line connected to the men in the pits. The two soldiers died instantly when an electric charge traveled from the point of contact to the phones they held in their hands.[4]

By the time the regiment had been notified of pending action on April 4, Bill Hackett and the third platoon of Company C were as ready as they would ever be. Their primary concern was not engaging the enemy itself, but the terrain over which the coming struggle would occur. Captain George F. Earle would write of the landscape:

"The difficulties of cracking the German's first line of defense could not be over-emphasized. The first and most obvious obstacle was the terrain. The hills were steeper than any the regiment had fought on. Lightly wooded with chestnut trees, they sloped downward although in many places they were bare rocky cliffs. On the gentler slopes and smaller summits, fields were cleared and small clusters of farm buildings huddled against the mountainsides. Between the mountains were deep, pine-studded draws with precipitous sides difficult to cross. The location and formation of the band of hills was jumbled and without apparent geographical pattern, so that individual hills and locations were difficult to identify."[5]

⚓

On April 14, two days after the death of U.S. President Franklin Roosevelt, the softening up of the German line in preparation for the assault took place. Four Air Corps "Thunderbolt" fighter-bombers bombed enemy positions. They dove close to the ground, setting several fires and wrecking serious damage to buildings along the mountain line with demolition bombs. Though the Germans were not surprised that the Allies were starting their move, they were nevertheless taken aback by the fact that the Allies were attacking so late in the morning.

From April 14 to 19, Bill Hackett fought in one skirmish after another. "This was it!" he would write, "After all the delays, the roar of bombs and artillery and the staccato bark of heavy machine guns sent ominous proof that the big drive was on! Then followed a bloody day—after scramble, from ridge lines, to hill towns, to hilltops, with hundreds of German prisoners of war moving to the rear with hands atop their heads."[6] Bill served in a platoon that originally consisted of forty-five men and saw action on, or occupied, Hills 860, 903, 894, 834, 810, and 569. But it was Bill's actions on Hill 293 that would win him the Silver Star, one of the highest awards the US Military can convey on a soldier. Only the Congressional Medal of Honor and Distinguished Service Cross exceeded the Silver Star and Bill was honored beyond belief when he learned he would receive the recognition.

Bill would devote but ninety-seven words in his diary to the action that took place on Thursday, April 19, 1945, but the memory of that day would remain with him till the end of his life. "During all the time which I commanded the Third Platoon, Company C," Bill recorded, "19 April turned out to be our grimmest day of battle, as the Germans fought on with great determination and tenacity. After encountering heavy fighting all day, we approached high ground toward evening."[7] Bill left the town of Merlano in the morning, in attack formation with the Third Platoon in the lead. They encountered heavy sniper fire during the first two miles of terrain. On the outskirts of the town of Mongiorgio, the infantry was working beside tanks to continue the Allied advance. On the east side of the village, Bill and the other members of the Third Platoon, charged into one bombed-out building after the next. As carefully as possible, they cleared one house after another, sweeping through town at a snail's pace. The soldiers worked their way around the town near Venerano where two squads were pinned down.[8]

A multitude of men were seemingly trapped. The soldiers of the Third Platoon were pinned down in a ditch of adequate size. Behind them was a pine forest and to the front was a wooded draw with Hill 293 rising behind it. In addition, the last few houses in town were situated on the edge of the forest, and these structures were enemy occupied. Germans were hidden behind the trees in the draw, picking their targets carefully and lobbing grenades towards the ditch. One of these grenades bounced off the back of Pfc. Venar Riddle and rolled away. Rifle grenades were next, followed by enemy artillery fire that set the forest ablaze. With growing concern, the American forces were desperately seeking a way to break out and achieve a more strategic location.

Captain Earle writes:

"Three men made a break. They had heard Sergeant Provelaites directing them to run for the houses. When they got to their feet, however, they started straight down the hill for the houses the Germans were in. They saw some Germans down there, but at first mistook them for friendly troops. They were within fifty yards when they noticed the German uniform. Seeing their mistake, they turned and ran for the other houses to the left, where the sergeant was. The Germans then fired, hitting Pfc. Arnold E. Riippa in the back of the neck. They all kept going, however, and made the house. Riippa was taken to the cellar and treated, and the Italians, huddled in the cellar for safety, fortified him with wine."[9]

It was under these conditions that Lieutenant Hackett made his move. While in charge of Third Squad, he realized that he and his seventeen men were in a position just forward of the ditch in which many of his fellow platoon soldiers were trapped. Bill led his team around a bend to the right of the main ditch, directly between the pine forest and Hill 293. Standing orders were to take the hill and he was determined to reach the objective. Hunched over slightly with rifle in hand, Bill led the quick charge up through the draw, shooting the Germans they encountered there.

Hackett would always remember that at this point in the battle, the most shy and introverted member of his team held his rifle over his head and screamed for his colleagues to join him. "Hey fellas!" he hollered, "Stick a feather in your ass and head for the high ground!" Bill couldn't believe that this kid, who was skinny as a bean pole, was personally taking on seasoned soldiers of the Wehrmacht. According to Bill, the youth returned to his calm, shy mannerisms shortly after the attack.

Between the pine-dotted draw and Hill 293, there was a smaller hill that commanded a fair view of their objective. Sergeant Stephen Scullen instantly recognized this site as a key fighting position and erected his machine gun on the spot. During these set-up procedures, the Third Squad encountered serious enemy fire. Bill grabbed a pair of binoculars and spotted a German machine gun nest perched atop Hill 293.

"There! There! Over there!" Bill yelled. Sergeant Scullen turned his machine gun to bear on the enemy position. Scullen's neutralizing fire made quick work of the German gunner and the men of Third Squad were soon scrambling up Hill 293 itself. When they reached the forward slope overlooking the river road below they encountered more enemy troops but were able to force their surrender. Just when it seemed as if they could have a well-earned rest, a hail of bullets began to rain down on them. Bill turned and saw that Germans were holed-up in sniper positions in houses down at the bottom of the hill. The men of Third Squad dove into the old German positions on the summit of Hill 293.

"Talk about F.U.B.A.R!" Bill remarked above the fire. About this time, a German Lieutenant suddenly appeared from out of the woods on the hill. Before squad members could gun him down, the enemy officer dropped his fully loaded machine gun over the bank and formally surrendered himself to Lieutenant Hackett. Pfc. Richard Zimmerman immediately picked up the discarded weapon and turned it on the enemy positions below. "Enemy fire," Captain Earle would write, "still pinned the squad to their holes. It was impossible to get back behind the hill. The German officer was put on the hillside, and told to tell the others in the houses below to surrender. He refused, but the enemy stopped firing when they saw he was a German. During this lull in the firing the squad was able to withdraw from the exposed slope."[10]

Hackett then ordered Sergeant Scullen to take his gun over a cliff face that was protected from enemy fire. The sergeant made a quick rappel and set up a firing position from the smaller hill in between Hill 293 and the enemy-held structures. Scullen had a better shot from this particular vantage point and he anxiously waited for any German soldier to reveal his position.

A second German officer suddenly appeared near the summit of Hill 293. This officer, with hands held high, surrendered to Bill and promptly informed the Americans that twenty more Germans were supposed to relieve him at any moment. This news came as quite a shock to Bill as he had hoped to maintain possession of the hill until reinforcements could arrive. Even the possibility that an enemy squad was en route to the summit caused the Americans to re-evaluate their situation. Bill had his men work their way back to the true summit and climb into the trees that were clustered on the crest. He hoped to ambush the enemy. Bill left one American behind in the bushes to guard the prisoners of war. The rumored German patrol never materialized and Bill's squad lost valuable time that could have been better spent fortifying their position.

Then, an incident occurred that made Bill furious and distraught at the same time. In a German-held building below Hill 293, an arm appeared out of a window, brandishing a white flag. Their message was clear and Pfc. Fred Zarlengo, up on the hill, left his position and began to descend the forward slope. As he waved the would-be German prisoners up he was shot dead by a sniper. Bill was furious. He couldn't be sure exactly where the fatal shot had come from but he believed it probably came from the same window that had just held the white flag of surrender. Bill knew there were no rules in warfare but the white flag was one of the oldest and universally understood symbols. The fact that the Germans may have used it in order to pick off an easy target enraged him.

Bill set up a 500-yard defensive line with his remaining men and awaited reinforcements. Within the hour, elements of the First Platoon scaled the peak to render their assistance.

Captain Earle describes the action:

"...The 1st Platoon in support under Lieutenant James H. Penrose had been swung around to the right of the wooded hill to approach the town and hill from the north. Company headquarters, the mortars, and the 1st Squad of the 3rd Platoon followed. They came under machine gun fire while still half a mile east of the objective, and had to advance one man at a time until they reached a draw that gave good cover. They were held up there as they approached a house, when a machine gun opened up on Lieutenant Penrose, Staff Sergeant Gilman, and the two scouts out in front of the platoon. A BAR was quickly set up in the rear, and covered the withdrawal of the four men. The platoon then worked their way further to the left under some sniper fire from C. Lezza to the north, but got into another draw leading down to the objective. They were hollered at by Hackett's men up on the objective [Hill 293] who spotted them at this time, just as they came under some scattered artillery fire. They were able to work down the draw and join Hackett's men on the reverse slope of the objective and secure his precarious defense. Lieutenant Hawk's 2nd Platoon, and the rest of the 3rd Platoon arrived at about 1900, completing the assembly of the company."[11]

—— ◄+►— ——

The following morning, April 20, a muster of Third Platoon revealed a staggering figure. Of the original forty-five members in Bill's platoon, only twenty-one remained. Bill was stunned. In six short days, his platoon had been depleted by over fifty percent.

For his combat leadership and 'gallantry in action on 19 April 1945,' Bill was awarded the Silver Star. Major Harold F. Miller would pen the letter that would accompany Bill's medal. In part, it read: "Second Lieutenant Hackett, unwilling to halt the assault, led his platoon past the tanks, and onto the platoon objective. Then, in spite of heavy resistance, he started the assault of the company objective. Advancing into the small village, he encountered a hail of small arms fire, which pinned his men down. Still determined to press onward, he rallied what men he could, and with one rifle squad and a machine gun squad fought his way forward to commanding ground, took the company objective, and held it alone for several hours until the arrival of other elements of his company. By his inspiring leadership and aggressive tactics, Second Lieutenant Hackett greatly expedited the offensive, and earned the confidence of his men. His heroic conduct in the battle, and his gallant disregard of safety to press the attack forward, are truly worthy of the finest traditions of the United States Army."[12]

After the action on Hill 293, Bill's platoon was transported by truck to the village of Muffa. There, they erected a road block and prepared to join the massive Allied sweep across the Po River Valley. The village itself was ideally suited for such an attack. To its back were the mountains and valleys, which the Allies had just overrun. In the forefront, just north of town, were the railroad tracks that connected Bologna with Modena. Farther north lay the fertile Po River Valley stretching to the foothills of the Dolomite Alps.[13]

The following two weeks were a blur to Bill. Continual troop movement, periodic engagements with the enemy, and the ever-present stress of not knowing what tomorrow would bring all seemed to blend together. "We were caught up in a bloody exercise which seemed to have no end," Bill would later write. "Casualties diminished my platoon to sixteen men by the time fresh replacements caught up with us on 23 April. Our First Battalion was the first unit to break through the Apennines, where we spilled out onto the flatlands of the Po River. We made our way across the valley against diminished organized resistance by the men of the German Army, who were riding in any kind of vehicle or walking a route march past the wreckage of their military units."[14]

From Muffa, Bill and his men traveled northeast to Calcara on the banks of the Samoggia River.[15] From there, it was on to Bastiglia by the Panaro River. The journey was made on the backs of tanks, trucks and even the occasional commandeered Fiat motorcar.[16] They traveled by day or night, depending upon the most recent intelligence. The move to Calcara, for instance was actually out of the way but enabled the men to bypass a significant number of enemy troops in the process.

Bombing runs on the part of the Luftwaffe exploded a series of Allied ammunition dumps, adding to the burning wreckage. Hundreds upon hundreds of German prisoners of war were being marched to the rear of the battle lines. Burning buildings and vehicles illuminated the night sky. When Bill was riding on the back of a tank he could clearly see the faces of the enemy enlisted soldiers. He noted that many of them actually seemed pleased to be captured, relieved by the knowledge that they would be able to ride out the rest of the war and survive. In sharp contrast, many of the German officers, entrenched in their own propaganda, were hopelessly convinced that the Allies would execute them within the hour.

Bill would recall the events of April 23: "After crossing seventy-five miles of this terrain, we came to the southern bank of the mighty Po River. Engineer assault boats were brought to us, and we paddled our way across the 400-foot stream to the north shore near San Benedetto. Our crossing was subjected to long-range machine gun and sniper fire, shelling by 20mm anti-aircraft guns and 88mm artillery time fire, which put an umbrella of shrapnel over our heads. On reaching the north shore, we consolidated our position."[17]

Four days later, Bill and his men reached the shores of beautiful Lake Garda. Surrounded by the majestic Dolomite Alps, the Lake Garda region was home to several villages and towns that would see serious action in the days to come: Spiazzi, Caprino and Pesina. Bill's company traveled east for four miles along the Garda Coast and erected defensive positions throughout the surrounding hillsides.[18] Vast numbers of enemy troops were attempting to flee the region by way of the Brenner Pass and the men of the Tenth were ordered to cut this avenue of escape.[19]

The village of Spiazzi would mark Hackett's last battle. Company A, just east of his position, was engaged in a serious fight with the Germans in and around the town. Hackett was ordered to have his platoon of Company C support Company A during this conflict. Before dawn, his men crept up a hillside behind the village in an attempt to surprise the enemy with a classic flanking maneuver. The men of Company C ran down the opposing side of the hill and as the Germans were facing the opposite direction, they were caught completely off-guard. After heavy resistance, the Allied troops took over forty prisoners of war and had killed an estimated seventy members of the Wehrmacht.[20]

On May 2, Bill learned that the German Armies in Italy had unconditionally surrendered to the Allies and five days later, Germany herself would follow suit.[21] In three weeks, the men of the 10th Mountain Division had broken through Nazi lines of defense, and had entered the Po River Valley. Bill wrote that, "Fighting elements of our 10th Mountain Division formed the spearhead for the 5th United States Army in its 150-mile offensive from the Winter Line to the north end of Lake Garda in the Julian Alps."

After Bill was awarded his Silver Star for his actions on Hill 293, he was notified that he was to receive two Bronze Star Medals, one for Meritorious Achievement in Ground Operations Against the Enemy, and another for Heroism in Ground Combat. Bill had been nicked twice under fire, once by flying shrapnel and another time by a bullet. "Neither," Bill would write, "damaged me enough to impair my performance of duty, so I continued in command of my platoon." Bill asked his superior officer not to submit his name for Purple Heart consideration.[22] Five short months after graduating from Officer Candidate School, Bill earned a combat promotion to First Lieutenant of Infantry, by Special Order Number 149 from Headquarters, US Fifth Army.

Though honored to receive such recognition, Bills was deeply saddened by the deaths of the men who had fallen in battle beside him. Only two of Company C's six officers survived. The regiment had suffered nearly eighty-eight percent casualties and only nine men remained of the original forty-five in Bill's platoon. The numbers spoke for themselves.

⊷ ▣◆▤ ⊶

There were lighter moments in Europe for Bill Hackett. After the cessation of hostilities in Northern Italy, US troops were relocated to regions they would occupy during the tense period following the cease-fire. The First Battalion of the 87th Mountain Infantry, of which Bill was a member, was moved west and camped on the outskirts of the town of Brescia. The town had a reputation as a hot bed for fascists. Members of the Third Battalion were moved farther north to Solda, a ski resort at the base of the Dolomite Alps. Members of their K Company quickly discovered a large cache of champagne and cognac in a nearby warehouse. General George P. Hays, the division commander, seized the goods and had them transferred to his supply department aboard eight deuce-and-a-half trucks. These spirits were soon be distributed to the troops along with their daily rations.[23]

About this time, the First Battalion received orders to move east to the vicinity of Udine. General Hays, realizing his trucks were off transporting the champagne, had to do some fast-talking in order to officially delay his men's departure. Within days however, the troops settled in the town of Plezzo in the valley of the Isonzo River. Once there, the officers were temporarily quartered in the Albergo Plezzo Hotel. A quaint, red brick U-shaped structure near the center of town, the Albergo towered five stories above its neighboring buildings. Overlooking a spacious flagstone courtyard, the hotel was capped with an ornate cupola.

One evening shortly after their arrival, Bill was drinking champagne and cognac with several battalion officers, including Dick Powers. As the evening progressed and stories were exchanged, Bill was asked to share some of his mountaineering adventures. Bill talked about headwalls and dangerous glacial crossings but mostly, he spoke of his passion and love of first ascents—to climb, conquer and stand where others had not. Getting caught up in the moment he proclaimed that he wanted to make a first ascent that very evening. Dick Powers assumed he was talking about tackling some technically challenging peak in the nearby Dolomites but Bill had other plans. He cast his gaze up to the roof of the Albergo Plezzo and announced he had found his goal.

⎯⎯ ⊨⊹⊯ ⎯⎯

"I was just a rookie at this mountaineering stuff," Dick Powers recalled over a half-century after the event, "but with the aid of the sauce that we had consumed, I volunteered. Base camp was established appropriately enough in a rest room on the ground floor."[24] Looking out the window of the rest room, Bill and Dick spied the courtyard and water fountain outside. Nearly thirty Yugoslavians were milling about the yard, oblivious to the two figures peering out from within the hotel. Night was falling and Powers knew their ascent would occur under the cover of darkness. Garbed in their olive-drab uniforms and waffle-soled Bromonti boots, Bill and Dick crawled out the window and grasped the nearby metal down spout. This led the men to a ledge on the second of five stories. "We were not equipped with any of the technical niceties of standard mountaineering gear," Powers would recall, "We didn't have any ice axes, pitons, ropes or hammers. We would traverse along the ledge from one drain spout to the other and then shimmy up to the next ledge." In this manner, they slowly made their ascent from floor to floor, using lie-back techniques to ascend the drain spouts. They would wedge the front of their boots in the small area where the metal spout met the red brick wall. Their feet would remain in position as long as their hands and arms pulled while their feet pushed in the opposite direction. When they gained the 18-inch wide masonry ledges above, they would place their backs against the brick wall and shuffle their feet from side to side in order to reach the next drain spout. Powers would recall that he never looked down but that Bill had, reporting that their ascent attracted little attention from the crowd below.

"I don't know to this day how in the devil we ever got up over the roof's overhang," Powers recalled. "It didn't hang out more than about two feet or so. Bill probably went up first and then hauled me up after him."[25] There was a strong metal gutter lining the roof's edge and the men used this hold to assist in their ascent.

The roof's eaves proved to be the crux of the route, followed by a slate roof angled at a moderate 30-degree slope. From here the climbers reached the top with relative ease. At the summit was a 4x4-foot level platform that held a large ten-gallon glass jug. The glass itself was roughly half an inch thick and was covered with ornate rattan latticework. Powers thought it resembled similar work he had seen on Chianti bottles.

The men congratulated themselves on reaching the summit and then held a meeting as to how to proceed. They decided unanimously to 'bomb the Jugs', their target, the unsuspecting Yugoslavians in the flagstone courtyard over fifty feet below. Dick was elected bombardier and carefully slid back down the roof to the edge of the building. He peered over the edge to the yard below and provided direction to Bill who was waiting higher up on the cupola. Dick waved his hands and called, "Bombs away!" Bill gave the large jug a nudge and it immediately left its perch, rolled down the slate roof and, according to Powers, seemingly vaulted into space. "It got a pretty good head of speed before it reached the gutter," Dick fondly recalled, "and it flew like a projectile out and down into that courtyard. It went off like a bomb!" With a horrendous crash, the jug shattered into hundreds of pieces, showering the crowd with glass. The Yugoslavians ran for cover, screaming and yelling, unsure of what was unfolding. When asked whether the make-shift bomb hit anyone, Powers replied, "O' God no...fortunately, otherwise we'd still be over there!"

As soon as Bill and Dick saw the crowds fleeing the vicinity, they realized the seriousness of the situation and sobered up pretty quick. "Let's get out of here!" Dick cried. Everyone below was so concerned with gaining cover that they failed to look overhead at the climbers beginning their hasty descent. Dick grabbed the strong metal gutter and swung his legs out over the edge of the roof. Quickly grasping the nearby drain spout, he began to climb down using the same lie-back technique he had used to make his ascent. They made remarkable time considering they had no rope for rappels. Within minutes they had safely descended five stories and entered the courtyard they had recently bombed.

"The jug had been filled with vinegar," Powers recalls with a grin, "and now the courtyard reeked of the stuff. It smelled like a pickle factory! The vinegar had splashed all over these people and they were startled, scared and angrily running around." Bill and Dick surveyed the damage and in the midst of the crowd was John Hordechuck, a Second Lieutenant from A-Company. The Lieutenant was down on his hands and knees with his hands clasped together and seemingly in great distress. Bill and Dick approached him and realized the officer had had his share of cognac. The officer kept repeating, "Why Hordechuck, *why* did you do it? Speak to me, speak to me!" It became apparent that Hordechuck, in his cognac-altered mind, had convinced himself that he had committed suicide by jumping from the roof of the Albergo. Bill and Dick took one look at each other, grinned and then grabbed the Lieutenant under each arm and led him away to grab some much-needed coffee.

In the ensuing years following the war, Bill and Dick would share many more glasses of cognac and reflect upon their adventure at the Albergo Plezzo. "How did the owners of the Albergo get the jug of vinegar onto the roof? How long had it been there? And for what purpose was it placed there? These were just some of the questions and minor mysteries of the evening that continued to entertain Bill and Dick for decades.

CHAPTER IV

Operation
White Tower

*"The tremendous precipices which guarded its summit from
almost every angle were mute evidence of why no one has yet succeeded
in climbing it by any side save the northeast."[1]*

—Dr. Bradford Washburn

In the fall of 1945 when Bill Hackett returned from Italy, he
decided to resume civilian life. It seemed to him, though events were
to prove him wrong, that he could better pursue the grand passion of
his life—climbing—if he doffed his Army uniform. He separated from
the service on October 22 and a week later celebrated with a one-day
marathon, climbing Mounts Democrat, Cameron, Lincoln and Bress;
all peaks in excess of 14,000 feet. Over the course of the winter his
mountain fever, put on hold by the war, had given him no peace. His
next goal was to conquer the tallest mountains in Mexico. He wasn't
getting any younger and his wife, Naydene, who probably understood better than he his compulsion for high peaks, kissed him and
sent him on his way. On May 8, 1946, Hackett departed Los Angeles
with another climber by the name of Sandy Wheeler.[2]

For Bill, taking a vacation did not mean sitting around sipping drinks by the poolside. Wheeler shared Hackett's passion for
arduous and challenging vacations and their adventures in Mexico

were a textbook example. On May 11, they arrived in Mexico City, and without even pausing to acclimate, they set out for Popocatépetl, a volcano rising 17,520 feet.[3] This, the second-highest peak in Mexico, dominated the skyline beside Mexico City. In their eagerness to summit, their fast pace brought on a great deal of nausea, and the men were limp as rags by the time they reached the top. Nevertheless, within two days they were scrambling up Nevada de Toluca (15,170 feet).[4] This particular ascent proved more difficult than Bill originally expected. "We got on the wrong summit," he would write with a smile. "And we had to race the dusk as we crossed two miles of spiky pinnacles on the summit ridge."[5]

On May 14, they rested, so to speak, by driving to the foot of Orizaba (18,700 feet), the highest mountain in the country. An agonizing day on mule-back took them short of the peak, and the following day they made the last of the climb on foot. Their guides, Cristofano and Ricardo, who Bill said were informative as well as entertaining, led them on their journey.[6] That left Hackett and Wheeler with only one big Mexican peak to scale in their marathon, a foolish schedule Hackett vowed never to repeat. After a day's rest following Orizaba, the two started up Ixtaccihuatl, a 17,340-foot peak known as *The Sleeping Woman*. Hackett and Wheeler picked up a guide, Trinidad, and drove to the base of "Ixta" at 13,000 feet, sacking out at dusk.[7]

Early to rise, the trio was on their way at 3:45 the following morning. They decided to take the southern route, a decision that meant they would be forced to drop in elevation before starting upward again. Their climb was a long and grueling march. At 15,000 feet, they began the interminable job of breaking trail in the soft snow, often sinking past their knees and trading leads. Wheeler, Hackett and Trinidad finally reached the large iron pipe cross that marked the summit near 11:00 AM.[8]

Conscious of a change in the color of the sky, which might signal threatening conditions, the climbers quickly left the summit. Hackett said later, "It was most fortunate that we did! On the latter part of the descent, we just happened to be near a rock overhang, which undoubtedly saved our lives. An afternoon storm hit us with hailstones the size of lemons. We would have been finished if we had not found the protection of that rock. We reached the car at 6:00 PM, having spent fourteen hours, forty-five minutes on the climb."[9]

In eight feverish days, Wheeler and Hackett had climbed the four highest peaks in Mexico, which included the third, fifth and sixth highest on the continent. There had been only one full day of rest and relaxation in Mexico City. Later, when Bill reflected on the hyped-up energy that had driven him and Wheeler to ascend four unfamiliar mountains in record time, he would state:

> "It was stupid of us. Our reckless hurry, as if demons were chasing us and would swallow us whole if we did not keep up our frantic pace, was typical, I think, at least for me, of discharged soldiers who were in a hurry to catch up with their missed lives. The fever that was in us could have taken many forms, and it did. I know that friends of mine who were in the Italian campaign with me did foolish things when they took off their uniforms. Some squandered their mustering out pay on the gaming tables, high with excitement, spurred on by a wildness they gave into and didn't understand. Others drove cars they bought too fast and were lucky they didn't kill themselves or hurt somebody else. It was a tense time for all of us. Our youth and the fact that we had survived the war were our only excuses and our forgiveness."[10]

By the fall of 1946, glad to be home with his wife, but bored with civilian life, Hackett was ready to return to Army life. He was immediately assigned to Camp Carson, Colorado, to teach mountaineering and skiing to the 38th Regimental Combat Team.

Around this time, Hackett heard that a Dr. Bradford Washburn was undertaking another expedition to Alaska's Mount McKinley, the highest peak in North America. Bill's childhood dream had been to scale two of the earth's greatest mountains—Everest and McKinley. Everest's summit was still virgin territory in 1946, and thousands of miles away in Nepal. Washburn however, had organized an expedition to McKinley once before and had numerous connections in Alaska and the Yukon. Washburn *might* be able to provide the ticket to one of Hackett's dreams and Bill, never the shy one, set about achieving his goal. He sent a letter to Washburn and in the cable he included his climbing resume and reasons why he wanted to accompany Washburn.[11] Washburn was impressed with Bill's letter and accepted the young mountaineer's application for membership.[12] When Bill received word that he had been accepted he was ecstatic and enthusiastically began to escalate his personal training program.

Hackett learned that he would serve in several capacities during the expedition. He was officially aboard as the US Army Ground Forces Observer and Representative and Washburn put him in charge of testing cold weather gear. Hackett's skill as a climber would also be an asset to the team. He wrote home to his parents that one of his greatest dreams just might become a reality—McKinley!

⊷ ⇥⊹⊨ ⊶

For centuries, Native Alaskans stood in awe of the highest mountain in their territory. The Aleuts called it *Traleika*. The Susitnas referred to her as *Doleika*, which means 'the big mountain.' The great peak had always been *Denali* to the Athabascans, the Native Americans of the Yukon and Kuskokwim regions. It wasn't until 1896, that the name McKinley began to appear on maps of the Alaskan Territory. William Dickey was a young prospector panning for gold within sight of the mountain. Other prospectors had referred to the peak as 'Densmore's Mountain', but Dickey decided to name it after William McKinley of Ohio. McKinley's bid for the presidency was the first news of the outside world Dickey had received while leaving Alaska. The prospector was also prophetic when he claimed Mt. McKinley was the highest mountain on the North American continent. Even as late as 1896, the general consensus was that Mount Saint Elias was the highest peak. It wasn't until two years after Dickey left Alaska, that Americans discovered the true grandeur of McKinley. That summer, George Eldridge and Robert Muldrow made the first triangulated calculations to reach the conclusion that she stood at 20,464 feet. They were only off by 144 feet.[13]

By the end of the Second World War, only three teams had successfully reached the true summit of Mt. McKinley; The Stuck Expedition (1913), led by the Archdeacon of the Yukon, Hudson Stuck, The Lindley-Liek Expedition (1932), led by Alfred Lindley and

Harry Liek, and the United States Army Alaskan Test Expedition (1942), led by Col. Marchman of the US Air Force. Bradford Washburn was a key member of this latter expedition and made his first trip to the summit during the venture. In October of 1946, Washburn began organizing his second expedition to the great peak.[14]

As the director of The New England Museum of Natural History in Boston, Dr. Bradford Washburn was, and remains, a scientist, cartographer, photographer and explorer. He was in a unique position to organize extensive exploration efforts in the northern territories as he had led or been a member of sixteen previous expeditions in Alaska and the Yukon Territory. Washburn had additionally made photographic and mapping flights over McKinley for the National Geographic Society in 1936. Six years later, he had climbed to her true summit by way of the Muldrow Glacier Route. As a result, he was an ideal candidate for the leadership position of a team with more clearly stated goals than all preceding expeditions.[15]

In 1947, RKO Radio Pictures was slated to run a motion picture entitled, *Operation White Tower* and, for publicity purposes, contributed the hefty sum of $25,000 towards the expedition. Climbing gear, camp tools, food, fuel and a wide variety of supplies needed to be procured. Washburn contacted Earl Norris, a well-known dog team driver from Anchorage, and organized the transportation issues.

The purposes for the expedition were varied. Hackett outlined their objectives:

> "To establish and maintain a cosmic ray research station at Denali Pass, 18,150' to be operated by a University of Chicago representative. Moving pictures were to be made on and around Mt. McKinley with a 35.-mm Mitchell commercial camera. Two professional cameramen were to be assigned this task. An extensive survey program was planned since most of the area was unsurveyed. Geological specimens of every type found on the mountain were to be collected since little was known of its structure. Glacier motion stations were to be occupied to determine the rate of glacial flow, and representatives of the Army Ground

Forces and the Army Air Forces were to test cold weather clothing and equipment."[16]

·—·—≡+≡——·

The members of the expedition were some of the most talented individuals in their respective fields. George Browne of Marin County, California, was the son of famed McKinley explorer, Belmore Browne. His father had led expeditions to the mountain in 1910 and 1912, helping to dispel the belief that Dr. Frederick Cook made the first ascent of the peak. Belmore Browne was also an accomplished artist who passed his talent onto his son. George would serve as Washburn's expedition artist in 1947. Robert W. Craig, of Seattle, Washington, would act as Assistant Leader and serve as meteorologist. He was a member of the Seattle-based Mountaineers and the American Alpine Club. William C. Deeke, of Wood-Ridge, New Jersey, would be one of two professional photographers on the team. James E. Gale, of Elmendorf Field, Alaska, would act as a climber, observer and representative of the 10th Rescue Squadron. G. Robert Lange, from Melrose, Massachusetts, would serve as Washburn's assistant during survey work.[17] Grant H. Pearson was no stranger to Denali. He came to Alaska in the winter of 1925, with $2.00 in his pocket. As a U.S. National Park Service observer and representative, he had made an ascent of McKinley as a member of the Lindley-Liek Expedition.[18] William M. Sterling, of Hollywood, California, would be the designated correspondent. Hugo T. Victoreen, from Chicago, Illinois, was considered one of the key members of the team, as he would be the University of Chicago's Representative for cosmic ray research, one of the primary goals of the expedition. Barbara P. Washburn, Dr. Washburn's wife, would act as expedition recording secretary and climber. George H. Wellstead, of Brooklyn, New York, was the second professional photographer added to the roster.

Due to the US Office of Naval Research's pronounced interest in cosmic ray research, Washburn was able to enlist the assistance of the 10th Rescue Squadron at Elmendorf Field, Alaska. Authorities there agreed to provide air support for the upcoming expedition.

By March 28, 1947, all of the team members were assembled at the air terminal in Anchorage. Through Washburn's connections, a warehouse owned by the 10th Rescue Squadron was procured.

During the following two days, expedition members packed food and equipment that were scheduled to be dropped to the team while on the mountain. Each package had to be packed under strict specifications. Every parcel had to meet rigid pre-arranged height and weight requirements—nothing could be left to chance. There would be no expedition representative left behind to oversee these aerial drops. Tags would tell squadron personnel the contents of the packages and when and where to drop them. There were six stacks of parcels, two for each of the higher camps. Another stack would be used for 'free fall items.' The final stack was devoted to fragile objects requiring special handling and mini parachutes. Hakon Christenson, a well-known Alaskan bush pilot, flew in most of the equipment to Base Camp. Flying a ski-equipped aircraft, he landed on Muldrow Glacier near McGonagall Pass. It took over a dozen trips to bring supplies and personnel up to base camp.[19]

On March 31, the first of two aerial reconnaissance flights took place. An Army C-47 lifted off into a cloudless sky reaching an elevation of 23,700 feet. The airplane flew completely around the mountain making a pass over the summit of the North and South Peaks. The cargo door was removed in order to allow for better pictures of the terrain below. Temperatures in the cabin reached minus thirty-one degrees Fahrenheit. From this flight, members were able to get a close-up look at the route they would be taking in the weeks to come. On the northern slopes of the mountain, Muldrow Glacier came into view, stretching some thirty-nine miles. Karstens Ridge, named for Harry Karstens of the 1913 Stuck Expedition, was also visible.[20]

On April 6, the second flight occurred. Bags of dried salmon and tallow were dropped to Base Camp. These were provisions for the dogs that Earl Norris would be bringing up in a few days. The plane then flew counter clockwise through Gunsight Pass and down Muldrow Glacier. Another circuit of the mountain was made at the 15,500-foot level and the team enjoyed a rare view of Wickersham Wall.[21]

Between these two flights, on April 1, expedition member Robert Craig and Sgt. Red Solberg of the Eielson Ranger Station took another flight to Wonder Lake. The plane, heavily loaded with supplies barely made it over the 7,000-foot pass leading to the lake. Craig was impressed with the view, writing, "Mt. McKinley was particularly impressive with its battlement-like approaches from the south and tremendous ice cliffs on the north. The secondary peaks and glaciers themselves would offer fine climbing. Peaks to the southwest of McKinley, near Mt. Russell, look to be a granite uplift of finely chiseled spires, much like the southeastern coast range. The Kenai Range back of Anchorage is also impressive, though difficult of access."[22]

Craig and Sgt. Solberg installed a 60-watt radio at the ranger station in order to relay incoming messages. The U.S. Forest Service only had three-quarter-watt radios which did not carry enough output. The following morning, Craig started hauling food and equipment up from Wonder Lake. While en route, he heard a tremendous cracking sound from the north which stopped him in his tracks. Twenty-five miles away, an enormous avalanche was falling down a northern wall. It was nearly a mile and-a-half in width and sent an impressive cloud of snow thousands of feet into the air.

Back in Base Camp the same morning, the photographers arrived heavily loaded down with equipment. Bill Deeke and George Wellstead announced that their supplies were not all of the photographic equipment they would require—that even more would be coming! Though base camp was well stocked by April 6, Washburn didn't arrive for another three days.[23] He flew in on a 600 HP Norseman, accompanied by Mrs. Washburn, Hackett and Grant Pearson. On April 12, Jim Gale and Hugo Victoreen also arrived in an Army C-45 equipped with skis.[24]

By April 12, expedition members were getting impatient and were more than ready to stretch their limbs. Craig had returned to camp, snow houses had been constructed and a weather station had been erected. Craig, Lange and Hackett decided to make ascents of nearby Oastler and Gunsight peaks. Oastler was situated right next to camp while Gunsight was a full four miles distant. On the summit of Gunsight, they placed a survey marker. These peaks were four miles from camp along the north side of Muldrow Glacier. Later that evening, apparently not fatigued by the day's achievements, they made an ascent of McGonagall Mountain. Located behind Base Camp, this summit was reached just as the sun was setting. Hackett would write that he enjoyed the view of the Alaskan sunset.[25]

Earl Norris had left Mt. McKinley Park Ranger Station on the morning of April 11. He mushed a team of dogs to Wonder Lake at the 2,000-foot level where he rested for a day with Sgt. Solberg. Norris arrived at Base Camp on the 15th after traveling over 100 miles via dog sled in poor visibility. When he arrived in camp, he found Bob Craig and others moving supplies over the glacier. This work proved to be time consuming and tedious as hidden crevasses repeatedly made their appearance as the day progressed.

CAMP I

Based on a previous reconnaissance foray, Gale, Pearson and Hackett established an equipment depot four and-a-half miles above Base Camp. They labeled this store of goods *Cache 1* and recorded its elevation as 6,835 feet. On April 18, the expedition continued up the glacier to establish Camp I, 605 feet higher. Hackett would long remember this day as he endured the first crevasse fall of his career. He had been wearing a seventy-pound pack when he suddenly broke through a hidden crevasse and disappeared beneath the surface of the ice. He would record in his diary that he had fortunately been belayed on both sides. He found himself fifteen feet down in a hole, suspended in the air with no immediate means of escape. It would take his companions forty minutes to extract him from the trap.[26]

Bill wasn't the only member of the team to take the plunge. Bob Craig also fell into a similar trap and would later report to *The Mountaineers*:

"In the fall I dropped my axe, but stayed with my rucksack and snowshoes. I found myself uninjured except for bruises on each temple and bruised hips. Jim lowered a light line and I sent up my pack. When the line was let down again I looped the end and fished my axe from the bottom where the crevasse had narrowed down to a few inches. Jim lowered my crampons. I snapped my axe into a karabiner on my waist and worked up a few feet to an ice chockstone, which I mounted in a sitting position. After getting my crampons on, Jim (Gale) took tension on the rope and I started climbing out. Part of the way I was able to stem, but a good deal of the going required a semi-stem, cutting steps and alternate upward traverse. It was very tiring, but fortunately I was able to find a couple of good resting positions. I finally reached the edge, Jim gave me his hand, and I squirmed out."[27]

These pitfalls were certainly nothing new to Craig as he had helped rescue climbers before on Mount Rainier.

Camp I was established in the center of the largest icefall. As supply runs would need to be initiated, teams were organized to pack food and equipment from Base Camp to Camp I. These supplies were packed by expedition members as they moved between each depot. Snow huts were constructed, sixteen in all, which marked the first time in mountaineering history that such structures were used for climbing pursuits on McKinley. These huts were built at each of the main camps on the mountain. Thirteen were used for shelters; two for latrines and the final house was used for storage. Washburn and his men preferred the igloos to the tents, most especially during periods of storms or increased snowfall. Hackett would record that the noise of the flapping tents in the wind kept the men awake and that this was naturally not a problem when using the snow huts.

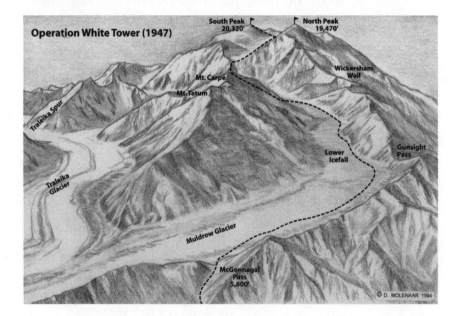

CAMP II

On April 29, Gale, Browne and Hackett continued up through the lower icefall and blazed a trail towards their planned site for Camp II. This section of the ascent was considered very tricky, as numerous crevasses were present, hidden by a thin layer of snow. The men had to cross snow bridges and locate a path wide enough to accommodate the dog team that would follow. George Wellstead and Bill Deeke, the expedition photographers, spent a greater portion of their day taking motion pictures of their fellow climbers. The weather was clear and Hackett and Pearson promised the photographers that there wouldn't be many days with such clear visibility. In order to avoid the avalanche hazards near the base of Mt. Carpe, the party kept to the other side of the glacier and proceeded north. A series of large crevasses were found in a gently rising hummock the team would label 'the Hill of Cracks.' After threading their way through this maze, they emerged on a level plane at the 7,200-foot level. Here they established Camp II.[28]

Bob Craig would note: "Entire party now all moved up to Camp II—The spirit of the group is very high...some of the members have been very cooperative taking loads even though not expected to—it is a real pleasure to work with such people." Hackett's diary reports similar feelings of friendship, the benefits of hard work and clear camaraderie among the men. This was Bill's first taste of serious, high-altitude mountaineering and he loved every minute of it. He had found his calling!

It took a greater part of the day to move supplies and equipment up from Camp I. Craig was correct in noting that nearly every member of the expedition was helping out with the transfer. The dog team could only carry so much, so every available man was fitted with a pack weighing between seventy to ninety pounds. According to Craig, from May 1 to May 6, the party ferried loads between the camps, stockpiling Camp II while weather permitted. Breaking trail grew increasingly difficult due to large snowdrifts. Even the dogs seemed to be slowing the group down, not pulling 'pound for pound.' On May 1, it was snowing so hard that visibility dropped to near zero, a complete whiteout with strong gusts of wind. On the 4th, Craig made three trips from Camp I to Camp II, carrying a ninety-pound pack each time. He reported it was a "grinding" day but that he was well pleased with the snow and ice conditions. Though burdened with a heavy pack, he felt comfortable hiking the distance between camps.

The evening of May 6 saw expedition members commenting on the shorter nights. It was not nearly as dark as it had been back in base camp or even in Anchorage. Evenings now were no darker than twilight.

CAMP III

On the morning of May 7, Jim Gale and Hugo Victoreen began the push for Camp III, near the head of Muldrow Glacier. The Muldrow, which Rev. Hudson Stuck would call "the highway of desire"[29] impressed Hackett immensely:

> "Muldrow Glacier is about half a mile wide at the cirque, the great amphitheater that is formed at the head. Here the great hanging Harper Glacier tumbles down from above. Every few minutes its movement gives the sound not unlike that of distant artillery. Very frequently great masses of ice and snow crash down the vertical rock walls below its overhanging snout giving the impression of a great waterfall. The billowing clouds of snow and pulverized ice blocks move with express-train speed and frequently travel for nearly a half mile beyond the head of Muldrow Glacier."[30]

Later that afternoon, Gale and Victoreen officially established Camp III at the 8,500-foot level.

Browne and Craig departed two days later, intent on finding rock specimens near the head of Muldrow Glacier. Their entire day was spent exploring while completely enveloped in a fog bank. They entered a heavily crevassed section and both men independently discovered hidden crevasses. They were able to extricate themselves and even managed to find the specimens they were looking for near the edge of one of the largest fissures. The men wisely decided to retreat and return to camp. Their sounding efforts also slowed their progress and it was some time before they were safely back in camp.

On May 12th, they set out again, this time for some much needed supplies. They packed loads over 100 pounds that day and set up relay posts along the route. They spent that evening cooking in Igloo 1 and then relaxing and eventually sleeping in Igloo 2.[31]

In the morning, Craig, Browne and others left camp to reach the 15,000-foot level. Deeke and Wellstead, the photographers, were also along for the trip. They shot moving pictures from the 11,000 to 12,300-foot levels. The early morning hours were pleasant enough and visibility was clear. By 10:30 AM however, a heavy fog enveloped the party and soon they encountered more difficult terrain. Craig wrote: "We were faced with a seventy-five-degree glare ice pitch at about 13,000 feet, up in which we cut large steps and at the top established a fixed rope. Above the pitch the going was quite good with alternate firm and drifted snow." On the return journey, the men slowed their pace and enjoyed the scenery. The sun was setting and the alpenglow on Browne Tower was beautiful.

CAMPS IV & V

While an Army C-47 was dropping supplies to Camp III, Hackett and Victoreen established Camp IV on a shoulder on Karstens Ridge. Here, at 11,000 feet, Hackett found a perfect site for the camp.

The following morning, Hackett and Victoreen set out again in an attempt to establish Camp V. Neither was aware just how much work would be required in order to reach this goal. Near 13,000 feet on Karstens Ridge, they discovered a doubled one-quarter-inch manila rope encrusted in ice. Washburn later confirmed it had been used on their 1942 Army expedition. At a position above this line, Hackett and Victoreen were able to unload some of their supplies. They established Cache 5 in a most precarious position. A 3000-foot fall to the Muldrow Glacier was on one side while a 5000-foot exposure was present on the other. This demanding stretch along Karstens Ridge was dubbed the *Coxcomb*.

Hackett later recorded his thoughts about the exhausting job of cutting footsteps in the ice on Karstens Ridge with characteristic frankness:

> "The standard and only route up McKinley starts from McGonagall Pass, climbs up the glacier, scales a snow wall to Karstens Ridge and then becomes a catwalk leading to three great plateaus, like mammoth steps below the twin peaks of McKinley. On the crest of the ridge, that day Hugo and I had to cut or kick 6,000 steps in the crusted snow. That's like taking 3,000 swings at a golf ball and 3,000 kicks at a football. When the mountain drops off 3,000 feet on one side and 5,000 feet on the other, it's not a comfortable job."

Hackett and Victoreen finally arrived at Parker Pass. At the 14,600-foot level, Camp V, or "Parker Pass Camp" was officially established. The Washburns arrived the following morning. Hackett was exhausted but did not share this fact with his companions.

CAMP VI

Jim Gale and Bradford Washburn established Camp VI at the 16,600-foot level on May 22—a remarkable accomplishment as the camp was fixed and constructed during one of the worst storms encountered during the expedition. This storm lasted a full nine days and Hackett, back at Camp V, vividly recorded his observations:

> "It struck with such severity at Camp V that the blowing snow nearly filled the igloo entrance. It was utterly impossible to see anything so we could grope our way the few feet from the tent to the igloo and would be completely covered with snow in the few seconds that we were exposed to the terrific winds. During slight lulls in the storm we could hear the wind against the cliffs on each side of the glacier above us. The roar could well be compared with that of a great waterfall

or the roar of the ocean. The winds were generally from the south but due to our topographical location with Browne Tower directly above us, and the entrance to the Upper Basin at Parker Pass with the east and northeast faces of the mountain exposed to view below us, the winds were apt to come from any direction. If one were caught in a gust that sometimes reached velocities of more than 100 mph it was similar to being sandblasted. It was impossible to see or to stand against and when cover was reached fine snow had penetrated every particle of clothing and had been driven almost to the skin. Snow became plastered on our faces and froze immediately, forming a mask, which was most painful. All of this occurred in a single moment of exposure to these horrible blasts."[32]

For the three climbers, spending nine days in a snow hut took its toll. Tempers frayed; random arguments blew up about all sorts of trivial matters. Mostly, the storm's three hostages avoided collisions by sleeping and reading. They had carried up four magazines and a detective mystery, *The Patients of Maigret*, by Simenon. Many years later Bill could still recite whole pages of that thriller. Toward the last days of the storm, he began to memorize it, perhaps to take his mind off the fact that the food was running low and his arguments with Victoreen were increasing in frequency. Barbara Washburn would oftentimes find herself acting as a referee between the two men, maintaining the peace and keeping the group focused on the tasks at hand. If anyone had cause for alarm it was Barbara herself. She had just married Bradford and this expedition was, in certain ways, an unofficial honeymoon. Now, up high on one of the toughest mountains in the world, her husband was trapped overhead in a storm with Jim Gale while she was below with Hackett and Victoreen. Since the radios were not working at the time, she was unaware that Bradford was safe (for the moment), out of the storm's fury and protected by an emergency snow shelter Washburn and Gale had hastily erected. Neither man could even extend their legs out and were forced to sit upright in the compact structure for two full days.

During two separate lulls in the storm, Hackett and Victoreen hurriedly transported equipment up to "Camp VI", Hackett's name for the diminutive structure Washburn and Gale had constructed. In comparing notes decades later, Washburn found it interesting to learn that Bill, ever the military man, seemed compelled to assign a name to everything they encountered. Most expedition members referred to the camp at Parker Pass, simply as *Parker Pass*. Bill, on the other hand, needed to call it Camp V. Again, Washburn and Gale never thought to call their uncomfortable shelter anything other than 'a miserable place to wait out a storm.' Hackett predictably called the site Camp VI and recorded it in his diary. What Washburn and others called "Denali Pass," Bill would call Camp VII. Washburn believes, as do many others, that it was simply the military training that Hackett was so accustomed to adhering to. Both Washburns recall that each time Bill would add or doff a layer of clothing; he would remove his only set of military collar devices and attach them to his new apparel. Dr. Washburn was puzzled and amazed that in such an environment as McKinley, Bill would take the time (or care) for such appearances. Over time, Washburn grew to understand that Hackett wasn't showing off for his fellow members, he was simply proud of the uniform he wore and took great pride in the fact that he was a representative of the US Army during the trip.

On their second return journey, the storm caught up with Hackett and Victoreen. They found themselves in virtual whiteout conditions. The climbers were separated by sixty feet of rope but were unable to see one another at times. Severe winds whipping across the glacier froze the surface, causing the men to break through the upper crust with every step. Hackett made his way through Parker Pass and eventually into the safety of Camp V.

On May 26, Bill awoke to clear skies for the first time in nearly a week. Accompanied by Victoreen once again, he set out for Camp VI. Before they had gone very far, another storm front moved in. The men bypassed Camp VI altogether and continued on up to the 17,400-foot level. Here, they dumped gasoline and equipment at a point they labeled Cache 6. With their task complete, they began their return march. A third of the way down, the storm intensified. The men waded through waist-deep snow in certain sections of the route. Hackett would state that it would take nearly as long to return, as it had to ascend.[33]

It was evident that Hackett and Victoreen made a compatible climbing team if not ideal tent mates. They had worked well together in fair and foul weather, independently, and more importantly, as a team. When a gasoline and food shortage became apparent at Camp V, these men were dispatched to retrieve the necessary supplies. On May 29, they radioed ahead and arranged a meeting with personnel from Camp III. Hackett and Victoreen would meet with a relief party high up on Karstens Ridge. Though winds were whipping over the mountain slopes, clear skies were present and both parties agreed to hold the meeting. Hackett and Victoreen began their descent after noon in bright sunlight. Craig, Lange and Browne departed Camp III near the same time.

The day's journey would be a difficult one for Hackett. He would write that though he could see the summit, a great plume of snow, half a mile long, was trailing over it towards the North Peak. On the ridge itself, strong winds brought similar snow plumes up from the Traleika side of the mountain. The winds had once again frozen the top layer of snow. With each step the men broke through the upper crust and then found themselves in waist-deep powder snow. They managed the best they could while fixing 350 feet of 5/16-inch rope. This line led from the top of the *Coxcomb* down to a point where 400 feet of rope had already been fixed. A mountaineer could then climb in relative safety, what had been the crux of Karstens Ridge only an hour before.

Hackett and Victoreen met up with Craig, Lange and Browne. The gasoline and supplies were exchanged and both parties turned to retreat to their respective camps. The winds had increased with such severity that Hackett would record, "…had it not been for the hand line we had installed, we would have been blown off the ridge and into the abyss on the Muldrow Glacier side."

Gale and Washburn established Camp VII at the 18,200-foot level on May 26. On an exploratory trip only 150 feet above camp, Washburn found a yellow cargo parachute in between in the rocks. He recognized it as one he had used five years earlier. On this same foray, Gale and Washburn explored Denali Pass, the saddle dividing the north and south peaks.

CAMP VII

As May 30 dawned, Hackett knew a beautiful day was in store for the expedition. It was one of only two completely clear days during the time the team spent on the mountain. Barbara Washburn, Victoreen and Hackett made their move to Camp VII in the afternoon.

In the first few days of June, Hackett began to take notice of the changes associated with increased altitude. He wrote that it was taking an average of two or three days to acclimatize to the camps at higher altitude. He also noted increased irritability, a loss of appetite and even nausea among his fellow team members. "These minor ailments," he wrote, "were overcome after a short while. Many lost their taste for chocolate candy, chocolate beverage, and greasy foods such as sardines and bacon. It was also found that not a great amount of food was consumed at one time, but food seemed to be required at quite frequent intervals throughout each day."

Dr. Washburn would recall that Grant Pearson, the veteran of the group, believed he was having trouble with his heart. "My heart's thumping," Pearson informed the group, "in a way I've never heard it *thump* before."

A brief window of fair weather in late May had enabled an Army B-17 to make several drops to Camp VII. Expedition members from Camp III and V also took advantage of the favorable weather conditions. They made the lengthy journey to Camp VI and immediately started reinforcing the igloos there for the storms they felt certain would come. On June 1, 100 mph winds blew over Camp V. These winds carried off a good portion of Victoreen's cosmic ray research equipment that had recently been dropped via parachute.[34] Victoreen and Sterling spent the next five days working on the remaining equipment.

The morning of June 6 was fairly clear and it was decided to make an attempt for South Peak, the true summit. A majority of the party roped up and began their ascent toward Denali Pass. This particular stretch of the route had never been used before. Washburn and his men were the first mountaineers to see Mt. Foraker and Mt. Hunter from this vantage point. At 19,250 feet, Grant Pearson was forced to retreat. The heart palpitations that had plagued him for a day were the official reason for his return to camp. A successful member of the 1932 party, Pearson regretfully would not be making a return trip to the summit slopes.

The remaining party members, the Washburns, Gale, Craig, Browne, Lange, Deeke and Hackett continued to ascend. They climbed west of Archdeacon's Tower onto a large plateau. Roughly 400 feet below the summit, Washburn called for a quick but necessary meal break. While eating, Hackett looked to the west and saw that the weather was beginning to turn. The summit region of Mt. Foraker, fifteen miles away, was slowly disappearing underneath a lenticular cloud cap.

Just prior to 4:00 PM, Washburn and his team reached the true summit, becoming only the fourth expedition in history to do so. Barbara Washburn became the first woman to ascend the great peak. This marked one of many summits the Washburns would achieve together, both literally and figuratively. Hackett, overjoyed at achieving one of his life-long dreams, was deeply impressed with the view the summit afforded. To the south he noted the 10,000-foot drop-off and the fact that cloud cover blanketed virtually every minor peak less than 10,000 feet in height. These clouds merely appeared to be fog from their elevated position. George Browne had the unique experience of seeing a point 200 vertical feet below the summit. It was here that his father, Belmore, had been turned back in 1912.[35]

Hackett and Lange broke out the surveying instruments they had packed to the summit and erected a hasty station. Washburn took his angles as quickly as possible as 30 mph winds were now blowing in from the south. The party stayed on the summit for nearly an hour and-a-half in temperatures below negative twenty-five degrees Fahrenheit. Their retreat to Denali Pass was hurried as the winds were increasing—another storm was approaching.

June 7 dawned and Hackett looked out his tent flaps to clear blue skies. The storm had passed over the mountain sometime during the night, leaving a dead calm. Washburn, celebrating his birthday, and others decided to take advantage of the clear skies and set out for the North Peak. Washburn, Hackett and Lange were the first to leave. They cut a thousand steps in the ice for those who followed and set a fixed rope in order to assist Mrs. Washburn, Craig, Gale and Sterling who were an hour behind. Dr. Washburn, Hackett and

Lange ascended to the top of a prominent ridge and then descended to reach the plateau separating the south and north peaks. "This brought us" Bill would write, "to the base of the final pitch. We reached the west end of the summit ridge where we looked down upon Wickersham Wall dropping 15,000 vertical feet below us, the second greatest precipice on earth. We continued on to the summit by following a heavily corniced ridge, arriving at 2:30 PM, the second official ascent of this 19,370-foot peak."

Mrs. Washburn, Craig, Gale and Sterling arrived an hour later. They found Washburn observing and Hackett recording angles with the surveying instruments. So calm were the conditions that Washburn set his angle logbook down and the pages didn't even flutter! The party stayed on the summit for nearly three hours, enjoying the clear weather, sunshine and impressive view. Washburn took his new bride aside and informed her that, "If you pushed a basketball off of here, it would fly over 19,000 feet before it stopped bouncing!" While Washburn recorded angles, Lange and other members of the party took photographs of South Peak, some two miles away.

Washburn kept all seven members of the summit party together during the descent to Camp VII. They reached camp near 7:00 PM, having completed what only the Lindley-Liek Expedition had accomplished fifteen years earlier—the summits of both peaks![36]

Washburn then gave the order to begin the official retreat down the mountain. Gale, Lange and Victoreen remained at the high camps in order to continue their cosmic ray research. The rest of the expedition carefully made their way to the mid camps. In between some rocks near Parker Pass, expedition members left a sizable cache of food for the party left behind. Bill would note that this particular cache was located in the same rocks that had held similar supplies for the 1932 and 1942 expeditions. This cache was marked with two attached tent poles and a three-foot high rock cairn. Another tent pole was centered in this rock pile and near its base, Hackett left a thermometer owned by the American Alpine Club.

If Washburn's summit party had found conditions on North Peak ideal, they found the exact opposite during the descent of Karstens Ridge. With ninety-pound packs, members descended the steep *Coxcomb*. During a 7,000-foot descent to Camp III, party members cautiously placed every step, sinking up to their calves or thighs.

Washburn, quoting Bob Reeve, recalled, "It was as cold as the heart of an elderly whore!"

At Camp III the decision to halt for the day was announced. They had originally planned on descending further but the group felt they had done enough for the day. Hackett took this opportunity to reflect over the previous twenty-seven days. He and his companions had spent those weeks above 14,800 feet in temperatures ranging from negative two to negative twenty-nine degrees Fahrenheit!

On June 15, four days after arriving, Washburn and his team departed Camp IV and continued their descent and camped for the night. The following morning they left for base camp at McGonagall Pass. Along the way, Hackett was pleased to see greenery again after seventy days on the mountain. The twenty-one mile hike over tundra to the ranger station at Wonder Lake was uneventful yet pleasant enough for party members. They arrived at the station in the early evening hours of June 18.[37]

Browne, Hackett and the Washburns remained at Wonder Lake while the bulk of the expedition returned to Mt. McKinley Hotel in Anchorage. Lange, Gale and Victoreen, who had been left behind in Camp VII, returned to Wonder Lake on June 30. Their cosmic ray research was complete and they shared their initial findings with Brad Washburn. The remainder of the expedition returned to Anchorage where they individually booked flights to their respective homes.

The members of Washburn's 1947 Mt. McKinley Expedition had every reason to be proud of their accomplishments. Rarely in the history of Alaskan mountaineering had so many of an expedition's pre-set goals been accomplished. They made successful ascents of South and North Peak, a cosmic ray research station had been erected at Denali Pass, moving pictures were taken of expedition members and route conditions, geological specimens were retrieved for future study, Mrs. Washburn became the first woman to summit the peak, and more extensive surveys of the mountain were undertaken.

For Hackett personally, his testing of cold weather clothing, food and equipment were of great benefit to Washburn and the team as a whole. This venture also marked the first of Bill's five expeditions to the mountain. Washburn would remember Bill's services and call upon them again.

CHAPTER V

The White
Sentinel

*"Out across the Chilean plain and over the Pacific Ocean, lay the shadow
of Aconcagua, 200 miles long. As we stopped to watch, the sun slowly
rose behind us. Finally the shadow vanished and the sun hit us
like a hammer-stroke."[1]*

—Bill Hackett

On the outskirts of the village of *Puente del Inca* in western
Argentina, Bill Hackett entered the Andinistas Cemetery. Dedicated
to mountaineers who perished on nearby Cerro Aconcagua, the continent's highest peak, the cemetery made Bill uneasy. He was particularly drawn to the gravestones marking climbers from his own generation: Newell Bent, an American who succumbed to altitude sick-
ness at 19,700 feet in 1936; and Señor and Señora Juan Jorge Link,
who died in 1944, the victims of a blizzard near the summit slopes.[2]
No stranger to the concept of fallen comrades, Hackett was nevertheless moved by the simple plot of earth reserved for those who had
held similar ambitions.[3]

Hackett reflected on the myriad events that had brought him
to this site. Flushed with the success of the 1947 White Tower expedition on McKinley, he had decided to turn his attention to other high-
altitude peaks. He gave serious consideration to making an ascent of
Chimborazo in Ecuador. At 20,703 feet however, this non-technical

ascent would only add 383 feet onto his personal altitude record. What he wanted was a peak that would provide a significant elevation gain, bolster his climbing record, have a historical significance, and provide a route that intrigued him personally. Bill's thoughts turned to Cerro Aconcagua in Argentina. This peak would add over 2,500 feet to his record and more importantly, it was the highest mountain in the Western Hemisphere. This train of thought alone sparked his interest. Had anyone ever made successful ascents of both McKinley and Aconcagua?

Hackett broached the subject with Don Onthank, a former President of the Mazamas. Together they began researching the issue, Onthank in Oregon and Hackett in Georgia. Their research indicated that no climber, American or otherwise, had ever stood on the highest summits of both peaks. Keeping this information to himself and a few trusted friends, he continued his research to be sure of the facts. He had his wife Naydene, who was fluent in Spanish, translate club journals from Latin American publications. Together, they spent over three months researching and came to the same conclusion. No single climber had ever achieved the highest points in North and South America. It was as if his decision had been made for him.[4]

Cerro Aconcagua, at 22,835 feet, is the highest mountain in the western hemisphere and is located in Argentina near the Chilean border. Her very name reveals the fact that even the ancient Incas recognized her geographical importance. The local Indians referred to her as 'Aconca-Hue,' meaning, "it comes from the other side." When the Incan Empire arrived however, they named her *Ancocahuac*, the White Sentinel. When word of this great mountain reached Europe, a German mountaineer named Paul Gussfeldt took up the challenge of organizing and leading an exploratory expedition. In 1883, he departed Santiago with few provisions and even fewer men. During his journey he began to recruit muleteers to his ranks by telling them of buried treasure high on the mountain's slopes. Gussfeldt crossed the Andean crest and set up his base camp on the north side of the mountain. Leaving his porters in camp, he went ahead to reconnoiter a route to the upper slopes. Along the way he discovered a human skeleton lying against the rocks, an apparent victim of a blizzard. Gussfeldt would launch two separate attempts to reach the summit from this vantage point. Surprisingly, his first effort was more fruitful than the second, reaching in excess of 21,000 feet on the Northwest Ridge. For one reason or another, his porters retreated for the low-lands, leaving Gussfeldt alone, ill-equipped and taking opium for an abscessed tooth. The assault would have to be abandoned. Having met with failure only a thousand feet short of his goal, Gussfeldt was unable to console himself with the fact that he had blazed an approach trail and reconnoitered the route that would soon lead to the summit itself.[5]

The first confirmed ascent of Aconcagua was accomplished in 1897, the result of a fierce yet friendly rivalry. Edward Fitzgerald, an Englishman, undertook the leadership of a seven-month expedition to Argentina and the White Sentinel in particular. His contingent, in marked contrast to Gussfeldt's, was well equipped, disciplined and contained one of the most recognized European Alpinists of the day; the Swiss guide, Matthias Zurbriggen. When Fitzgerald arrived in South America in the fall of 1896, he was surprised to learn that he would meet with stiff competition for the summit of Aconcagua. A team of German mountaineers had high hopes of following in Gussfeldt's footsteps. This team believed the efforts of their country-men fourteen years earlier would lead them to victory. The Germans would follow Gussfeldt's already established route while Fitzgerald believed a more practical approach lay farther south, up the Horcones Valley to the northwest face. Both expeditions were simultaneously attacking the mountain, yet neither could easily monitor the progress of the other due to the intervening ridge. After five attempts to reach the summit, Zurbriggen finally achieved the prize, alone, on January 14, 1897. The Germans, who had set up base camp near the same skeleton Gussfeldt had discovered fourteen years earlier, were plagued by foul weather. They eventually abandoned their attempt and retreated back to Santiago.[6]

In the fifty-two years following Zurbriggen's first ascent, only twenty-nine of forty-three expeditions had successfully reached the summit. All of these teams, with the exception of one, had followed the Northwest Ridge Route. In 1934, a Polish team completed an ascent of the glacier on the mountain's northeast slopes.

Though Hackett thrived on establishing new routes, he reluc-tantly made the decision to attempt the standard Northwest Ridge. The reason for such a decision was simple: he had arrived in

Argentina *alone*, having the original intention of making an ascent with Piero Chiglione. A member of the successful 1934 Italian Aconcagua Expedition, Chiglione had to back out of the venture and Bill was forced to look elsewhere for a companion. Major Edward Mueller, a fellow Army Officer, was a competent mountaineer who shared Hackett's newfound fascination with the Andes. Unfortunately for both officers, Mueller was transferred for further training and unable to join the expedition. It appeared as if Bill would be heading south alone.

After obtaining leave from the 3rd Army, Hackett had taken a series of free or low-cost military flights to South America. He had arrived alone but hoped to enlist the assistance of members of the *Club Andinista Mendoza* or officers in the Argentine Mountain Troops. On February 7, Hackett presented his letter of introduction to Lt. Colonel Nicolas Plantamura in Buenos Aires. The Colonel, military *Aide de Camp* to President Juan Perón, had been the first Argentine officer to summit Aconcagua fifteen years earlier. In a matter of minutes, Bill's charm and enthusiasm secured him full military support of his venture. The Colonel promised mules, provisions and more importantly, the assistance of the Argentine Army.[7]

Hackett left the Andinistas Cemetery with four men Colonel Plantamura had persuaded to accompany him: William van Ditmar, Jr., a Dutchman and active member of the *Club Universitario*; Alejandro Cassis, an Italian and member of The Andean Club of Mendoza; Francisco Ibanez, a military cadet at Mendoza's academy; and First Lieutenant Jorge J.C. Mottet who served as a Liaison Officer. Colonel Plantamura had insisted that the Argentine Ministry of War assign an officer of the mountain troops to accompany Hackett, and Mottet was the natural choice.

Standing five-foot eleven and weighing roughly 160 pounds, Jorge Mottet was not an immediately striking figure. He had thin, angular facial features and his ears were slightly larger than normal. His eyes, at times, seemed too close together and his high cheekbones and pointed chin were greatly accented when he smiled. The only physical characteristics he shared with Bill were a high forehead and a neatly trimmed mustache. Though not physically imposing, he possessed incredible strength and endurance. He was an expert skier and taught this skill to the mountain troops under his command. He had made a successful ascent of Aconcagua a year earlier, and Tupungato, a 21,490-foot peak farther south, in 1946. His broken English was often difficult to understand and as a result, Bill communicated with him mainly through sign language.[8] Mottet's guidance, physical strength and humor would be of great assistance to Hackett in the weeks to follow.[9]

On Valentine's Day, the morning after paying their respects at the cemetery, Mottet led Hackett, Cassis and van Ditmar up the slopes of nearby *Banderita Sud*. A minor peak rising 12,631 feet, *Banderita* would serve two purposes; a helpful training ascent to strengthen their limbs; and a vantage point from which to get a better look at their main objective—Aconcagua. The lower slopes of *Banderita* were nothing more than a slag pile but towards the summit they encountered Class IV climbing on stable rock. When Bill reached the summit his vision turned to the north and he saw the sheer south face of the White Sentinel some twenty air miles away. Noting its "massive grandeur," he resolved to depart for her the following morning.[10]

Within twenty-four hours, Hackett became agitated by his teammates' apparent lack of punctuality. As a career Army officer, used to rising early, it distressed him to see his companions still asleep when an 8:00 o'clock reveille had clearly been issued.[11] More importantly, Bill knew the river they would have to cross would be swollen in the afternoon due to sunshine melting the glacier higher up the valley. It took nearly two and-a-half hours to get the expedition members onto the trail and heading for their goal. The following morning the men were also two hours late. This tardiness would be a problem that Bill would never fully understand, let alone resolve.

The party consisted of nineteen heavily laden mules, the five climbers and seven additional individuals. There were two sergeants, Ramon Miguez and Lucas Serrano; four enlisted soldiers, Florentino Cortez, Fidel Garcia, Francisco Lopes and Gregorio Sosa. The twelfth member of the party was a civilian, one Señor Corbella. Bill was in the lead, keeping a close eye on the mules ferrying their supplies. When they crossed the *Rio Horcones* the swift-moving water pushed against the sides of the mules, causing the water to rise on one side. Bill wanted to ensure the provisions he had brought all the way from Georgia remained dry. It wasn't so much the equipment he was concerned about, but rather the rations: tomatoes, peaches, butter and tea. Of special interest was the case of beer, purchased in the expectation of a successful summit assault.[12]

The caravan of mules was led up the Horcones Valley, through the river and eventually up another ford of the *Rio Horcones Inferiore*. Bill alternated between hiking and riding a mule. He was impressed with the sheer walls of the valley, the very walls Sir Martin Conway had called "rugged and ruinous, like the shattered crest of a falling castle."[13] If the party had departed camp when Bill had origi- nally intended, they would have spent half their day hiking under clear skies. As it was, the sky grew overcast near noon and afternoon showers eventually caused the team to stop for the night at 10,800 feet, merely nine miles from *Puente del Inca*. They set up their tents in a slightly sheltered area now known as Confluencia Camp, a level plain where the Horcones Valley and the run-off from the Lower Horcones Glacier converge.

On the morning of the sixteenth, the caravan continued their journey up the valley. The first eight miles were level and pleasant to traverse and Hackett could spend less time watching his foot place- ments and more on the scenery around him. As the miles passed by he was afforded clear views of *Mt. de los Dedos*, *Mt. Catedral* and *Mt. Cuerno*. Afternoon clouds began to obscure these lower summits how- ever and by the time the expedition passed an abandoned base camp, snow had started to fall. This camp, known as *Antigua Plaza de Mulas*, had been used by several of the expeditions following Fitzgerald's established route. Mottet advised Hackett that a slightly higher base camp could be established on a level plain called *Plaza de Mulas*. To reach this site the mules would have to be led up a steep pitch and through a labyrinth of rock fall debris. Mottet assured the team that favorable ground was just ahead.[14]

At 13,800 feet, *Plaza de Mulas* was a level and spacious shoul- der of rock that could accommodate several expeditions at once. The mules were unloaded and the provisions were laid out. Ten of the mules were moved into a man made rock corral. Sergeant Miguez, accompanied by three soldiers, brought nine of the mules back down the Horcones Valley. They would descend to *Puente del Inca* for the remainder of their supplies and return to base camp the following afternoon. The firewood that had been carefully brought up the valley was now put to use in a stone kitchen that had been constructed by a previous expedition. After supper, the flags of the United States and Argentina were simultaneously raised over base camp.

Hackett awoke the following morning to clear skies and an air temperature of negative four degrees Fahrenheit. Though the team knew they needed to rest for a day in order to acclimate, they couldn't help but explore their new surroundings. Of particular interest was the Horcones Superior Glacier. Mottet, Ibanez and van Ditmar accompanied Bill up to the main icefalls. Here they studied some of the world's finest examples of *nieve penitentes*, large ice structures towering nearly fifty feet high. Bill would later write to a friend: "Great boulders were perched atop thin columns of snow looking as if some giant had carefully placed them there. The Andean sun had done this, melting down the wintry snows and transforming them into an icy fairyland." It was an enjoyable day but Bill could barely wait for the chance to continue the ascent.[15]

On February 18, ten men and thirteen mules departed base camp, bound for higher ground. The rock they traversed was as uneven and unstable as that in the valley below. The mules, sure-footed at lower elevations, seemed to be having greater difficulty as the journey progressed. The altitude was beginning to affect the beasts as well as the men. Their ascent was too rapid, in fact, and some of the men suffered as a result. When they stopped for the night, they discovered Mottet had led them up 7,200 vertical feet![16] The Argentine officer had chosen the *Refugio Plantamura*, a wooden shelter, for their evening quarters. At 20,997 feet, Bill had already exceeded the height of McKinley and therefore, every step forward would only add to his personal altitude record. He was pleased with the site and thought it would prove to be an ideal launching stage for the summit assault. Another day or two at a lower camp might have enabled other party members to visit the upper slopes. As it stood, several of them were beginning to suffer from the effects of the thinning atmosphere. "No great amount of food was consumed (that night)," Bill would later note, "Since the appetites of all members were retarded by the altitude. Early in the evening, I moved van Ditmar into the Refugio as he was quite ill from the effects of the elevation." Serrano and Cassis, who shared another tent nearby, were also feeling ill. In marked contrast, Hackett spent a comfortable evening alone in his tent, remarking that he had a very restful evening and looked forward to the summit assault.[17]

⋯ ⋯ ≡◆≡ ⋯ ⋯

In the morning, Hackett checked the weather. There wasn't a cloud in sight and there was only a moderate breeze from the west. The temperature was negative seventeen degrees Fahrenheit. Bill took a moment to appreciate the moment. The shadow of Aconcagua extended far into Chile to the west and the weather seemed perfect for climbing. At 7:00 AM, he emerged from the tent and started to wake his companions. There were no plans for the day other than resting up for a summit attempt the following morning, weather permitting. At some point during the next three hours, while the expedition members ate breakfast, Bill made a decision that would affect them all. With the presence of fair weather, he had decided to make his summit bid.

If Hackett was hoping for a unanimous burst of applause, it was not forthcoming. Serrano, Cassis, Ibanez and van Ditmar all had to force-feed themselves. Cassis was even temporarily snow blind. They each stated they would be unable to continue, at least for the present day. Only Mottet and Serrano, calmly sipping cups of hot Ovaltine, were ready for the final push. Mottet, more than anyone else present, knew just how close their camp was to the summit.[18]

The national flags of the United States and Argentina were carefully rolled and stowed for the journey ahead. Bill double-checked his clothing and equipment, as did Mottet and Serrano in the confines of the shelter. Together, they departed camp and headed for the upper slopes. Near the outset, they were plagued by the unstable rock, which makes up the greater portion of the mountain proper. Even when they reached a lengthy stretch of ice their progress was delayed. Hackett had to cut steps in the ice for the men who followed. This task caused the fingers on Hackett's right hand to show the initial signs of frostbite. Mottet had to massage Bill's hand on several occasions in order to restore circulation.[19] During this portion of the ascent, Bill took the opportunity to look to the west. He would later claim that the view he beheld was reward enough for making such a journey. "Out across the Chilean plain," he would write, "and over the Pacific Ocean, lay the shadow of Aconcagua, 200 miles long.

As we stopped to watch, the sun slowly rose behind us. Finally the shadow vanished and the sun hit us like a hammer-stroke."[20] With the intensity of the sun, Bill thought it strange that it was still seventeen degrees below zero!

Serrano had to stop suddenly. He found the altitude too much to handle and reluctantly asked to be left behind. It was agreed that he would wait where he was for the summit party to return. As Hackett and Mottet passed the 22,000-foot level, they were conscious of the fact that Hackett had just passed the previous American altitude record held by J.G. King, a man who made five attempts to reach the summit. "(Mottet and I) then entered a large couloir," Bill wrote, "filled with enormous stones, all resting dangerously near the angle of repose. The elevation began to have great effect upon us, and we were forced to rest after every five or six steps. I was in good condition physically as my strength was holding up well, and before realizing it, I found myself well in advance of Mottet."

When Hackett arrived on top of the summit ridge, he paused to get a better look at his surroundings. He glanced below him to make sure Mottet was still advancing and safe, and then looked towards the southeast. He could look straight down the 10,000-foot South Face to the Horcones Inferiore Glacier. Bill hiked up an additional 150 feet and saw the true summit a short distance away. Here he paused to wait for Mottet. Hackett would acknowledge that he was personally feeling the effects of the altitude at this point. He found himself staggering and had to concentrate before placing every step. Mottet caught up with him and they turned to look towards the true summit. "That's it!" Bill exclaimed. The two walked arm-in-arm for over fifty feet.[21]

At 6:00 PM, February 19, 1949, they reached the summit together. With the Western Hemisphere far below them, they shook hands and then embraced. Though Bill was conscious of the mountaineering feat he had just accomplished he nonetheless found himself yawning. He had never felt so tired before in his life.[22] While Mottet located the summit register book near a cairn, Hackett started taking pictures to record the moment. The flags were unfurled and each man in turn held them aloft in the high winds. Bill even left a smaller American flag inside the register box for posterity. Mottet removed an Italian flag, one Bruno Caneva had left behind on a previous ascent. Mottet apparently wanted the ensign as a souvenir. When it was time to sign their names in the log, Hackett found it hard to pen his name and his signature seemed to wander all over the page. As he had retrieved some rocks from the summit of Mt. McKinley, he knelt down to do the same in Argentina.[23]

After spending only twenty minutes on the summit, they turned to begin their descent. The ice corridor that Bill had easily traversed during the ascent was now a formidable obstacle. "The descent of the couloir," he remarked, "was one of the most tedious and tiring jobs I can ever recall, for to pick our way through this maze of rocks without upsetting some seemed interminable." The work was even harder for Hackett as he had frozen three fingers. They were now beginning to thaw; a pain too many mountaineers from Bill's generation had to endure. After they were clear of the couloir and on more stable terrain, their descent rate became more rapid. They arrived at the Plantamura Shelter and rested briefly. Their teammates had departed camp, as planned, several hours earlier.

They arrived in Plaza de Mulas Base Camp near midnight, some five and-a-half hours after leaving the summit. They had ridden mules partway down in order to speed up the nearly 9,000 vertical feet required to reach base camp.[24] They were met with a hero's welcome from the remaining expedition members. The case of beer was opened and the team readily polished it off in record time.[25]

After returning to *Puente del Inca*, Hackett and his team had continued on to Mendoza. From there he and Mottet took a plane to Buenos Aires and then a cab to the U.S. Military Attaché. They met with Argentine Defense Minister, General Humberto Sosa Molina. When Hackett emerged from that meeting, he had another scheduled for the following morning with the President of Argentina, Juan Perón. At this informal meeting, Bill had presented the president with the American flag he had carried to the summit and exchanged pleasantries.[26] On March 2, Hackett found himself sitting outside the White Room of the Governor's House. Though Mottet was at his side, Bill was anxiously awaiting a second audience with Perón. Bill was at a loss to explain why he had now been summoned a second time. He thought everything had gone well at that earlier meeting. Why would Perón call for a second?

The summit team was dressed in their finest military uniforms. Mottet's white Argentinean Army uniform only accentuated his slim build. His epaulets seemed too long for his shoulders and his high-collar shirt revealed he had a small neck. Bill was in his standard Army uniform, complete with the 10th Mountain Division patch on his right shoulder.

"Here we go." said Bill as a side door opened up. He and Mottet were ushered into the White Room.

Hackett was amazed at the number of government officials present at the ceremony. In addition to the president and Evita Perón, there were the Ministers of the Executive Power, chiefs of the armed forces, heads of the diplomatic missions, military, air and naval attaches of different American missions and representatives of their Congress and Supreme Court. Bill recognized some faces from the US Embassy as well. Argentine General Sosa Molina then approached Hackett and Mottet with outstretched arms. He proceeded to decorate them each with the Gold Condor, Argentina's most coveted military mountaineering decoration. Bill was the first foreigner to receive such an honor. Evita and President Perón then welcomed the climbers.[27]

President Perón, dressed in a light blue silk suit, gave a speech that moved Bill both as a soldier and a mountaineer:

> "Lieutenant, the feat that you have just accomplished on Aconcagua has two meanings for me, which concern me in a personal way and as an Argentine official. That is why I want to combine the two acts in this opportunity, giving you two souvenirs; one in the name of a great movement, which I lead, and the other in the name of General Perón, as you, a man of the mountains. In the first sense, we usually give this *Medalla Peronista*, with which we want to reward the acts, which honor man in his fight against nature and for the perfection of mankind. That is why I wish that this medal will always remind you of having climbed Aconcagua in the Argentine Republic, which makes you the friend, companion and comrade of all Argentine mountaineers, and which especially presents you before our country as a man of enterprise always near to our hearts. And now to the personal part. I myself am an old mountaineer. Among my

souvenirs from the mountains I kept my old ice ax
with which I climbed Mont Blanc and which I used in
all my trips through the Argentine mountains. I
thought that it could be in no better hands than in
those of the American comrade, and he can use it in
the American mountains as a reminder of the
Argentine mountains and that it may serve to unite
more each day the mountaineers of both countries. I
wish that this ice ax may accompany the Lieutenant
with the same safety and good luck it has accompanied me for many years in our mountains."[28]

Hackett, a man normally prepared for any contingency, was
left speechless.

Later that same afternoon, Hackett was reclining aboard a
Pan-American Constellation, bound for Montevideo. He couldn't
help but replay the events of the previous four years in his mind:
service in the 10th Mountain Division, Operation White Tower and
now his greatest achievement—Cerro Aconcagua and the attainment
of the highest summits in both North and South America. For a man
who had diligently studied the history of mountaineering, it gave
him a great sense of satisfaction to be *making* history. He additionally took pride in the fact that his most recent adventure had been his
brainchild, from inception, organization to execution. In the Army
there were always plenty of superiors. On McKinley there was no
denying that Dr. Washburn was in charge. On Aconcagua however,
Bill called the shots, and the results of his efforts went further than
even he first imagined. As the first climber in history to achieve the
highest summits of North and South America, Bill began to wonder
how he could top such a feat.

In a letter to a friend, Hal Burton, Hackett described his
adventures on Cerro Aconcagua and that he had set himself the
goal of the Seven Summits—the highest peak on each of the seven
continents; "I still have a lot of mountains to go up. There are five
more continents on my list of high spots—Australia, Antarctica,
Europe, Asia and Africa. In Australia, the biggest peak is Kosciusko,

only 7,328 feet high. In Antarctica, it is Thorvals Nilssen (Vinson Massif), 15,400. In Europe, the topmost point is on Mt. Elbrus, 18,450 feet. Unfortunately, that's in Russia. In Africa, Kilimanjaro rises to 19,717 feet from the Equatorial jungles. And, in Asia, of course, is Mt. Everest, which nobody has ever climbed. If my luck holds out, maybe I'll get them all. If not, I'll still keep trying for new mountain records. It's the hardest kind of work around, but I think it's the most worthwhile." Hackett had therefore pioneered the Seven Summits dream over three decades before Dick Bass and Pat Morrow made headlines achieving it.

━━◆❈◆━━

CHAPTER VI

The Dark Continent

*"The mountains of Africa are like no other I had ever seen.
The surrounding bushland seemed to stretch for miles and then suddenly
these peaks would rise to incredible altitudes. The contrast between the ice
and the jungle was fascinating!"[1]*

—Bill Hackett

In 1950, after numerous close calls in the mountains, Bill Hackett thought his number might finally be up. During a flight from the island of Terceira to French Morocco, he encountered some of the worst air turbulence he had ever experienced. He was aboard a U.S. Army C54, heavily loaded with cargo, bound for Craw Field on the northwest coast of Africa. Standing in near darkness, grasping canvas straps hanging from the overhead of the compartment, Hackett attempted to maintain his balance. The plane lurched and yawed so much that he was continually tossed about the interior, tripping over sacks of mail and non-perishable provisions. The plane would drop fifty feet in elevation on occasion, sending anything not tied down flying about the compartment. The other passengers, mainly military dependents, fared far better than Bill. Wives and children of American servicemen were huddled together in the center of the compartment. As a result, only those on the exterior of the ring were pelted with debris. Flashes of lightning repeatedly illuminated the

interior of the cabin. During one of these brief periods of illumination, Hackett noticed a group of sailors near the back, apparently
unconcerned with all of the activity. For a flight that was technically
free, Bill was definitely paying a price for his transport to the
Dark Continent.[2]

There was another sudden flash of light, quickly followed by
a thunderous noise. When they eventually landed and the exterior of
the aircraft was inspected, crewmen discovered the nose had been
struck by lightning. It was an inauspicious beginning to one of Bill's
most memorable adventures.

There was quite a commotion near the entrance to the Kibo
Hotel in Marangu, Kenya. Bill was busy checking the contents of a
half-dozen equally weighted loads for his porters to carry. Natives
looked on in amazement as this silly American repeatedly lifted the
sacks and boxes to ensure they were properly balanced. Hackett was
not in the best of moods. His hired hands were running late, remind-
ing him of his sometimes sluggish companions on Aconcagua. He
learned that many of his current porters were tribesmen from the
local villages, hired by the staff of the hotel to accompany tourists to
the high camps of Kilimanjaro. Mrs. Annie Breuhl, the owner of the
hotel, had dispatched her head porter to round up his colleagues in
the nearby village. With a cigarette dangling from her mouth and a
glass of whisky in one hand, she watched Bill try to make headway
with the natives. She was completely entertained. "Look yank!" she
finally called out, "You're not even going to make it to base camp the
way you're going!" Mrs. Breuhl was kind enough to provide Bill with
a list of fifty Swahili names and phrases that she felt would be useful
to him in the week to come

"Time means little to these people," Hackett would say, "and
the concept of schedules is alien to them." When the team was finally assembled, he started a round of introductions with the use of
hand gestures. He discovered that his head porter, Daudi Jonathan,
was an experienced guide with several ascents to the high camps.
Siara Kisaka would act as cook and Mariko, Sitefano and Eliangiringa
would perform general guide duties and ferry the bulk of supplies.[3]

Mrs. Breuhl, Hackett would recall, had one of the most frank and honest personalities he would ever meet during his travels. She and her late husband had migrated from Germany several years earlier. They established the end-of-the-road hotel. Small, clean and rustic, it served its purpose. Rough and tough, she swore like a trooper, chain-smoked and liked her booze. Bill enjoyed the time he spent with her and missed her cooking soon after departing the hotel.

There was a secondary reason for Hackett's eagerness to hit the trail. He had met two novice British climbers the previous evening and their conversation naturally turned to Kilimanjaro. Bill had played it smart and let his drinking companions speak their minds. It became apparent to him that these climbers, though well meaning, were no mountaineers in the true sense of the word. Bill was polite and amicable but did not divulge the fact that he was also heading for the great peak. He bid farewell to his companions and took every precaution to avoid contact with them again. He did not want to offend them, but he simply didn't need to be held back by a pair of novice hikers. He had a strict schedule to keep if he intended to climb Mt. Kenya as well.[4]

With the exception of continual tardiness, Hackett couldn't have asked for a better team of porters. All five were from the Masai and Wanderobo tribes that lived in the region. Daudi Jonathan, the head porter, appeared to resemble his role. Just under six feet in height, he was broad shouldered and carried himself well. His head was always held high, revealing sharp and authoritative features. Siara Kisaka, the cook, was the eldest of the porters. Soft-spoken and always ready to lend a hand, he was one of the most popular members of the group. The three porters: Eliangiringa, Mariko and Sitefano, were in their early twenties, eager to please and make a name for themselves, Sitefano being the most energetic of the trio. He was confident in his abilities and as eager to proceed as Bill himself. Dressed in simple yet practical cloth shorts and shirts, the porters carried heavier coats for the upper camps. Siara was the only one who wore sandals, the balance of the party opting to make the ascent barefoot!

"Just a moment," Bill said to his new friends, "I want to check something out. Load up and I'll be right back." With that said, he jogged around to the back of the hotel and scrambled up to the summit of a small hill no more than forty feet in height. When he turned around to face south, he could see right over the thatched roof of the hotel. In the distance, he could see Kilimanjaro and the summit of Kibo in particular. If everything went as planned, he would stand on her summit in a few days and look down upon the hotel, adding yet another of the Seven Summits to his record. Only one thing concerned him. He noticed that there was a considerable amount of snow crowning the upper reaches of the mountain.[5] Hackett wasn't simply after the summit, he wanted to explore Kibo Crater and climb both the smaller summit and Mawenzi if time permitted. With these goals, he believed he would need the assistance of at least one of his porters. Seeing their lack of footwear, Bill grew concerned that he alone would be making a bid for the summit.

Twenty minutes later, Hackett was a world away from the comfort and amenities the hotel had to offer. He and his men were walking along a wide dirt trail bordered by native huts. Cultivated plots of earth surrounded these houses and farmers acknowledged their passing with either a nod or simple smile. Hackett stopped at the last hut as he spied some bananas. He purchased a substantial amount of the fruit and ate several during the following three miles. Still not satisfied, he chewed on sticks of sugar cane. As they continued their march, the path ahead narrowed to only a few inches and within a mile they were in the jungle proper. This was dense equatorial forest with shoulder-high fronds and lianas that brushed their limbs as they walked by. Water droplets fell from overhead ferns and fed the lush undergrowth. Bill noticed elephant tracks through the underbrush but wasn't too worried about wildlife encounters. He and his men were making so much noise walking through the jungle they even scared away the nearby blue monkeys. Bill's only concern at the moment was avoiding the Giant Groundsel; a sizable plant crowned with rows of thorns and spiked leaves. These plants towered eight to ten feet off the forest floor and sometimes drooped to one side. Hackett had been warned to avoid these and other such obstacles along the approach march.[6]

As the team continued to make their gradual ascent up the mountain's southeast slopes, they passed through the equatorial zone and entered the higher ericaceous region. Marked by more sparse foliage, Bill found this belt of vegetation more appealing for several reasons. He could now avoid the troublesome root system that had caused him so many slips and stumbles and he could see more of his surroundings due to the decrease in trees and ground cover. He liked the odd contrast between the alpine meadow and desert terrain. Acacias and thorn bushes were standing right next to stretches of heather and grass. The land was getting dryer, that much was certain, but the men's feet would slide from an area of dry broken soil right into mud puddles. Hard-packed earth was slowly turning into the rock and scree Hackett was more accustomed to.

At 6:00 PM, they arrived at their evening camp. The Bismarck Hut, constructed by a German team years earlier, lay at the edge of a clearing near the 9,000-foot level.[7] The hut was a sound, stone structure with a corrugated metal roof. Within its walls were two sleeping quarters, a spacious kitchen, tables, benches and a wood burning stove. Fresh water was provided by a nearby spring. A secondary hut was reserved for the porters and a communal outhouse was an added luxury. Siara started preparing a supper of pumpernickel sandwiches, boiled eggs and tea. During the course of the meal, Hackett continued to review his objective.

At 19,341 feet, Kilimanjaro had an impressive altitude but offered few technical difficulties. The Breach Wall, a sheer rock face on the mountain's western slopes was the most demanding route the peak had to offer. This wall was still virgin territory in the mid-twentieth century, but Hackett decided to forgo a first ascent attempt and follow an already established route.[8]

As usual, Hackett had thoroughly researched the history of mountaineering on Kilimanjaro. In the mid-nineteenth century, reports of snow near the equator had reached the halls of London's Alpine Club.[9] This was met with great skepticism at first. Exploration of the Andes had proven the existence of snow near the equator but European climbers refused to believe Africa held peaks high enough to keep a mantel of snow year-round. By the 1880s several Christian missionaries had made the ascent to the saddle between Kibo, the true summit, and Mawenzi, a smaller yet just as impressive volcanic cone. In 1889, German geographer Hans Meyer organized an expedition to East Africa. With sixty-five porters, he marched to Marangu near Kilimanjaro's southeastern slopes. Once there, he took a smaller team up to the saddle and higher camps. When they reached Kibo's crater rim, they hiked to its highest point and called it Kaiser

Wilhelm Peak, a name still in use when Bill arrived in Africa sixty years later.[10]

On Wednesday morning, February 8, Bill finished a cup of coffee outside the Bismarck Hut. Mariko and Sitefano were busy gathering firewood to be used for fuel above timberline. Hackett led the team single-file for three and-a-half miles through dense foliage. Though he was an experienced outdoors man, Bill nonetheless found himself tripping over roots and stones. He was amazed that his bare-foot companions appeared to have little trouble navigating through the bush.

When Bill had approached large peaks in the past, there were other mountains nearby to occupy his vision. This was not the case in Africa. Kilimanjaro stood alone and aloof, rising over 15,000 feet above the surrounding territory. As a result, Bill's attention was drawn to the bush land surrounding him. During this portion of the ascent they would cross four streams while ascending through ever thinning brush. Hackett particularly enjoyed this section as he ate oranges and bananas while the porters continued to gather firewood.

At 1:20 PM, they arrived at Peters Hut at the 12,500-foot mark.[11] The team was more impressed with this location. There were four corrugated huts, two of which held wood paneling. Bill chose the smaller of the two units to spend the night. This structure had a few bunks that he could stretch out on. The porters occupied a third hut and the smallest unit was used as an outhouse.

Hackett had a pleasant evening meal. The skies, which had been overcast during the day, began to clear and revealed an impressive sunset. Siara had prepared steak, potatoes, gravy and pumpernickel bread with marmalade. Bill enjoyed this fare while bringing his diary up to date. When he was unable to finish everything on his plate, Siara consumed the scraps so as not to waste any food.[12]

When Bill retired for the evening, he bade his companions good night and entered his hut. He strung a makeshift clothesline from one end of the structure to the other, hanging his socks and other articles of wet clothing on the line in order to dry. He had great difficulty in falling asleep as he had convinced himself that he was hearing noises from outside the cabin. When these unidentified squeals appeared to be closer, and in fact, within the confines of the shelter, Bill sat upright and reached for his flashlight.

Daudi, Siara, Mariko and the rest of the porters were sitting around the campfire for warmth. They were planning to retire in a few minutes but they waited to make sure their employer was comfortable. To their amazement, Hackett flung the door to his hut open quite suddenly. Cursing and mumbling something under his breath, he tossed two sizable objects near the edge of the fire. The porters recognized them as two large rats with broken necks. "Now I can sleep!" Bill retorted to no one in particular, slamming the door behind him.[13]

In the morning, Hackett was eating breakfast when he noticed Mariko was grabbing his chest. Bill asked if he was feeling well and Mariko merely complained he was having trouble with his heart. It was apparent that the young man was having heart palpitations, brought on, no doubt, by the increased altitude.[14] Bill offered to have the man remain behind but Mariko insisted on proceeding. Hackett assigned him a lighter load and retained a constant vigil over him on the path ahead. Only a mile from the hut, Mariko stopped suddenly and knelt down. Bill rushed to his side. It was agreed that Mariko was ascending too fast and so, he was ordered back to the hut to rest and acclimate. The loads were redistributed and the party continued the ascent.

Hackett was very impressed with the rock saddle that separated the Mawenzi and Kibo volcanic peaks. They were now at an elevation, which would not support plant life. He and the men enjoyed corn on the cob while taking in the view. In the distance, on the lower slopes of Kibo, they saw two small structures. One was Kibo Hut, their current objective.

Near two in the afternoon they approached the 16,000-foot mark and the Kibo shelters. As before, Hackett had first choice of accommodations and selected a cabin that would normally house four. He had the use of a table, two benches and a wood stove that had surprisingly seen much use. He ate some jam sandwiches while watching the porters set up in an adjacent hut. Bill advised the men that as soon as they had set up camp they should rest for the remainder of the day. They needed to conserve their strength for the final push to the summit.

Dinner that evening was one Hackett would remember for years to come. He had shown Siara how to use his Coleman stove and pressure cooker. The porter was amazed and overjoyed to witness such culinary advancements. While his child-like wonder of modern innovations made Hackett chuckle, something happened that caused Bill to be struck dumb. Daudi, his head porter, suddenly announced he wanted to accompany him to the summit.

"I don't know my friend," Bill eventually responded while pointing at the porter's bare feet, "I'm not sure you're ready for the ice and snow." Whether Daudi understood Bill's words was unclear, but his employer's finger pointing relayed a clear message. The porter held up both hands, as if to advise Bill to remain seated. He then darted into the nearby cabin. He emerged a moment later with a rucksack. From its confines he produced a pair of German climbing boots, leftovers from the Second World War. Hackett laughed aloud and then nodded in agreement—Daudi would be allowed to complete the ascent.[15]

On Friday, February 10, Hackett woke Daudi at 1:45 AM. Together, they quietly begin preparations for their summit bid. Breakfast consisted of boiled eggs and bread. While eating, they stuffed rucksacks with provisions and equipment. Bill stuck his head out the cabin door in order to check the weather and was greeted with a cloudless sky, filled with stars and a half-moon. It would be a cold ascent, he thought to himself, best to dress in layers. After helping Daudi shoulder his pack, Bill glanced at his watch. It was 2:30 and time to start the final march.[16]

For the next hour-and-a-half, they made their way up a steady slope of scree and loose boulders. Bill hated this 1,500-foot stretch of rhomb porphyry lava. For every step forward he slid backward several inches. Using his ice ax as a walking stick, he did his best to maintain his balance. In the decades to follow he would refer to this stretch as simply, "not to my liking," but at the time he could only curse and complain about the terrain. Most of his words were lost on Daudi as he spoke only rudimentary English. The porter, with his prized German Army boots, rarely spoke but when he did it was to warn his companion of loose boulders or a particularly nasty pothole.

The climbers sought a brief respite in Hans Meyer Cave, an alcove that Bill recognized from some climbing literature he had studied before arriving in Africa. Both men sat with their legs drawn up to their chests in order to conserve body heat. A moderate wind from the west, combined with the chilled damp air made the men shiver uncontrollably. Within a few minutes, Hackett noticed his feet were going numb. It was only then that he realized that his bent knees were constricting the blood flow to his lower limbs. It was time to keep moving.[17]

The terrain ahead grew steeper. Another 1,500 feet of loose rock brought them to Gillman's Point on the eastern edge of the summit crater rim. The view from this vantage point was fantastic! To the east the first signs of the pending sunrise appeared over the black crags of Mawenzi. To the southeast lay the plains of what is today, Tanzania. Though the skies remained clear, mist enshrouded the view to the west. The only object to arise above the fog was the rounded bulk of Kibo, Kilimanjaro's true summit.

It was a strange contradiction to be so cold after suffering the heat of the bush land below. Hackett became aware that he hadn't brought enough clothing to ward off the chill. There was far more snow at these higher elevations than he had at first anticipated. As a man accustomed to continual movement in the mountains, it must have been difficult for him to sit still during any delays in his well-laid plans. He and Daudi were forced to remain at Gillman's Point and await more sunlight. They waited a full twenty-five minutes before Hackett felt confident enough that the journey ahead would be adequately illuminated.

They left the edge of the crater rim and began to cross the summit crater in a clockwise direction. Though the terrain ahead was even more tiresome than that previously encountered, Bill enjoyed it thoroughly. Lengthy stretches of scree would oftentimes disenchant him but presented with a series of varying natural obstacles at high altitude was always his forte. Weary of the loose gravel, he jumped at the chance to use the ice and snow that he was more accustomed to. Within ten minutes however, he changed his mind. After he and Daudi waded through waist-deep fresh powder, they realized it was only impeding their progress. More annoyed than angry, they switched back to the rock gendarme known as Bismarck Tower.[18] Sharp, two to three-foot vertical steps were easily hurdled but when a sudden descent of equal elevation was required, the pair of climbers ran into trouble. While attempting to gain better footing, the heels of their boots would dislodge large flakes of rock and send them both to their knees or buttocks. Such poor quality of rock reminded Bill of conditions he had encountered on Mount Hood back home. Only now he was dealing with an added 7,000 feet of elevation!

At 7:50 AM, Hackett and Daudi arrived on the summit of Kibo, the highest point in all of Africa.[19] Hackett had become the first climber in history to successfully reach the summits of the highest mountains on three continents. This achievement was foremost in his mind. Before he snapped even a single picture, his immediate concern was locating the summit logbook to record his ascent. Daudi found the locker among some sizable boulders. Bill opened the small metal trunk and retrieved the large leather volume that was stored within. He entered his name and handed his mechanical pencil to Daudi. The porter happily made his mark.[20]

Daudi Jonathan had every reason to be happy. On an economic level, he would be able to charge his clients more money for similar journeys. His friends could prove they had been to the high camps but only Daudi could document that he had reached the summit. Such an achievement would also ensure that he retained leadership of any further ventures on the mountain. Hackett was pleased to discover his porter could now support a family on his future earnings. As for Bill himself, he was well aware of what this particular summit would mean back home. He had gained acceptance into the tight-knit league of high altitude mountaineers with his ascent of McKinley three years earlier. After Aconcagua, he gained more respect for organizing and executing a high altitude ascent. Yet here on the Dark Continent, Bill Hackett had clearly announced his presence as well as his intentions. Climbers from the Seattle-based Mountaineers to London's Alpine Club would now have to take notice of the upstart American. His dream of reaching the Seven Summits was clearly taking shape.[21]

At times it seemed as though there were two Bill Hacketts. One was a true mountaineer who was thrilled with new and engaging climbing endeavors, while the other was a self-professed *Peak Bagger*. Hackett's primary reason for traveling to Africa was to achieve its highest summit and continue working towards his mountaineering goals. The true climber inside however craved the second highest, and yet far more fascinating peak—Mount Kenya, 120 miles to the north. As soon as his primary objective had been obtained, he quickly set about achieving the second.

Mount Kenya had an incredibly brief but rich history of mountaineering. The local Kikuyus considered the mountain the resting place of Ngai, the god of all creation and called her *Kerenyaga*, "the Mountain of Brightness." They considered the snow on her sides an unnatural, spiritual substance as it disappeared from sight as soon as you brought some down to lower elevations. When Hackett arrived in British East Africa in 1950, the mountain had rarely been climbed since the first ascent in 1899. As far as African scholars can tell, the indigenous people made no attempt to scale its heights. These included, but were not limited to the Wanderobo hunters, the Masai, or the Wakikuyu. They saw no purpose in deliberately entering a region that presented even harsher elements than those encountered in the bush land below. The mountain's isolation changed overnight in the summer of 1899, when Halford John Mackinder, a reader in Geography at Oxford University, led a massive expedition to the base of Mount Kenya.[22] Mackinder and his Italian guides Cesar Ollier and Joseph Brocherel not only achieved the first ascent of the highest point on the mountain, but would go on to name its two highest summits after prominent members of the Masai tribe—Batian and Nelion. British climbers, Percy Wyn-Harris and Eric Shipton (whom Bill greatly admired) were next on the scene, making the second ascent of Mount Kenya thirty years after its initial conquest. Shipton had arrived in the region to work on a coffee plantation while Wyn-Harris had been involved with the government of Kenya as early as 1926.[23]

Bill Hackett and guide, Raymond Hook approached Mount Kenya via horseback and covered over eighteen miles of bush land on Valentine's Day, 1950. They rode through stretches of open country prior to entering thick forests of dense bamboo. Hackett felt it necessary to duck on occasion and hug the horse's mane to avoid being swept off his saddle by low hanging branches. Game trails interlaced the dense growth, and their present trail became narrow and at times, seemingly non-existent. They rode up into the Burguret Valley where they encountered giant groundsel and lobelia flourishing. With five additional miles of open terrain behind them, they came upon Two Tarn Hut at 14,800 feet.

Located on the shore of one of two lakes, the rustic cabin had been constructed and owned by the Mountain Club of Kenya. From this location, climbers could embark on a wide variety of rock scrambles on and around Mount Kenya. Arthur Firmin of the Mountain Club of Kenya had organized an ascent of the mountain and Hackett had been able to join this team. When Bill arrived at Two Tarn Hut, Firmin introduced him to the brothers, James and Mickey Moore, Irene Pereira, David Wilson, Lorna Constantine and Dr. H.C. Perry. They had started their journey a day earlier, but had taken two days to cross the eighteen miles of jungle that Bill had just covered in a day. Over tomato soup, stew bread and tea, the group became acquainted. They shared their tales of high-altitude adventures and plans for future conquest.[24]

The following morning, Hackett awoke to find the air temperature a balmy twenty-nine degrees Fahrenheit. Accompanied by Wilson and Moore, Hackett hiked to Midget Peak and climbed on excellent fourth and fifth class rock. Here, they found some old slings and hardware that Bill was convinced had been left there by Shipton and Wyn-Harris. The day's outing was perfect for acclimating, although not completely necessary for Bill as he was still in great shape from his recent ascent of Kilimanjaro.

On Thursday, February 16, the entire group made their way up to the Top Hut, 1,000 feet higher than the two tarns. After initial scrambling on the southeast side near the Curling Pond, the team broke steps across Lewis Glacier to the base of the southeast ridge. Wilson turned back at this point but the balance of the team continued on. The glacier's steeper icefall was ascended to a point where they could clearly see off the northeast side to the Gregory Glacier. From here, they continued to climb to the summit of Point Lenana at 16,300 feet.[25] Bill was greatly pleased with this, one of Kenya's lower summits, as the position provided spectacular views of the main peaks themselves and the surrounding territory.

Hackett awoke the following morning at 4:45, ready to begin his push for the true summit. Moore, Wilson, Pereira and Hackett departed the Top Hut dressed in their best cold-weather parkas. As it was still night, they used flashlights to illuminate their traverse of the Lewis Glacier. By the time daylight appeared they had reached the rock bands higher up. The party roped-up and proceeded cautiously, careful to limit the amount of rocks they dislodged as they might strike their colleagues below. Bill was thrilled with such terrain, noting in his diary, "The first part was free hand...the going became progressively difficult with great exposure-Mackinder's Crack, Rabbit Hole, Shipton's Crack, Rickety Crack, Amphitheater, etc."[26] Bill Hackett was clearly in his element.

When the party reached the top of Nelion, Kenya's lower summit, snow had already started to fall. At 17,000 feet, with a fair amount of snow being deposited on the rock shelves beside them, it was difficult to believe they were in equatorial Africa! Rather than inherit certain risks by attempting the slightly higher summit of Batian, the climbers voted to make an immediate descent.

At this point, Hackett suddenly realized no one had brought any runners with them in order to facilitate rappels! There was a moment of awkward silence while they searched their memory banks to determine how such a mistake could have been made. Apparently no one had been assigned to the task and in the sleep-deprived atmosphere of their pre-dawn start, a proper inventory of equipment had been overlooked. They had but one 125-foot nylon rope among them! Hackett did some mental math: elevation of the summit, elevation of the Top Hut, and the length of rope. The answer came quickly—1,200 feet to descend with a maximum rappel of sixty-five and-a-half feet and no runners! 'Time to get creative' Bill thought to himself. Using a knife, the climbers cut a three-foot section of their rope to use as their first runner. This left them with 122 feet of remaining rope. Since a rope needs to be doubled in order to retrieve the line after a rappel, the first runner enabled the party to make a safe rappel of sixty-one feet. The climbers would then need to find a relatively safe position to rig their second rappel and cut another three-foot section of rope. Now, with 119 feet of climbing rope available, they were able to safely execute a fifty-nine and-a-half foot rappel. Again, a stable position would need to be found for the third rappel. This pattern was repeated over and over for nearly thirty rappels: cutting three-foot sections of the line for runners while rappelling on an ever-shrinking length of climbing rope! Though incredibly time-consuming the pattern nevertheless provided the safest method of descent for the four cold and tired climbers. It would take them five hours to descend a mere 1,200 feet. When they finally reached safety, Bill had but twenty-five feet left of his 125-foot climbing rope!

During one of the many military hops Hackett would take to return to the United States, he reflected on what his adventures on the Dark Continent had brought him. First and foremost was his successful ascent of Kilimanjaro, which added a third continental peak to his growing resume. This achievement made him the first climber in history to make successful ascents of the highest summit on three continents. He had additionally made several new friends at the Mountain Club of Kenya and been exposed to a wide variety of new and exciting cultures. With the exception of reaching Kilimanjaro's summit, Bill believed the most exciting moment of his venture was when he and his companions found equipment left behind by Shipton and Wyn-Harris. Decades later, when Bill entertained Shipton in his Portland home, he was thrilled to be able to share stories of equatorial mountaineering with a climber he greatly admired.

CHAPTER VII

The West
Buttress

*"The valley walls, sheer rocky ridges, towered above us on both sides.
We flew between a rough floor of glacial ice and a solid ceiling of dark,
gloomy fog 2,000 feet above us. It was like flying through a gigantic tunnel.
However, the cloud ceiling seemed nearly level, while the glacier climbed
steadily. If the two met, we would be out of luck."[1]*

—Dr. Bradford Washburn

In 1951, Dr. Bradford Washburn employed the use of aircraft
to successfully ascend Mount McKinley from its western flanks. All
previous expeditions had used McGonagall Pass, Muldrow Glacier
and Karstens Ridge to reach to the upper summit slopes. As early as
1936, Washburn felt he had discovered another possible route to the
summit via an immense rock formation known as the West Buttress.
In July of that year, he made a series of photographic flights over the
mountain for *National Geographic Magazine*. After analyzing the photographs from this venture, he was struck by the technical-free
approach from the western side. In 1947, he published his belief that
a practical route had been found in the *American Alpine Journal*. Two
years later he flew over the western slopes of McKinley in order to
assist the Office of Naval Research in selecting a site for future cosmic
ray research. The only logistical problem Washburn could foresee was
the extensive approach march from the lowland tundra to the upper
Kahiltna Glacier. He felt that landing a ski plane on the glacier itself

might solve this problem. In 1951, Washburn heard through climbing associates that mountaineers from Denver, Colorado were preparing an expedition to Alaska. The director telephoned their leader, Dr.
Henry Buchtel, vice-president of the American Alpine Club, who
readily agreed to join forces. Dr. Buchtel had been working with Jerry
More, Barry Bishop and Dr. John Ambler for nearly a year and welcomed the multitude of services Washburn could provide. With two
other hastily placed calls, Dr. Washburn was able to enlist the services of Bill Hackett and Jim Gale, his friends from the 1947 venture.[2]

The 1951 West Buttress expedition was divided into two main
groups in order to cover all of the pre-set scientific and mountaineering goals. Four members would fly to Lake Chulatna and from there
to the Kahiltna Glacier. The second party of four proceeded north by
rail to McKinley Park Station and from there they would board trucks
to Wonder Lake. Both teams would link up at a central base camp high
on Kahiltna Glacier to continue their ascent and scientific studies
from that location.

The expedition had three clear-cut goals. First, they would
attempt to determine if Washburn was correct in believing that the
West Buttress offered a shorter, safer path to the summit. Dr. Marcel
Shein, Head of the Department of Physics at the University of Chicago,
hoped this goal might be reached as he dreamed of fixing a cosmic ray
research station high on the mountain's western slopes. Second, to
study the geology of the western buttress. Third, to continue the survey and mapping program that Dr. Washburn and his museum had
been working on for years.[3] Dr. Buchtel and other members of the team
hoped to explore and map the physical structure of the western side of
the peak. This work was backed by the University of Denver and The
New England Museum of Natural History. The team naturally hoped to
reach the summit via the West Buttress as this new route would open
up the western slopes to scientists, geologists and climbers alike. If the
upper slopes were barred for any reason, Washburn wanted to at least
adequately photograph the region for future study and to assist others
in making the final bid for the summit.[4]

Buchtel had run into some initial logistical troubles but once
Washburn was on board it seemed as if Alaska bent over backwards
to accommodate the man. Washburn's reputation for Alaskan exploration had been firmly secured after fifteen years of research,

exploration and climbing.[5] Hackett and Gale, the men Washburn had selected to join the expedition, were also afforded Alaskan courtesies and cooperation. Bill was immediately granted a two-month period of detached service from the offices of Headquarters of the United States Army. Jim Gale, a civilian working for the Alaskan Air Command, was granted authorization to join in order to support the scientific arm of the expedition. Grant Pearson, a member of the 1932 and 1947 expeditions, was now the Superintendent of Mount McKinley National Park. He was able to cut through a lot of bureaucratic red tape and grant authorization to make the attempt on the untried western side of the mountain. A close, personal friend of Washburn's, Dr. Terris Moore had become the President of the University of Alaska. Moore would not only provide his personal Super Cub 125 airplane for the journey to Kahiltna Glacier, he offered his skills as pilot as well. Moore had not only climbed McKinley with Washburn in 1942, but also the mighty Minya Konka in 1932.[6]

"Belt fastened tight?" Moore shouted to Dr. Washburn as they sat in the former's two-seated single-engine aircraft. Just 100 miles northwest of Anchorage, the plane bumped along the gravel runway at Lake Chelatna. "Okay! Here we go!" with that the plane lifted off and banked towards the mountain.

"We were off," Washburn would recall, "on an adventure which already had my heart pounding with mixed feelings of excitement and, I must admit, a certain amount of apprehension. Terry Moore, who was going to try to land me on Kahiltna Glacier, is not only an experienced bush pilot but was also president of the University of Alaska. If we could land successfully, he was to leave me there with a small radio, camped on a smooth snow plateau. After this it should not prove too difficult to fly in to the glacier camp my first three companions, Dr. Henry Buchtel, James E. Gale, and Captain William D. Hackett. With the radio I could tell them before they even took off what the weather was like at my end of the line."[7]

This flight would mark the first attempt to land an airplane on Kahiltna Glacier. Ice seracs, open fissures, hidden crevasses and even an avalanche were just a few of the natural obstacles Moore would need to overcome in order to pull the stunt off. Moore had his plane modified to accommodate aluminum skis that were raised with hydraulics above the wheels. These skis would be employed for glacier landings while the standard wheels would be used for the gravel runways that were cropping up all over Alaska.

Of this historic flight, Washburn would write:

"Beneath us as we flew, the surface of the ice was at first so broken that nothing could possibly have landed there, not even a helicopter. The glacier's snout was buried under masses of rock and gravel. Some boulders were as big as bungalows, piled helter-skelter in heaps more than a hundred feet high. The valley walls, sheer rocky ridges, towered above us on both sides. We flew between a rough floor of glacial ice and a solid ceiling of dark, gloomy fog 2,000 feet above us. It was like flying through a gigantic tunnel. However, the cloud ceiling seemed nearly level, while the glacier climbed steadily. If the two met, we would be out of luck.

Ahead, the valley made a sharp bend to the right. As we turned the rocky corner, a great rift split the clouds as if by magic. Before us soared the thrilling virgin peak of Mount Hunter, white beneath a mantle of fresh snow. Looking back, we could see the dark, evil tunnel from which we had just emerged. The valley floor below was now much higher, and a snow blanket covered the rough ice. We were flying about 2,000 feet above the glacier, but our altimeter showed us to be 5,500 feet above sea level. Ahead the valley twisted abruptly to the left, the turn hiding the spot where we hoped to land. Every minute or two Terry swung the plane a bit so we could check our avenue of retreat. Until we sighted good landing snow we could not afford to let our black tunnel close up behind us.

As we neared the turn, Kahiltna Glacier became a veritable cataract of ice, two miles of it so rough it would have been utterly impassable on foot except along its edges. A tiny patch of blue sky appeared above, and a shaft of sunlight began to move slowly across the glacier toward the spot where we wanted to land. We followed it, circling, for it was moving only half as fast as we were. At this "spotlight" crossed the valley, we took our chance. The snow below us appeared perfect—no bumps, no hollows, no crevasses. Terry Moore cut the throttle, lowered the flaps, and before I could believe it we were skimming the glacier. Then we settled for a perfect landing."[8]

After only an hour's flight, Washburn had been transported forty miles and deposited on the Kahiltna Glacier, a full one-third of the way up the highest mountain on the continent! Washburn exited the aircraft just as the sun was beginning to set on the horizon. As Moore would need every available moment of sunlight, there was no time to lose. Together with Washburn, he hurriedly unloaded some supplies and turned the plane around till it faced downhill. Moore extended his hand and Washburn readily shook it in true appreciation and friendship.

"So long, partner." Moore simply stated prior to departure. Within the span of only a few minutes, Moore had landed, unloaded and taken to the air once again.

"I heard the drone of the motor for a minute or two," said Washburn. "Then it died away, and I was alone, 7,700 feet up in the heart of the Kahiltna amphitheater, close under McKinley's flanks. It was so quiet I could hear my heart beat."[9]

In a few hours, Moore was making a return journey with Dr. Buchtel aboard. Washburn was able to pick up the radio traffic between Moore and Talkeetna on his radio set.

"N-1088-A to KW034," Moore's voice sounded over the radio. "Can you see or hear me? I'm flying through drizzling snow about five miles below your camp."

"Landing conditions marginal," Washburn reported back. "Ceiling 300-500 feet, absolutely calm. I've marked a runway." Washburn's runway was merely a path in the snow, dotted with every available dark object he had at his disposal. Within a few minutes Buchtel and Moore had touched down. After the doctor's provisions were unloaded and Moore had again taken to the air, Washburn noticed that the weather was turning for the worse. Bill Hackett and Jim Gale, who would have been Moore's subsequent passengers that evening, would simply have to wait for a break in the weather.

＋－＝＋＝－＋

The second team of four, those approaching the mountain by the ground, consisted of Barry Bishop of the University of Cincinnati, Dr. John Ambler of Denver, Geologist Melvin Griffiths of the University of Denver, and Jerry More of Dartmouth University. More (no relation to pilot, Terry Moore), would report the following to the Colorado Mountain Club:

> "It seems hard to realize that tomorrow we will leave
> civilization and start the last and most important leg
> of a trip that has been over a year in the planning.
> From the front of our cabin, which is about 2,000 feet
> in elevation, the tundra stretches for fifteen miles to
> the small hills, which form the base of the mountain.
> These hills are about the size of the 14,000-foot peaks
> in Colorado. Behind these hills a gleaming white

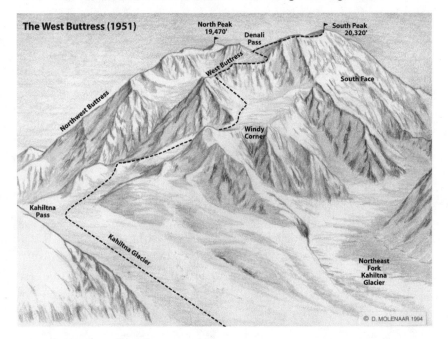

The West Buttress (1951)

pyramid soars 20,278 feet above sea level in a fantastic jumble of ice crevasses and vertical glaciers. This is
Mt. McKinley, rising higher above its base than any
other mountain in the world. The northern face is
almost vertical, and it is beyond belief and certainly
beyond description to tell you how a 17,000-foot face
of a mountain looks from only thirty miles away."[10]

On June 23, these four men, accompanied briefly by Carl
Anderson, departed Wonder Lake and led a packhorse train across
the McKinley River downstream to the mouth of Muddy Creek.
More would write that, "The horses were prime examples of biting,
kicking, Alaskan fury, and a drenching rain whipped across the tundra reducing our spirits to less than zero. For three days we battled
rain, roaring glacial streams, thawing tundra, and ferocious mosquitoes to reach the western flank of McKinley." The pack train
reached a position just below the snout of Peters Glacier, setting
camp in a grove of spruce timber. In the days to follow, they continued up Birch Creek to the junction of Crosson Glacier and a
small tongue of ice leading westward from Peter's Pass near the
5,400-foot level.[11] A four-mile ascent over Peter's Pass necessitated
a series of switchbacks, which seemed to add nearly 50 percent to
the distance of their day's journey.

On June 28, Barry Bishop and Jerry More made the first ascent
of Peter's Dome. More would humorously recall, "Peter's Dome is a
rather gentle name for a peak that required the entire day to climb.
We started on a gravel ridge, which slid at every step and then on to
a 50 (degree) knife-edge of snow and ice. At noon we dug a small hole
in the snow to gain partial protection from the savage wind while we
sipped some warm tea, which we had placed in our thermos bottles
that morning. After a bite of lunch we continued, but the wind-driven
snow now all but hid the mountain, and we sank up to our knees at
every step. By mid-afternoon we reached the summit, which meas-
ured 10,550 feet, and placed a piece of yellow parachute silk on a pole
which would later be used as a survey marker."[12]

Bishop and More now had to catch up with Ambler and
Griffiths who had gone ahead and pushed the route forward to the next

camp. Dr. Ambler, in a successful attempt to motivate his friends, had deposited Tootsie Rolls every 100 yards leading from the base of Peter's Dome to the next camp! Bishop and More happily followed the trail.

On June 30, Bishop, Ambler, More and Griffiths made a successful ascent of the Peter's Basin Headwall, encountering horrible conditions along the way. Their legs would penetrate an upper breakable crust and then sink into deep powder snow. Underlying all this was a layer of steep ice. After resting from their labors, they hiked to Kahiltna Base Camp to rendezvous with Washburn and the others.

⸺ ⸺◈⸺ ⸺

Base camp would be established near the 10,300-foot level. The camp had been carefully selected and Hackett was well pleased with the site selection. He and Jim Gale had each taken their turns aboard Terry Moore's plane and thoroughly enjoyed the journey. They immediately set about expanding the camp that Washburn and Buchtel had initiated. Their three Logan tents were erected just below Kahiltna Pass, a shoulder on the mountain that separated Peter's Glacier from the Kahiltna. An additional tent was hurriedly pieced together and a snow house was created to serve as a latrine.[13] Gale then used a three-quarter-watt radio to establish communications with the Civil Aeronautics Administration stations in Talkeetna and Minchumina. He needed to confirm that an aerial supply drop would proceed according to schedule the following morning.

Hackett would only manage a few hours of fitful sleep that night. His efforts to rest were shelved when a C-47 from Alaska's 10th Rescue Squadron flew overhead prior to the morning reveille. Bill recognized the fly-by, as a signal that the supply drops would commence any minute. After a few moments to gather some warmer clothing, he emerged from the tent and looked skyward toward the plane. It had already started dropping five packages with the assistance of parachutes. When these had safely reached the ice field, the plane began to drop a series of bundles and bags containing the bulk of the expedition's supplies and provisions. Thirty-nine bundles free fell from the aircraft, all landing within 300 feet of camp. "The pilot," Washburn would recall, "somehow missed the red cloth marker laid out on the snow 100 yards away. We realized with sudden horror that bundles and boxes flying out the open cargo door were streaking directly for our tent! They showered around it, one making a deep crater less than five feet from the tent in which Jim Gale was talking on the radio. It was his own bag of personal Equipment!"[14]

"Hey," Gale screamed into the radio, "for heaven's sake, watch where you're throwing that stuff! Throw it at the *marker*, not the tent!"

"Mighty sorry, fellows," came the reply over the radio, "We see the marker now. It won't happen again!" Washburn, Buchtel, Hackett and Gale all helped to retrieve these supplies and ferry them in to camp. Hackett couldn't help but notice that another sizable bundle had landed only five feet from his own tent! Had he been sleeping and had the load fell shy of its present position; Bill would have been rudely awakened. The four climbers then spent the remainder of the day sorting through photography equipment and organizing their supplies.[15] Hackett, who thought that Operation White Tower was a large expedition, was amazed at the number of supplies Washburn and Buchtel had assembled. There was the standard gear; tent poles, pegs and nylon rope, survey markers, birch-wand trail markers and sleeping bags, but these items did not capture Bill's attention. What brought a smile to his face was when he spied enough wood to build a small tool shed, 500 pounds of Birdseye frozen foods, forty-eight loaves of bread and even a complete King Salmon! Bill had never eaten so well on an expedition before and never would again.

The historical significance of the previous half-hour was not lost on the men. Washburn would write:

> "It had been a breath-taking half-hour. We had not yet had breakfast, but more than a ton of supplies had already been delivered at our front doorstep from a warehouse 130 miles away. In the old days it would have taken a twenty-horse pack train and three wranglers weeks to move this load from Anchorage to the lower end of the Kahiltna Glacier, forty-four miles below our camp. From there to where we sat, it would have been such a prodigious job of back packing to move these same supplies that we shuddered even at the thought."[16]

On the morning of June 23, Bill stuck his head out of his tent to observe the weather and what he saw caused him to groan in disappointment. Snow was falling so heavily he could barely make out the nearest tent. He had been looking forward to a day of climbing but instantly realized the foul weather meant a day of manual labor in camp.

Washburn, Buchtel and their fellow climbers spent the day bringing order to the chaos of supplies strewn about camp. In the mess tent, they sorted their food rations for the higher camps to come. The sheer number of bags and boxes was staggering. These provisions would need to sustain the team, as well as the secondary team fast approaching, for a period of six weeks at high altitude. Once their rations were in order they turned their attention to the climbing equipment. Bill re-inspected their nylon and manila ropes as well as the 607 bamboo trail markers. Snow pickets, pack boards and snowshoes were all certified for use.[17]

In the evening the weather cleared and Dr. Buchtel made the decision to descend the glacier for more equipment and provisions. The men suited up and donned their pack boards for the descent. When they arrived at a lower cache, Buchtel took a brief rest. When he looked around this small depot at 9,000 feet, he noticed certain medical supplies that were surely needed back at Base Camp. He advised Washburn that he would carry these supplies back up the glacier. Washburn, Hackett and Gale continued their descent to Cache 1, a thousand feet lower in elevation. The majority of provisions found at this site were evenly distributed among the men. A certain percentage of food was left for the geologists that would be coming shortly. With packs exceeding seventy pounds, Washburn and his men turned to begin the five-mile journey back to base camp. Bill had no complaints however, as he was pleased to be climbing again and the air temperature had warmed to a more comfortable eighteen degrees above zero. They arrived in camp before noon and Buchtel was able to welcome them with coffee and cocoa.[18]

The following morning, Washburn, Hackett and Gale became the first climbers in history to reach the snow-covered saddle—Kahiltna Pass. A colossal cornice was hanging over the lower Peter's Glacier, 3,000 feet below. Washburn led the team up the northeast ridge of a peak they originally called *Prime Z*, for use in surveying. Snowshoes were doffed as the slope was too steep and snow conditions were growing increasingly poor. The wind had picked up as soon as they began their ascent of this smaller sentinel. When they reached her summit they erected a seven-foot bamboo pole and tied strips of red nylon on its head. Here, they built a snow house only a few yards from their survey station so the men could get out of the elements and warm themselves when their fingers grew too cold to work the theodolite. Washburn recalls that on the summit of this peak, which they called *Peak Z,* the temperature 'grew absurdly warm.' Washburn and his men considered forty-degrees Fahrenheit balmy and they stripped down to their work shirts. They descended to a saddle where they rested briefly. A diagonal traverse of the southeast slope was then undertaken and they reached base camp as the air temperature began to plummet.[19]

Earlier that same morning, Washburn, Hackett, Buchtel and Gale had departed camp on snowshoes, bound for higher ground. Near the 11,000-foot mark they donned crampons as ice conditions warranted. Gale and Hackett took turns breaking trail for an additional thousand feet. The natural path a climber would take appeared to take a sharp left turn. A rock rib, free of ice and snow, formed a col between a corner of the West Buttress and a snow platform they called *R-Triple Prime.* Due to the high wind velocity in this area, Hackett dubbed it "Windy Corner," a name it has kept during the subsequent half-century. The climbers cached some gear in between the rocks and then continued up the mountain for further reconnaissance.

On nearly every high-altitude expedition, team members oftentimes wonder if they will accomplish their pre-set goals on schedule. Washburn and Buchtel were well pleased with the survey work accomplished thus far. Bill, on the other hand, was a man who thrived on continual movement and action. To remain inactive in camp was very difficult for him to endure. He had arrived with the expedition's advance party in order to ensure they had adequate time to complete the survey work. Officially, an ascent of the West Buttress was a secondary goal, one to be attempted should weather and schedule permit. Bill was naturally proud to have played a role in the survey work but it was no secret that he craved the summit. The Muldrow Glacier Route he had taken in 1947 had been established by pioneering climbers before him. He had also used well-established routes on Aconcagua, Kilimanjaro and Mt. Kenya. He missed making first ascents like he had in the Cascade Range. A possible first ascent of McKinley's West Buttress captivated his imagination as few routes had. No one had ever made a successful ascent of McKinley by a different route and this fact alone propelled him to want to move forward.

As mentioned before, the significance of the 1951 West Buttress expedition was two-fold; the first ascent of McKinley from the western side, and the first use of aircraft to ferry supplies, men and equipment up the mountain. Of the latter, no clearer example could be had than that shown on July 2. Both the air and ground parties had linked up in base camp two days earlier, and all eight climbers were setting down for their evening meal. Terry Moore made a landing with his plane, pulling up only a few yards away from the mess tent. Washburn was amazed that Moore brought him a letter from Boston that had been mailed only three days earlier! Moore even remained in camp for awhile, sharing dinner with his friends. Suddenly, he stood up and brushed some cracker crumbs off his lap.

"Good night!" he said, "It's five o'clock. I have only two hours to get back to Fairbanks for a faculty meeting!"[20] Washburn would later learn that, "(Moore's) meeting was 160 miles away and 9,650 feet below us on the other side of Mount McKinley. In a jiffy he was off over the pass and out of sight, making it back in plenty of time to shed his heavy clothes and parka, have a shower, and don a summer suit."

Washburn figured that the expedition had roughly ten days of supplies before they would be forced to return to civilization. The climbing plans were reviewed and it was determined that all eight climbers would be needed to ferry supplies up to an advance camp. For now, the geologists would need to set aside their objectives and assist the mountaineers. Even with the cooperation of Griffiths and the others, McKinley was known for its harsh weather and there were no guarantees that favorable climbing conditions would be encountered.

On the afternoon of the July 4, everyone bore sixty to ninety-pound loads up to Camp I, just past Windy Corner. Once there, they deposited their provisions in between the rocks. Ambler, Buchtel and Gale began erecting a Logan tent while the balance of the party descended to 12,000 feet in order to retrieve supplies cached there during the previous week. After the majority of provisions had been brought to Camp I, Bishop, More and Griffiths returned to base camp to continue their geological studies. All depot carries had been accomplished in poor conditions that afternoon and early evening. Winds increased and spin drift caused low visibility. Fortunately the bamboo trail markers, placed by Washburn and Buchtel, were fixed at intervals just shy of the length of a climbing rope so the lead man could reach the next pole before his partner lost site of the previous marker. In addition, so many trips had been made along this corridor; there was virtually no possibility of losing sight of the swath of footprints and postholes.

On the following morning, the general concern among the more avid climbers in the group was the state of the weather. Poor conditions had turned into another full-blown storm during the night. When the men awoke they discovered snowdrifts had nearly covered the entrance to their snow house. Winds were in excess of sixty miles per hour and Bill was certain the storm would only intensify. The decision was made to construct a secondary snow house and a covered passageway, which would connect the two structures.[21] These new accommodations would not only expand the climbers' personal space during the storm but also provide emergency shelter should any one house collapse. During the course of the day the winds increased dramatically and Washburn contacted base camp to check on conditions below. Griffiths informed them that the anemometer had read eighty-one miles per hour during the apex of the storm. Washburn merely laughed and replied that the wind speeds at Camp I had reached ninety miles per hour on two separate occasions. Drifts became such a problem that snow in the Logan tent had to be shoveled out on three separate occasions.[22] Washburn would fondly recall a time when John Ambler crawled into the mess tent, his beard and mustache caked with ice, and said, "This kind of climbing is about 90 percent trying to stay alive and warm, and only 10 percent climbing!"[23]

The storm still raged during the following morning and the men knew they were pressed for time. As a result, Ambler and Gale volunteered to descend to Cache IV to retrieve more supplies. Back in Camp I, Hackett helped organize the packs the team would use for the summit assault. These preparations seemed prophetic when the storm suddenly died out near 3:00 PM. A half an hour later, Washburn, Hackett, Gale, Buchtel and Ambler departed for Cache 5 at 14,000 feet. As soon as their supplies were properly stowed

Washburn called for a retreat to Camp I. The winds and snowfall were
too heavy to continue and the storm showed every intention of continuing unabated.[24]

Jerry More clearly understood the pressure the men
were under:

> "Just to stay alive at these great altitudes involves a
> constant battle with violent storms and sub-zero tem-
> peratures; the rarified atmosphere causes even the
> simplest movements to become exhausting work.
> Thundering avalanches and hidden crevasses are
> always present and can completely wipe out an expe-
> dition. Such mountains are usually situated at great
> distances from civilization, and this presents complex
> problems in transportation and communication.
> Expeditional mountaineering in such circumstances
> requires the best climbers that can be gathered, and
> safety must be paramount in the minds of all. Since
> few men in a lifetime are exposed to such conditions,
> the mountaineer who accompanies such an expedi-
> tion usually feels that he must give his maximum,
> because of the party—and, especially, because of him-
> self. There are few who can realize the tremendous
> driving force that pushes a climber on, even after his
> body has all but given up and his brain, so numbed
> by lack of oxygen, fails to warn him to turn back."[25]

July 7 seemed to find the expedition filled with renewed vigor
and determination to reach the top. Washburn and Gale were in the
lead, reconnoitering the route. Ambler, Buchtel and Hackett followed, carrying what Bill would later call *punishingly* heavy loads.
Near Cache 5, these five men used quarter-inch rope to rough-lock
their snowshoes, providing traction on the steeper sections of ice.[26]
This steepening slope hampered their forward momentum briefly but
soon they were making a direct assault up the West Buttress. A decision was made at this point to divide the team. Washburn and Gale
would continue to push ahead, cutting steps for the team to follow.

Ambler, Buchtel and Hackett would descend to Cache 5 for more supplies. When these men returned, they exchanged their snowshoes for
crampons and started up the trail Washburn had previously prepared.
Roughly 500 vertical feet above Cache 6, Hackett and the others
found a suitable location to establish Camp II. Located beside the
lower lip of a bergschrund two miles outside of Camp I. Washburn
and Gale were not present but their prints indicated they had continued up the mountain, preparing the route even further.

Washburn would write:

> "For a thousand feet we plowed almost straight up the
> slope, still on *snowshoes*, until the breakable wind-
> blown crust and loose snow beneath it made going vir-
> tually hopeless. With snowshoes on, it was too slip-
> pery on the crust and steep side hill; without them,
> one went in waist-deep. For three hours we shoveled a
> trail two to three feet deep and over 200 yards long, till
> we got out of this miserable stuff. Then we hit a steep
> slope (40 degrees) up which we wallowed crotch-deep,
> but with a firm base far below the surface powder. At
> 2:45 PM, we reached the bergschrund at 15,400 feet, so
> exhausted we could scarcely even eat lunch."[27]

Hackett awoke on the morning of July 10, confident that he
would make his second ascent of McKinley that very day. He lay in
his sleeping bag and reflected on the events of the previous few days.
The men had fixed over 600 feet of rope up a 50-degree snow slope
above a large bergschrund just above camp. After reaching the summit of a col at 16,200 feet, they encountered mixed ice and rock terrain. Another 1,000 feet of similar work had brought them to the top
of the West Buttress. Further geological specimens had been collected for Griffiths and the University of Denver. Through poor visibility, the team had worked their way up to the saddle between the
north and south summits of the mountain. Here, they had established Camp III at nearly 18,000 feet, the highest shelter during the
expedition. The standard method of relaying supplies to this upper-
most camp was then undertaken.[28]

Washburn and Buchtel had every reason to be proud of their men. For several days it appeared as if the mountaineering aspect of the expedition would have to be sacrificed in order to accomplish the scientific objectives. Even when it appeared as if the men and proper resources could be devoted to the assault, foul weather had presented itself time and time again. In a matter of days, through poor ice and inclement weather, their team had forged a route up the West Buttress and were now poised to make the final assault on the summit. Washburn knew from his earlier aerial photographic work, that the crux of this new route would be encountered in between 15,000 and 17,000 feet. The most technical aspect of the ascent behind them, the team looked forward to what they hopped would be the culmination of their historic journey.

That Tuesday morning, July 10, was virtually cloudless. Only a small blanket of white clouds hovered around the upper reaches of the mountain's twin summits. Washburn, Hackett and Gale departed camp in the morning with only a few light loads; just what they needed for the day. A breakable snow crust led to deep powder and their progress was slowed as a result. They avoided a series of large crevasses and two sizable blocks of ice. Terraces filled with ice required extensive step cutting; thirty 'whacks' with an axe in order to allow a single foot placement. Though the going was never steep from a technical sense, one final pitch required fixed rope. Here, Bill saw a familiar sight. The thermometer he and his colleagues had left in 1947 was still firmly placed in the ice, registering a lowest recorded temperature of -59 degrees Fahrenheit.

This thermometer wasn't the only remnant of Operation White Tower. In 1947, Jim Gale, Bob Lange and Hugo Victoreen had left a food and clothing cache here and had it well protected from the elements. Now, four years later, Washburn and his men discovered that the supplies had been broken into and scavenged.[29] Documentation discovered within revealed that members of Walter Gonasson's 1948 expedition had broken into it. In the mountaineering community it is perfectly acceptable to use another party's abandoned supplies but any provisions not used must be protected from the elements for future use. In addition, the party who used the supplies left behind by others must *report* the fact that they used them so future parties do not bank on the cache for survival purposes. Gonasson's party apparently forgot to take either of these steps. His men had helped themselves to the supplies, in and of itself not a transgression, but failed to adequately cover up the cache and therefore ensured the destruction of the remaining provisions.

By now the affects of working at higher altitudes were beginning to show. Washburn himself was making minor arithmetic errors in his survey work. He would write:

"Up there, three miles above the sea, we began to feel the insidious effects of anoxia, or deficiency of oxygen. Anoxia increasingly impairs a climber's judgment, alertness, and will power the higher he gets. He becomes apathetic, careless and tends to put off doing important tasks, or does them sloppily. Worst of all, though he realizes his companions are affected by it, he is convinced that he himself is perfectly normal...our writing became less legible, and we began to make elementary errors in arithmetic. For this reason we carefully double-checked our surveying figures. Once, because of anoxia, we set up the theodolite tripod so high I had to stand on tiptoe to see through it. And anoxia made me so apathetic that I used it in that awkward position and made several silly errors, which fortunately were corrected later. Anoxia's ill effects can be reduced if a climber works slowly and rhythmically, without wasting energy. If carrying a heavy pack, he chances to stumble, it is often better for him to go ahead and fall than to expend strength in a stubborn effort to retain his footing. There is no known cure for anoxia except bottled oxygen, which is far too heavy and clumsy to use on McKinley."[30]

Washburn and his men found remnants of trail markers from their 1947 effort. Though many of them had their tops snapped off, they still remained fixed in place after four years, revealing the final stretch of their journey.

When the party reached the top of the southern, and true summit, there was yet another remnant of their previous expedition. Bill saw the eight-foot bamboo pole they had used to hoist their summit flag. For Gale and Hackett this was their second trip to the summit, and for Washburn this moment marked his third. The view was familiar but still just as fantastic as it had been in years past: Mount Spurr, Mount Hayes and Mount Foraker, all standing majestically without a cloud to shroud them. Washburn would write that, "...the whole amazing panorama to the east burst upon us. It was almost cloudless in every direction. Most impressive of all was the deep emerald green of the lowlands to the south and west. River after river sparkled in the afternoon sun, twisting off into the distance. As Archdeacon Hudson Stuck said after his first ascent of McKinley 38 years before, it was like looking out the very windows of heaven."[31] Jerry Moore would add that, "Only the mountaineer can know and understand the silent loneliness that crowns the summits of all great mountains."[32]

The West Buttress Route, which Washburn had foreseen from the air, had finally been established. Despite inclement weather the men had accomplished all of their primary objectives. Terry Moore had proved aerial landings on the Kahiltna Glacier could safely be performed, and that the climbing route itself only held technical difficulties between the 15 and 17,000-foot range. Washburn and Buchtel additionally showed scientists that the western approach to the mountain proved more suitable for scientific experiments.

Dr. Henry Buchtel, co-leader of the expedition, would provide Washburn with the following comments after the conclusion of the venture. "The 1951 trip up Mount McKinley was an unusual one. When I say this, I am not referring to the fact that I reached the top—which is, to my friends, the most remarkable fact about the enterprise. The trip was unusual because the route had been scouted entirely by air, no one having set foot on that side of the mountain before the expedition reached it, and because the party was brought in satisfactorily by two different routes and by two different methods of transportation. Most important of all, the entire party reached the top of the mountain and returned safely."[33]

On Halloween, three months after the conclusion of the expedition, Captain William Hackett walked into the office of his commanding officer and handed him his thirty-three-page report. This brief outlined for the US Army, how the expedition achieved their pre-set goals. Personnel, itinerary, weather, medical and equipment were all covered. Captain Hackett was one of the few members of the expedition that had continued to receive paychecks during his time on the mountain and Bill naturally wanted to thank his employer. He would state that he was always grateful to the Army for their time, expense and even their patience while he was up in the hills. Bill used government aircraft for free or low-cost flights around the world, he was continually granted paid leaves-of-absences, and he always, without fail, received his government check twice a month while he was off exploring.

Bill Hackett had his faults but ingratitude was not among them.

C H A P T E R   V I I I

The
Recalcitrant

*"Memory revolts from a purgatory of rivers, creeks, lakes, bogs, hills,
clumped tundra, and the curse of Alaska, the ever present cloud of mosquitoes,
many of which were so large we felt they somehow ought to be
harnessed to our advantage."[1]*

—Robert Anderson

W hen Bill Hackett returned to military duty after the West
Buttress expedition, he resolved to lead his own party to the summit.
He knew there would be several obstacles he would have to overcome
in order to obtain such a goal. He learned that the US National Park
Service had recently prohibited all access to McKinley by airplane
unless a given expedition could prove their purposes were   scientific in nature. Hackett could make no such claim but refused to allow
such an obstacle to stop him for long. He could have asked Dr.
Washburn to work with the authorities, but Bill craved the captain's
chair for himself. For organizational, logistical and climbing plans, he
wanted to ensure he was the undisputed leader, taking the blame for
any shortcomings but also sharing in the rewards. When Bill realized
he would have to lead a party over mile after mile of difficult tundra
to even approach the great mountain, his first instinct was to launch
an incredibly large full-scale siege-style assault of the mountain with
over twenty climbers and hired packers. Bill's love of the history of

mountaineering would override this initial decision and led him to the belief that he should lead one of the first lightweight expeditions to the summit with only a handful of climbers. Such an expedition, quite common today, had rarely been attempted on McKinley, and for this reason alone, Bill resolved to proceed.

Hackett then needed to determine who would accompany him to the summit. For this is how Bill's mind worked, he never thought in terms of 'who would make the *attempt* with me,' but rather, 'who would summit.'[2] Though he was unaware of it at the time, he had become a bit spoiled when it came to the ever-changing weather on mountains. True, he had endured incredible storms before but nothing so severe it would force a retreat from the mountain. He had seen success on every high-altitude venture he had been involved in: McKinley (1947, 1951), Aconcagua (1949) and Kilimanjaro (1950). Never had he met defeat on what he called, "The Big Ones." Such a success rate is rare even in today's climbing community where better equipment and supplies are employed. With summit success a forgone assumption, it is interesting to note his selection of climbing candidates. Robert Anderson was a twenty-eight year-old college student studying English Literature at Lewis & Clark College in Portland, Oregon. He had joined the Mazamas in 1947 and linked up with several members for climbing ventures throughout the Cascades. He had taken part in climbing trips to Glacier National Park and the Yoho region of southern Canada but his climbing resume, at that time, listed Mount Adams in Washington State as the highest point he had ever reached. At 12,276 feet, it was hardly a conquest that would endear oneself to a leader of a high-altitude expedition. In early 1952, Anderson was approached by Mazamas historian, Don Onthank in the club offices in the roof studios of the Pacific Building. Onthank advised Anderson that his good friend Bill Hackett was organizing an expedition to McKinley and would he, Anderson, be interested in joining? Anderson, who wanted to try his hand at expeditionary mountaineering, quickly agreed to the proposal. With limited funds available, he asked his employer at a local lumber yard for the time off and set about organizing transportation to Alaska. It is unclear why Hackett accepted Anderson's resume over more qualified candidates, but perhaps he understood that camaraderie and harmony within the team were oftentimes as important as experience and technical expertise[3]. Robert "Bob" Goodwin of Leadville, Colorado, often worked in Alaska for outdoor skiing venues. He additionally held odd jobs along the Kenai Peninsula. Ernie Baumann of Anchorage, Alaska rounded out the roster of climbers. He worked as a mechanical maintenance man for Reeves Aleutian Airlines, serving the Aleutian Islands.[4]

With a team of only four climbers in place, Hackett set about organizing the necessary supplies and equipment that would sustain them for such a journey. On Saturday, June 7, 1952, Hackett picked Anderson up at the airport and invited Goodwin over to discuss preparations.[5] Anderson was immediately impressed by what he saw. In the basement of Hackett's residence, Bill's wife, Naydene showed him supplies stacked nearly to the ceiling. "Bill," Anderson would report to the Mazamas, "...had been working out the details and accumulating food and equipment since the preceding fall. A neatly ordered sheaf of correspondence an inch or so thick stood as mute testimony to the amount of labor involved. A meticulous attention to detail pervaded his whole attitude, indicated in the manner in which he chose the food items. During the previous winter he and his wife, Naydene, selected various foods by testing their palatability, and eliminating brands of inferior taste and quality. The expedition's headquarters were located in the basement of the Hackett's residence at Fort Richardson. When I arrived, a week before our departure, the larger portion of the food and equipment had been purchased and stacked in rows along the walls. The quantity of gear we were going to carry up the mountain was appalling. But it wasn't until we had it all packed in waterproof bags and boxed that the enormity of the task we were setting out to do became apparent."[6]

Getting to their debarkation point for the assault on McKinley proved both entertaining and informative. On June 16, the team loaded up all of their supplies and equipment onto a boxcar owned by the Alaska Railroad. After saying farewell to friends that had come to see them off, the team boarded the train bound for the Mount McKinley National Park Hotel. During the journey, Hackett reclined in his seat and looked the part of a seasoned McKinley veteran. When the great peak came into view and Anderson started snapping pictures, Bill began to regale the group with stories from his two previous ventures on the mountain. The following morning, the team loaded

their supplies into vehicles to be transported ninety miles into the
bush land to a point within twenty miles of McGonagall Pass. From
this vantage point four men would need to ferry supplies for a month-
long expedition over many miles merely to step upon the Muldrow
Glacier, gateway to the upper slopes of McKinley.

Anderson would write:

> "Looking back from a perspective of time and dis-
> tance, the five days it took us to get all our gear to
> McGonagall Pass, lose none of their savor. Hackett
> had come out this way in '47 and in describing the
> terrain applied to it the term 'miserable.' This, we
> were quick to learn, was an understatement of the
> most disarming kind. In recalling it, memory revolts
> from a purgatory of rivers, creeks, lakes, bogs, hills,
> clumped tundra, and the curse of Alaska, the ever
> present cloud of mosquitoes, many of which were so
> large we felt they somehow ought to be harnessed to
> our advantage."[7]

Today's mountaineers who are quick to accept the timesav-
ing alternative of using bush pilots rarely experience the difficulties
early pioneers encountered en route to the mountain. The 1952
team had to relay loads not twice but three times over the same
twenty-one mile route. With heavy packs they crossed clumped, or
Tussock tundra that was made up of intertwined vegetation standing over a foot tall in many sections. These clumps stood roughly
six inches apart and considering the average man had a foot ten to
twelve-inches long, such terrain was difficult to navigate through.
Hiking was slow and monotonous. "No rhythm of movement is
possible," Anderson recalled, "and with heavy packs the effect is
like a perpetual stagger." In other areas, the men crossed through
black spruce and over thick layers of soil strewn with sphagnum
and related material. Underneath everything was permafrost,
ground that had remained frozen for centuries. The team clearly

noticed that the mosquitoes were most prevalent in the 3-4,000-foot elevations, large enough 'to bring a bull-moose down' they joked.[8]

To combat this 'morale-busting' terrain, Hackett had the men make shorter relay trips. This action helped the team in many ways; it acted as a pre-climb conditioning regimen, helped build camaraderie among the men as few had climbed together before, and finally, it helped raise morale. Bill would record that he and his men had crossed the McKinley River five times and forded eight minor streams during the course of a single day. Every now and then the group would hit upon a game trail and follow it for a few miles, increasing their speed while observing grazing caribou. From June 17–22, Bill would record countless round-trip ventures with full packs. He observed caribou, an albino wolf and noted every river, stream or alluvial fan he crossed. His McKinley diary entries are devoid of any emotion or historical tangent. He never discusses the topics of the day or what his companions felt about such a journey. It's as if he tried to cram as many facts as his 6x3" diary pages could hold and the more he wanted to say, the smaller he wrote.

On June 22, they arrived at McGonagall Pass at 5,800 feet, the standard launching point for assaults from the mountain's northeast side. Hackett had hoped to use food and supplies at the cache left here by Dr. Washburn's 1947 expedition, but grizzly bears had long since ransacked the cache. Tin cheese and some coffee were all they were able to salvage. Bill tried to bury an emergency supply cache at this location but in order to avoid a repeat visit from grizzlies, he deposited the supplies in a cleft in a hillside, covering it with small boulders. When they would return to this site a month later, they discovered that the bears were more determined than they at first anticipated. The cache 'had been wiped out.'[9]

As much as the men had found unfavorable conditions below, they were well pleased to greet the ice and rock of the mountain proper. In teams of two they would rope up and begin their ascent towards Camp I. As it was slightly warmer than normal for that time of year, snow conditions were not at their best, but Hackett would remember a marked improvement in unit morale that overrode such a minor setback. Anderson fondly remembered that Ernie Baumann would sing aloud while he hiked, recalling many German folklore songs and poems. Morale additionally improved the higher they climbed. Anderson would write:

> "The level and uncrevassed, the first several miles of glacier were still mantled in a heavy layer of winter snow, which, under the influence of warmer temperatures, was beginning to deteriorate. It was a sight to behold; the rapidity with which vast reaches of the dazzling white surface were turning to green blotches as the snow became saturated with water from its own melt. On our last relay across this area great changes had taken place, since our trip the day before. Little trickles became flowing streams surging to either side of the glacier. So we wasted no time in getting our equipment to the base of the first ice-fall at 7,000 feet."[10]

Anderson, on his first high-altitude venture, marveled at Hackett's skill in navigating over the glacier. Bill had brought a seven-foot bamboo pole with him and used this tool to probe the route ahead. There were an incredible number of snow-covered crevasses in the ice field and Bill wanted to ensure that each snow bridge could not only stand up to a single crossing but remain intact for some time. They even marked their route with dowel wands at suitable intervals, hoping the path would remain stable and intact in the weeks to come. The men wore their lengthy, trail-style snowshoes in order to stay on top of the snowdrifts. These shoes, which additionally helped them pass over smaller crevasses, also came with a price. With each morning the team could feel the strained and pulled muscles of their inner thighs.[11]

Hackett was also able to employ experience he had gained on his earlier high-altitude ascents. Where some climbers would push to stock the higher camps as quickly as possible, Bill held back and ensured each and every camp was properly stocked to sustain his men should a serious storm envelope the mountain. Well aware that the mountain was capable of creating its own weather, Bill wanted to leave nothing to chance. He knew that should any trouble arise or

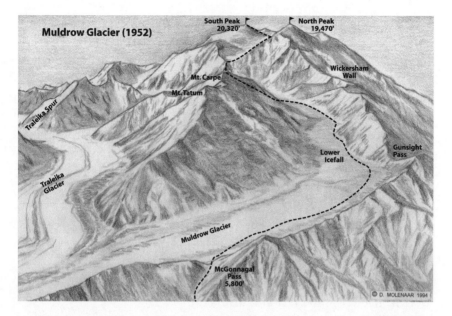

Muldrow Glacier (1952)

South Peak 20,320'

North Peak 19,470'

Mt. Carpe

Wickersham Wall

Mt. Tatum

Traleika Spur

Traleika Glacier

Lower Icefall

Gunsight Pass

Muldrow Glacier

McGonnagal Pass 5,800'

© D. MOLENAAR 1994

accident befall one man, there would be but three to assist. In many ways, Bill would have rather been confronted with a serious storm as he could at least console himself with the knowledge that progress could not be made that particular day. What really galled him however, was when warm vapor would settle over the Muldrow Glacier. As the vapor was the same color as the surrounding terrain, near whiteout conditions would exist. In this environment, trail finding was nearly impossible. Hackett told his men that things would be fine once they left "The Lowlands!" but such unstable weather plagued the expedition clear up to 15,000 feet!

The following week was a series of supply relays and establishing camps. Camp I was situated at 7,000 feet while Camp II was found merely 400 feet higher. More than once their progress was hampered by bad weather. Hackett and Baumann would play chess to pass the time, and Bill would record how many times they would play and even who won each match[12]. One incident that stood out for several members of the team occurred on the afternoon of June 27. While navigating through the ice field known as the Hill of Cracks, the men thought they heard the whine of an airplane. They stopped in their tracks and scanned the heavens. In the distance they spied a single-engine aircraft approaching their position. When the plane was close enough it banked slightly and Dr. Terris Moore was clearly visible at the controls. As a former climbing partner of Hackett's, Moore yelled out a greeting to his friend. Bill responded in kind, happy to see that his friend cared enough to check on their safety and progress.

The following day, June 28, the expedition encountered obstacles that seriously impeded progress. While climbing through the Hill of Cracks a heavy fog enveloped the team. The air temperature rose considerably and made snow bridges weaker and weaker as the day progressed. Goodwin fell through three separate hidden crevasses; his descent to the depths halted by the quick actions of his companions on each occasion.

"You're a crevasse magnet, Robert!" Bill would shout aloud above the sound of the wind. Baumann's snowshoes broke around this time, which necessitated an hour's delay while they were repaired. By the time they established Camp IV near 9,000 feet, they were in need of some rest and diversion.[13]

Terris Moore wouldn't be the only visitor to greet the team during their time on the mountain. That night, while the team ate supper, a weasel stopped by to the surprise of all assembled. Naturally, the topic of conversation turned to the rodent and why it would be running around at such an elevation when his food supply was clearly far below. "The fact that he knew his business was revealed the next day," Anderson would write, "as we, after several false starts, found the key to the ice-fall known as the 'Grand Serac.' There were his tracks, and, except for a few deviations, he had found, probably the only route through that tremendous ice-fall."[14]

"Well, this is a first!" Bill announced with a broad smile, "I've never been led by an animal on a mountain before." As much as the weasel had lifted their spirits and assisted their progress, the team had to be mindful of continual avalanches that occurred on both sides of the glacier. The warmer temperatures had loosened snow cornices and sent them raining down on the Muldrow with great frequency. Morale remained high and during the easier stretches of the ascent the men would engage in a game called PIG; similar to the game children play with a basketball. They would continually try to best one another with the most remote yet accurate facts and figures they had at their disposal. The questions ran the full gambit of knowledge; history, politics, geography, etc. 'Who was Henry VIII's third wife?'

'How many fathoms are there in 300 feet of seawater?' and 'who was the first western explorer to step foot in Ceylon?'[15]

Camp V was established near Karsten's Pass at 11,000 feet on June 29. Here, in the upper basin of Muldrow Glacier, the mercury in their thermometers finally began to plummet and reveal better ice conditions. That evening, the Scotch sail-silk tent fabric barely kept the cold winds out and for the first time the men had to don their long underwear and felt booties to combat a 7-degrees Fahrenheit air temperature. Anderson remarked that little to no thawing occurred above 12,000 feet and these booties were a luxury far exceeding their minimal weight.

Looking up at the mountain, Anderson was confronted with the crux of the route, Karsten's Ridge rising over 4,000 vertical feet! He would note:

> "Seen from Muldrow Glacier, the graceful lines of Karsten's Ridge gradually steepen in a series of undulations seemingly gaining momentum for its precipitous rush skyward, merging finally into the brown granite of Browne Tower. It is, however, only an interval in a long serrated ridge which rises at the junction of the Traleika and Muldrow glaciers and ultimately forms a principal buttress of the South Peak...Karsten's Ridge can be considered the crux of the entire ascent and its statistics are not out of keeping with the general dimensions of this fabulous mountain: in an estimated three miles it rises 4,000 vertical feet. It was our misfortune, though, to find it sheathed in a heavy layer of fresh snow."[16]

Normally a climber can deposit his snowshoes at the base of the ridge as stable crampon-snow can be found running the length of the ridge. Hackett made the determination however, that since they had encountered warmer temperatures below, he could not say with certainty what conditions would be found higher up. For this reason the team would bear their snowshoes up to the higher camps. Every time they tried to doff the shoes they would sink in fresh snow up to their hips and progress would come to an immediate halt.

Hackett in particular was pleased with the progress made on a single day, July 3. Four inches of new snow had fallen during the night and temperatures hovered around 10 degrees Fahrenheit. Bill had stuck his head out the tent flaps at 4:00 AM and saw promising weather overhead. He roused his troops and hurriedly packed to take advantage of the window of opportunity. 'We'll reach the top of the ridge for sure!' Bill remarked, trying to rally the men. Hackett would lead the way most of the day and soloed a difficult near-vertical pitch of ice and snow. He set fifty feet of fixed rope and reached 12,300 feet before being consumed by a heavy fog. The team labored all afternoon in what Hackett called 'the soup.' They established Camp VI nearby and retired for the night. Even Bill Hackett could rest easy that evening knowing they had done a full day's work.[17]

If Hackett was pleased with the day's progress he couldn't conceive of how much work would be accomplished in the following two days. Fair weather allowed the men to make a multitude of relay trips between camps in order to re-stock the higher positions. They discovered the cache at Parker Pass that had been left behind by the 1947 team. Bill had the pile inventoried, re-stocked and replaced in its position for future expeditions should they ever need its contents. "At various points along the ridge," Anderson would record, "we fixed hand lines of quarter-inch hemp and on one icy pinnacle added the third in a series dating back to 1942. On the treacherous slopes below the Coxcomb we anchored 400 feet of line for protection from wind-slab avalanches, which tend to occur there. Three shovel handles made anchor pins and we were glad to be rid of them." By the end of July 5, Camp VII had been established at 14,800 feet and was fully stocked, able to withstand a prolonged stay due to storms.

Every mountaineer who has spent any time at higher altitude will tell you that a price must be paid for every period of unbelievably fair weather. For Hackett and his team, this reckoning came on the morning of July 6. Anderson writes:

> "We had enjoyed two rare days of fine weather on
> the upper portion of the ridge but as we prepared
> lunch at Parker Pass the tent was suddenly rocked by

a volley of wind coming down the mountain. A glance outside confirmed our fears: clouds of snow-smoke were boiling into the air, being blown from the cliffs below South Peak. During the afternoon the disturbance intensified, manifesting itself in a storm, which raged across the upper 5,000 feet of the mountain for two days. Our camp was situated so as to receive only spasmodic gusts of wind as it eddied around the great walls of the peak, but these blasts were usually violent and would strike with a tremendous wallop. Borne on the wind were clouds of tiny, sharp snow crystals; the effect on one's skin has been likened to sandblasting. One encounter with it was enough to convince and all errands outside the tent were timed most judiciously!"[18]

The men spent the days making their lives as comfortable as possible under the circumstances. Anderson, suffering from an unknown stomach ailment, spent a majority of the time in his sleeping bag, taking his turn at the stove to prepare meals. Baumann continually prodded Hackett to play games of chess, but Bill was getting frustrated with the fact that Baumann appeared to be winning more games the higher they climbed.

"It's the altitude I tell you!" Bill would say, "As soon as we get back to the lowlands I'll kick your butt!" For Hackett himself, a couple days stuck in a 7x7-foot tent was nothing new. He reminded his companions that in 1947, he, Barbara Washburn and Hugo Victoreen had been trapped in the same region for nine consecutive days. Ever cautious when enduring such storms, Bill cut the men's rations to two meals a day in order to conserve their food supply. Both Baumann and Goodwin were suffering from altitude-induced headaches, which, they hoped, would be dispelled with aspirin.

There was no rhythm or schedule to keep during these periods of isolation. One moment Bill was checking the thermometer to see if they had broken their record for the lowest temperature and then he'd be busy disassembling the stove to replace the needle valve. Baumann, acting as a salesman, would proclaim the benefits of playing chess until Bill relented and played a game. An hour would go by where not a word would be exchanged and then, three hours of uninterrupted conversation would take place on a variety of subjects. They engaged in trivia contests to determine who would have to prepare the evening meals. When the wind died down however, the conversation invariably returned the task at hand—McKinley. Bill worked out some relay figures in a notebook and had the unfortunate task of informing his team that they would need to carry seventy-pound packs from their current position clear up to the summit.[19]

Over the following few days, the team took full advantage of the next break in the weather. Anderson was feeling better though Baumann was beginning to feel the effects of higher altitude. They made their way to Parker Pass, Harper Glacier and Denali Pass. Camp VIII had been established at 16,500 feet[20] and Camp IX, their highest camp, at 18,150 feet.[21] Temperatures ranged from negative four to negative ten degrees Fahrenheit but the team kept moving in order to remain warm.[22] Bill was very concerned about the wind gusts that exceeded seventy to eighty miles per hour. With seventy-pound loads in order to cut down relay trips, the men were top-heavy and were blown to the ground on many occasions. Anderson wasn't as concerned about the wind as he was the snow consistency and depth. "The conditions," he would write, "under which we crossed (Parker Pass) will remain forever etched in our memories—its snow structures running the gamut from wind-slab to hard-packed surface. For some distance waist deep snow was covered with a two-inch icy crust, which Bill had to break with his knees before slogging through. It took us two-and-a-half hours to go a scant quarter mile."[23] While navigating through such ice conditions, Baumann fell through a hidden crevasse and cracked two ribs. Anderson taped him up that evening and the team continued to press on.[24]

At 1:00 AM, Saturday, July 12, 1952, Bill awoke and crossed his fingers. He peeked out through the tent flaps and discovered the weather was 'somewhat favorable.' When he tried to rouse the troops he was met with initial hesitation. Goodwin threw-up the breakfast Bill had prepared for him. Baumann indicated that his headache was reaching astronomical proportions. Anderson, the self-professed recalcitrant, was having further troubles with his stomach and abdominal muscles. Anderson, not wishing to hinder the progress of his teammates, asked to be left behind in camp. In his own words, he states that, "Bill would hear none of it and after long, patient ministrations and many verbal proddings the recalcitrant emerged from his bag for the final dash to the summit."

They departed Camp IX at 4:30 AM, climbing south from Denali Pass. The way ahead was difficult not from a technical standpoint but three of the four party members were suffering from exhaustion. On a snow shelf near 19,200 feet, they were forced to stop as Goodwin was clearly showing signs of frostbite. They set him down and removed his boots. Bill instantly recognized the early signs.

"Damn Bob," Hackett said quietly, "This could take a while." With that said, Bill placed his friend's freezing feet under his parka and directly onto his bare stomach. Hackett would later say that in order to understand how cold this sensation was, you had to 'recall a particular time when your wife slipped into bed in the dead of winter and put her cold feet onto your own. Then take that feeling and multiply it by a factor of ten!' Every climber was suffering from the cold in one capacity or another but Goodwin's condition was, for the moment, Bill's only concern. When Goodwin himself stated that he was able to proceed, they suited up and continued the march towards the summit.

Only four hours after leaving camp, the party arrived at the highest point on the North American continent! One of the first lightweight parties on McKinley had achieved their goal. Anderson, who only hours before had asked to be left behind, could not believe his good fortune and marveled at the view below him. "So vast an area seen from so great a height of itself blunts the perspective, leaving the mind befuddled by a multitude of detail." Fortunately for the team, the fair weather had held. Bill's thermometer read 0-degrees Fahrenheit and only a slight breeze was blowing. They stayed on the summit for an hour, taking pictures, enjoying the scenery and each other's company after so many weeks of hard work. And then, as Bill had in 1947 and 1951, he took a last look around and began the journey home.

The expedition returned to the Mount McKinley National Park Hotel in only five days. Altitude headaches were gone, packs were light as supplies had been exhausted, and muscles were relaxed after descending to more level terrain. Only severe sunburns and sore toes from frostbite told the men they had physically been to the summit. They had been away for a month and were glad to be sharing beers with friends and plying them with stories of their venture.

◦◦◦ ◦◦◦

"I'm very proud that I took up the opportunity to do this," Anderson would recall in an interview half a century later, "I later became a park ranger in the Grand Teton National Park for two years but never encountered the same level of adventure or camaraderie as I did on McKinley in '52. Bill invited me to go to K2 with him in 1960, but I didn't have any money available at the time. McKinley was then my one and only opportunity for a high-altitude ascent."[25] Anderson also recalls that Bill would always keep him in the back of his mind, offering him climbing and occupational opportunities. Bill was influential enough to get Anderson a position as a civilian instructor for the US Army mountain troops based at Camp Carson, Colorado in 1953. He additionally sent Anderson a letter in 1960, offering him a teaching position in Bad Tolz, Germany. Though Anderson was busy raising a family in the states, he would always remember Bill as the man who took a chance on him and led him to the summit of McKinley.

WDHP

First ascent of Mt. Hood, 1933

WDHP

Camp Hale, Colorado, 1943

'The Boys of the Tenth', Glocknerhaus, Austria, July 1945.
Back Row: (L to R) Bill Andrews, Bob Swartz, Ed Alwieda, Chet Hallstead,
Lou Witcher, Karl Schnackenberg.
Front Row: (L to R) Kerr Sparks, Ray Beonard, Karl Stingl, and Bill Hackett

WDHP

'Operation White Tower', McKinley, 1947

Bill Hackett and
Barbara Washburn
enjoy a morning
cup of coffee,
McKinley, 1947

Grant Pearson,
Bill Hackett and
Jim Gale, McKinley,
1947

Top Left: Bill Hackett on the summit of Aconcagua, the Andes, 1949

Top Right: President Peron, Maj. Hackett and Maj. Mottet, Buenos Aeries, 1949

Right: Jim Moore, Perry Pereira and Bill Hackett, summit of Mt. Kenya, Africa, 1950

Below: Eliangiringa, Daudi Jonathan, Siara and Sitefano, Kilimanjaro, Africa, 1950

Top Left: Bill Hackett and Jim Gale as members of Dr. Washburn's first ascent of McKinley's West Buttress, 1951

Top Right: McKinley's West Buttress, 1951

Right: Bill Hackett and Jim Gale summit McKinley, 1951

Below: (L to R) Pilot, Dr. Terris Moore and climbers, Dr. Henry Buchtel, Dr. Bradford Washburn, Bill Hackett and Jim Gale. Kahiltna Glacier, McKinley, 1951

'A man in his element.' Grizzly
Peak, Colorado, 1954

Captain William D. Hackett,
United States Army, 1957

The Mt. Logan Massif, Yukon Territory, Canada, 1959

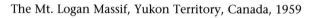

Top Left: K2: 'The Savage Mountain', 1960

Top Right: Boarding Alexander's Barge on the banks of the Indus River, Karakoram, 1960

Above: Porters crossing the turbulent Braldu River on a rope bridge, 1960

Below: The 1960 German-American Karakoram Expedition to K2. (L to R) Lüdwig Greissl, Dr. Wolfgang Deubzer, Günter Jahr, Bill Hackett, Herbert Wünsche, Captain Sharif Ghafur, Dave Bohn and Lynn Pease

WDHP

Top Left: House's Chimney, Abruzzi Ridge, K2, 1960

Top Right: Base Camp on the Godwin-Austen Glacier, K2, 1960

WDHP

Above: Camp III, Abruzzi Ridge, K2, 1960

Below: Establishing Camp I, Abruzzi Ridge, K2, 1960

WDHP

Top Left: Captain Hackett providing instruction at Fort Carson, Colorado, 1947

Top Right: General Omar Bradley (far right) inspecting Captain Hackett's troops, 1952

Below Left: Bill and June Hackett on their Wedding Day, November 19, 1989

Below Right: Bill Hackett on the summit of Sunshine Peak, Colorado. His last ascent, 1992

Above: (L to R) Dr. Terris Moore, Capt. Bill Hackett, Ernest Baumann and Dr. Frank Palmer after their plane crash on Mt. Spurr, 1958

CHAPTER IX

The Northwest Buttress

"Every movement requires effort—we all pray that good weather
will release us from this existence by morning."[1]

—Bill Hackett

Bill Hackett thoroughly enjoyed the challenges of organizing and leading expeditions and by the mid-1950s he rarely gave thought to joining trips led by others. A telephone call from his friend Dr. Bradford Washburn in 1954 quickly changed his mind. Washburn informed him that a group of Alaskan climbers was organizing an attempt on one of McKinley's most challenging routes to date—The Northwest Buttress.

By now Hackett was familiar with the history of mountaineering on McKinley and knew The Northwest Buttress to be virgin territory. He was aware that in 1903, Judge James Wickersham led a party onto the mountain's northern flank but had been rebuffed by the 17,000-foot high wall of ice that would later bear his name. "Our only line of further ascent," the judge would report, "would be to climb the vertical wall of the mountain at our left, and that is impossible."[2] Such a climb had all the elements that drew Bill to such heights: high-altitude, a virgin route, technically challenging aspects, and historical significance. Besides, call something *impossible* and Bill Hackett was sure to take up the challenge.

Fred Beckey, who would join the expedition at the last moment, described how this expedition was formed in his *Mount McKinley: Icy Crown of North America* (1993). Members of the Alaska Alpine Club had reviewed photographs and initial map drawings made of McKinley by Dr. Bradford Washburn. The director of the Boston Museum of Science had continually advised mountaineers about virgin routes on McKinley and when he believed the best time of the year was to approach such challenges. The Alaskan climbers met in Fairbanks and discussed two virgin routes they hoped to achieve during the 1954 climbing season. Both were immense buttress routes, one leading to the South Summit from the south while the other led to the North Summit from the northwest. It was this latter goal that initiated planning for the 1954 ascent of the Northwest Buttress.

Donald McLean, prime organizer of the expedition, described one of his primary concerns:

> "A major drawback of the northwest route was the late arrival of the sun on the northern slopes of the mountain, particularly early in the year. All but the peak would lie in shadow until 11 AM. The mountain, lying only three degrees south of the Arctic Circle, would have a considerably lower mean temperature for the month of May than for July when most expeditions tackle it. There was no telling when or where the winds would be worst. Perhaps the greatest attraction and greatest obstacle lay in the series of three rock outcrops along the ridge at 11,000, 13,000, and 15,000."[3]

McLean, a recent graduate from medical school, knew he would need a special team for such an endeavor, and he found some up-and-coming climbers from around the country. Charles "Bucky" Wilson of Fairbanks would act as co-leader of the venture. Wilson was a physics researcher working on theories of the origins of the *aurora borealis*, the Northern Lights. Captain Bill Hackett, in charge of training at the Mountain and Cold Weather Training Command at Camp Carson, Colorado, joined the expedition through the efforts of Dr. Washburn. Hackett, with three successful ascents of McKinley would bring a great deal of high-altitude experience to their ranks. In addition, he could take advantage of the opportunity by testing the *Walking Penguin* down sleeping robes and vapor-barrier sleeping pads for use in the US Air Force.[4] Henry Meybohm, a German skier, had initially been hired for ski patrol duty near Fairbanks, but was soon introduced to the mountaineering community. They quickly recognized his talents and noteworthy stamina. The fifth and final member of the expedition was three-time Alaskan expedition veteran, Fred Becky, a member of the Seattle-based Mountaineers and a rising star in the North American mountaineering community. Less than a month prior to departure, Hackett called Beckey and invited him to join the team. Though Beckey brought his considerable rock climbing experience to the team, certain members of the expedition feared that he might try to lead them on a nightmare route plagued with a host of technical rock obstacles. It was hoped that Hackett, a friend of Beckey's, would help reel him in and ensure the most practical route to the summit was pursued.[5]

On May 2, 1954, the five-man team reported to the Fairbanks Flying Service and boarded Hollie Evan's twin-engine Beechcraft. They flew 150 miles from Fairbanks to a frozen lake called *Minchumina*. It was a clear day and Mount McKinley, Beckey would recall, grew ever larger in the window. Once on the frozen lake, the team had to take turns flying in Dick Collins' Piper Pacer that was equipped with skis. Collins, who worked for the Civil Aeronautics Administration, made several round-trip flights in his 125hp aircraft; depositing the expedition on another frozen lake, this one near Straightaway Glacier on McKinley's northwestern flank.[6] Here, the team could see the entire length of their proposed route and marvel at the 18,000-foot elevation gain they would need to make in order to achieve their goal. One of the advantages of climbing earlier in the season was the lack of mosquitoes that had so plagued the 1952 team.

The first order of business was to ensure they had cached enough food for their return journey. The men suited up, donned their packs and snowshoes, and tramped across four miles of ice and snow with nine days worth of supplies. They reached a moraine and deposited their supplies on top of an eight-foot boulder. The expedition would spend their first night near here at 3,400 feet.

Starting on the morning of May 3, the team began their trek to gain altitude and better access to the base of the Northwest Buttress. Several gullies forced them to follow a snow-filled moat that ran parallel to the glacier but the reflecting sun heated the men up so fast they were elated when they reached the cooler temperatures near Crosson Glacier. After dinner that evening, several members of the party repaired their snowshoe bindings while discussing past alpine adventures.[7] Hackett and Beckey had climbed together before but never with any of the others. Likewise, the climbers from Fairbanks had spent time together in the hills but rarely with outsiders. Beckey and Meybohm got along well together and, in fact, a month after the conclusion of the McKinley expedition, they climbed together with Heinrich Harrer; making the first ascent of nearby Mount Hunter.[8]

May 4 brought continued progress. Beckey would write:

> "By the next evening we had climbed from 5,800 feet into 8,200-foot Peters Pass and descended the sastrugi-covered slopes of Peters Glacier.... We established base camp well out or reach of avalanches on a patch of flat sastrugi that had survived the blasts of the wind. Surrounding us in the great basin was the dirty tone of neve (old snow from the previous year). Casting a glance sideways at the overwhelming Wickersham Wall, which rose to the summit of the North Peak in an unbroken and dangerous sweep, we were relieved that the Northwest Buttress did not seem to present a particular ice avalanche hazard."[9]

McLean was also impressed with the terrain, remarking; "Only one mile ahead lay Cook's Shoulder, a gigantic white mass, studded with patches of pressure ice in innumerable pastel shades of green and blue. It was broken by fields of seracs and icefalls, by a headwall and great yawning crevasses, couloirs streaked with ava-lanche debris and topped off by a huge pyramid of rock."[10]

During the following two days the expedition divided into two teams and concentrated on reconnaissance efforts. Beckey and Hackett explored a path leading to the southwest. They climbed to an elevation of nearly 10,000 feet, but rock of inferior quality was found. Scanning higher they spied several pitches clogged with suspicious-looking ice. McLean and Wilson fared no better, finding deep snow drifts atop solid ice, a notoriously dangerous combination.

Once Hackett and Beckey were back near base camp, they donned snowshoes and tramped out a suitable landing area for Collins to land his plane and re-supply the team. The following morning every member of the party pitched in to assist in the final preparations for the landing strip. No one could predict that this strip would never be used.

Richard and Jeanne Collins were flying their Piper Pacer towards base camp in order to land and provide the expedition with further supplies. They were accompanied by another plane of similar design, which acted as cover for Collins. Both planes dropped in altitude to make an initial pass over the camp to inspect the terrain below. Hackett, Beckey and the rest of the team were having breakfast in a Logan tent when they heard the whine of an airplane engine. Hackett stuck his head out of the tent, spied the plane passing overhead, and watched as Collins seemed to disappear.[11]

"Hallo!" Bill said aloud while putting down his food. "What do you make of that?" There were shrugged shoulders and looks of puzzlement on some of the faces of his colleagues. There had been neither sign nor sound of a crash but everyone agreed Collins had passed extremely low to the ground. Looking in the general direction of where they had last seen the aircraft, they spotted his cover plane making a few circles higher in the air. Then, inexplicably, the cover plane took off. There was an awkward moment of silence as each climber tried to make out what had happened or whether anything had happened at all. On one hand it was clear that Collins had flown low to the ground but on the other, the flight path wasn't *so* low as to cause immediate concern. 'Nothing I haven't seen Don Sheldon do on many occasions' Bill thought to himself.

In addition to the down suits and sleeping pads Hackett was testing for the Air Force, he was examining the use of white felt Army boots. Though oversized, one could wear several pairs of wool socks inside and most climbers agreed that the boots were quite warm and a welcome addition to the expedition. There was one serious drawback however, one Bill was all too ready to acknowledge—the sheer size of the boot hampered one's movements while wearing crampons.[12] Bill donned a pair of these boots for the first time before he and his companions departed up the glacier in the direction they had last seen the plane.

No sign of the Collins' or their aircraft were found.

Expedition members returned to the Logan tent to continue their breakfast. In less than an hour, Dick and Jeanne Collins suddenly made an appearance in camp, surprising everyone! Wilson even accidentally kicked over a pot of tea he was heating. The pilots had been forced to crash-land when they encountered heavy down drafts. They landed abruptly and ended up upside down less than a mile from camp. The crash site had been obscured by undulations in the ice.[13] Hackett was amazed that neither the pilot nor co-pilot were injured. He was even more astonished to realize they had hiked nearly a mile over the glacier without the protection of ropes! A few members of the expedition had dropped partway through hidden crevasses the day previous but had been roped up and easily extricated. Dick Collins had been able to radio for help before the battery in his radio died. They would just have to wait to be picked up.

Before the expedition could continue, the safety of the Collins' would have to be ensured. With a window of fair weather, they could be picked up in a matter of hours but Beckey and Hackett could clearly see the signs of a pending storm front on the horizon. This three-day storm was one of the most interesting and severe storms Hackett would ever endure. McLean would write that, "Warm winds eventually came well in excess of 100 m.p.h., sweeping the glacier cleaner than ever." Hackett would note in his diary that, "Chunks of ice and snow [were] being blown horizontally."[14] Fred Beckey, who has certainly endured plenty of storms during his career,[15] had this to say about life in camp:

> "We turned the French tent around and prepared for
> a violent, crowded night, one that promised no
> sleep. Rather quickly, thoughts turned from the
> Buttress to survival. With the high wind sweeping

the glacier cleaner than ever, it seemed safer to crawl than walk when outside the tent...I was glad that we were at 7,000 feet, in the lee of the main tempest, rather than on the exposed 18,000-foot summit plateau. We avoided answering the 'call of nature' except when absolutely necessary."[16]

The five climbers and two pilots were crowded into three tents. One was a standard, four-man Logan tent with a central pole while the other two were of French design. Wilson and Beckey spent a good portion of the night bracing the pole in the Logan tent.

The storm lasted three days, and only when the skies cleared could the team begin to evacuate their downed pilots. McLean and Wilson accompanied the Collins' down the glacier to the frozen lake. A last inspection of the downed plane revealed that it was still upside down, but now the $7,000 uninsured aircraft was missing a wing and the right side landing gear was completely smashed.[17] The climbers spied a reconnaissance airplane overhead, apparently scanning the valleys below. Wilson and McLean used a signal mirror but failed to grab the attention of the aircraft. It was decided that a better signal would be needed. Members of the expedition cut down some trees farther down the mountain and used the logs to spell out the word LAKE in six-foot letters. They additionally created an arrow pointing towards the lake itself. A signal fire was used to grab any would-be rescuer's attention. Finally, four days after crashing onto McKinley, a helicopter crew from the 74th Air Rescue Service picked up the downed pilots.[18]

Once the safety of the Collins' had been ensured, the climbing team could once again turn their attention to the Northwest Buttress. An inventory was taken to confirm that they had enough provisions for the assault. Fair weather had enabled the team to receive critical airdrops from pilot Ginny Wood, whose husband was climbing the mountain from the south side. On paper, the supply and logistical plans seemed to barely coalesce. The men would need to work quickly, efficiently, and with few mistakes.

Beckey, Hackett and Meybohm were able to provide a serious breakthrough as soon as they were out the gate. The best way of reaching the top of Cook's Shoulder was a subject under much debate but the trio eventually decided to climb it the old fashion way; by cutting thousands of steps in the ice.[19] McLean, quite proud of the advance the team had made, described the terrain and initial portion of the historic route:

> "It was a glassy staircase of precarious steps chopped 80 percent of the way, 2000 feet up. Beginning in a snow couloir on the left or northern slope of the shoulder, it then went to the right across a small triangular plateau about midway and eventually zig-zagged straight up the western crest of the shoulder. Two fixed ropes were established, both of which were taken up higher with us a few days later after we had finished the relays. The ice steps deteriorated badly in the sun, but we did not anticipate interval melting above 11,000 feet. Beyond the 10,500-foot cache lay a cockscomb, the cornice of which fell straight off on the north, directly over the little plateau at 9,000 feet. Sitting astraddle this knife ridge during delays was like riding a horse!"[20]

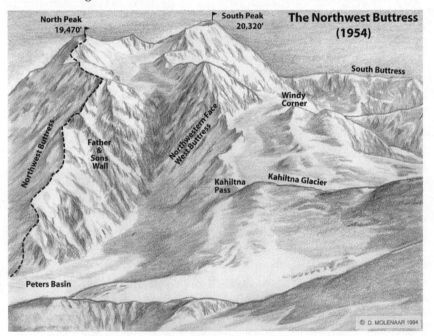

Just above this knife-edge crest, Camp I was established. Under the circumstances the position of the tent site was ideal as it was protected by the high winds that continually scoured the mountain slopes. This 'windless oasis' as they called it, stood roughly 300 feet below and slightly to the left of the ridge. While Hackett and Meybohm began erecting the Logan and French tents, Beckey wanted a more stable shelter. Should a storm like the one they encountered on May 7 present itself again, Beckey wanted more than a mere bolt-hole to dart into. He dug a sizeable snow cave that could comfortably accommodate a small climbing party.

Hackett would later say that he was quite impressed with Beckey's performance on McKinley. The latter's decision to take the time and expend the effort to build a suitable snow cave at Camp I was just such an example. Such a move, according to Hackett, demonstrated the type of patience and determination that were needed to climb a massive mountain like McKinley.[21] Another example can be found in Bill's diary entry for May 11, where he describes their daily loads as "miserably heavy"[22] Bill Hackett, a man not unfamiliar with carrying oversized packs, marveled at the fact that Beckey could not only bear his share of the load, but additionally carry extensive camera equipment in order to film footage of their ascent.

On May 13, Beckey and McLean made the next serious territorial gain by pushing the route up an immense black pyramid of rock. Bill dubbed this technically challenging site 'Abruzzi Ridge' and it proved to be the central crux of the Northwest Buttress.[23] In his report to the American Alpine Club, McLean would state that, "Fred and I selected the right side of the rock ridge leading up 1,000 feet to the right-hand side of a great rock pyramid. This ridge...we found to be of reddish brown schist cracked in all directions but with a favorable dip for climbing. The slope began at about 20 (degrees) but steepened as we reached the pyramid where there was actually an overhang in places. We climbed unroped because of the severe exposure and treacherous nature of this loose rock, sometimes frozen, sometimes not."[24] Beckey and McLean additionally set fixed ropes up some of the more difficult rock towers, in order to make sure that the balance of the team could follow in relative safety.

The following morning they continued to stock and clean up the route while continuing to push forward. Everyone reached the summit of the pyramid and in the days to come they established a camp at 12,500 feet as well as a food cache. Nearly a thousand feet higher, the men encountered another rock barrier they labeled appropriately, Pyramid II. "Not knowing what lay above," McLean would state, "...we traversed around it to the left, across a great sloping cirque. We could see above us the long serrated ridge which we had just skirted, while the steepest portion of the Wickersham Wall, looking very bad, lay in profile to our left." Up ahead of them the men encountered a large, snow-filled couloir leading up from the cirque back to the northwest ridge. It would take a full six hours of hard climbing to surmount it. They had to chop steps in the ice up the entire length of the chute. Here, at 14,200 feet, McLean was impressed with the natural beauty the ridge presented, writing:

> "The ice chips here would skip and slide down to the *Tuluna* Icefall, 6,000 feet below us. The rock on the ridge had changed to black schist, especially dark in contrast to the overall whiteness of the snow. Here, well above the clouds, which obscured everything below 13,000 feet, stood only Denali and Denali's wife, McKinley and Foraker, alone and serene. The clouds, like a greater Niagara, poured down from central Alaska eastward between these two peaks, reaching as far as the Kenai Peninsula, where they simply evaporated upon reaching the sea."

As they had studied aerial photographs of the Northwest Buttress prior to their departure from Fairbanks, expedition members knew that they were now at the base of the last remaining technical obstacle along the route-rock pitches near 14,800 feet. The team took advantage of another three-day spell of fair weather, climbing steadily up the granite face. Along these speckled orange granite rock walls, Beckey placed the first pitons into Mount McKinley, forty-one years after its first ascent.[25] Bill would note that some of this climbing was extremely difficult and would force them to change into crampons every other pitch. They'd be going strong for some time only to be confronted with schist so steep that snow and ice would not adhere to its surface. With forty-pound packs, laden with ropes to be fixed, the men would need to hold onto the rock with one hand while removing their crampons with the other.[26] By the end of the day, May 19, they had fixed over 400 feet of rope, cached loads at 15,600 feet and located a site for Camp III.

Life in camp would alternate from chaos to complete lethargy. In Camp II for instance, everyone pitched in on the material maintenance of their tools and supplies. Beckey repaired the leather waist loop on his ice axe; Meybohm sewed his trousers up while Hackett sewed up his long underwear that had torn. Hackett also cut the elk top sole from Meybohm's felt boots in order to give him better traction on rock. For entertainment they played Hearts with a deck of cards Mrs. Collins had provided them, played chess or read books they had hauled up the mountain. Beckey was engrossed in an Edith Hamilton book on Greek mythology while Hackett selected, *The Sex Habits of American Women*. At night the men would exchange stories about women they had known, cars they had owned, and what adventures they wanted to embark on in the future.[27]

The journey between Camps II and III, though not too technical in nature, proved interesting to all assembled. In the morning the men divided into two rope teams and leap-frogged their way up towards Camp IV. A solitary eagle flew overhead while they took a break for a much-needed meal. The entire team then roped up on a single 220-foot line and climbed the steepest portion the buttress had to offer. McLean stated that it was fortunate the cliffs had been fixed with rope the previous day, "otherwise, with the new snow it might well have proved impassable." When the team reached Camp IV they unloaded their packs and began setting up tents for the night. At some point, Wilson realized they brought food and stoves but neglected to pack the necessary pots to cook with. Two climbers were selected to rappel back to Camp II, retrieve the necessary cookware, and climb the steep wall a second time!

Attempting to climb back up to Camp III from the lower camps proved more tiresome and difficult than the team had at first anticipated. Both Beckey and Meybohm's feet were showing the first signs of frostbite. Beckey would recall that he had to sit in the

snow during a break, remove his own boots and warm his feet up
inside his down jacket. Hackett recorded in his diary that most of
the men had to have their feet warmed during this repeat ascent.
Wilson and McLean, who were the first climbers to ready themselves in the morning, were selected to break trail. They found
themselves kicking steps up the snow couloir for over four hours in
order to reach the saddle at 14,200 feet. All of the steps the expedition had created over the previous few days were now filled with
sixteen inches of new snow! Wilson and McLean even used a shovel to clear portions of the trail that had been easily traversed only a
day earlier. McLean and Hackett would expand on the site designated as Camp III, while colossal ice avalanches roared down the
Wickersham Wall in the distance.[28]

On May 23, while en route to Camp IV, Wilson suffered a fall.
He was climbing a near vertical pitch when his foot slipped on the
snow and down he went. He fell only six to eight feet before he was
yanked to a halt. Beckey had been belaying him from above and
Hackett, from below. Fortunately, Wilson had been the middleman
on a three-man rope team. Wilson credits their belaying with saving
them all from a 4,500-foot fall. As soon as he found himself dangling
on the rope, he reached out and grabbed hold of a protruding rock on
the wall. Beckey would note that, "Wilson was not really shaken, but
winded from the effort of lifting [his] body and pack with one hand
at an elevation of 15,500."

By the time Camp V was established at 17,400 feet, everyone
was feeling the effects of the increased altitude. Wilson and McLean
were suffering from incredible headaches while Beckey was experiencing bouts of nausea. Hackett's diary indicates that he and
Meybohm were fairing well, for the time being, but that he knew it
was only a matter of time before he too, fell ill.

McLean records his memories of Camp V:

"We all reached the new cache at 17,000 feet...decid-
ing to place Camp V there early in the evening because
the weather had closed in. We purposely had carried
only the Logan tent above Camp IV. To set up camp
here at 17,400 feet on a moderate slope, we were
obliged to cut a six-foot platform, the inner wall of

which was four feet high. In a way, it was unfortunate that we had such excellent weather because we had climbed so fast that we had not become acclimatized. Three of us suffered headache, nausea, and vomiting. I administered to each an intramuscular injection of Acth-Ar-Gel, a pituitary hormone which stimulates secretion of the adrenal cortex and is known to be of exceptional value in stress conditions."

── ═◆═ ──

May 26 saw an increase in activity as the expedition finally reached the Great Plateau of McKinley's North Peak. Wilson would state that climbing that day 'was a bitch!' Beckey, repeatedly doubling-over and vomiting, was somehow able to summon reserves and continue up the mountain fully burdened! At 18,500 feet, Camp VI was established and everyone piled into the Logan tent for some much needed and well deserved rest. Icefalls, rock cliffs and a host of other mountaineering challenges had been overcome and now, after nearly a month's worth of hard work, they were poised for making an assault on North Peak.

When Hackett awoke on Thursday morning, May 27, 1954, his observations of himself and his teammates were not reassuring. According to Bill, Wilson threw up his breakfast, McLean was enduring a splitting headache and appeared 'punchy,' and even Beckey was still not up to speed. Sticking his head out of the tent flaps, Bill observed that the skies were overcast. All signs pointed to a day of rest but everyone agreed that it was time for the final push and achieve their goal—completion of the Northwest Buttress. "On the morning of May 27," Beckey would record, "Wilson paid for the previous day's effort with dizziness and vomiting. Some hot tea was comforting and helped combat the bitter cold outside the tent. All of us had spent poor nights because of the cramped space. Donning all the clothes we could muster, we laced boots, tied into the ropes, and started for the North Peak, but then the weather closed in. After a long rest in the tent, we began again, this time making an easy two-hour ascent to reach the top at 6:45 PM."[29]

It is interesting to note that after working nearly non-stop since May 2, most of the summit party had little to say once they reached the summit. Hackett's diary merely states, "...reached summit of North Peak, 19,450', 6:45-cold and semi-cloudy. Took pictures and descended to meet others...." Beckey would add that, "The hoped-for view was murky." Even McLean, who provided the American Alpine Club with a very detailed article, would state, "Grant Pearson (McKinley veteran of 1932 and 1947) had asked us to travel down the northwestern ridge for approximately a quarter of a mile to look for evidence of the [1910] sourdough's pole or its guy-lines, which once stood on the last rock outcrop of the north ridge. But with foul weather brewing we gave up this highly desirable quest."

After the summit teams had returned to the Logan tent at Camp VI, conversation turned to their next objective: the south, and true, summit of McKinley. The team had enough food and fuel to last two to three days but all they needed to complete their ascent was a single day of favorable weather. From the evening of the 27th to the morning of the 31st, the expedition was holed up in Camp VI. Each morning they would awaken to find hoarfrost covering their sleeping bags. This would naturally melt and dampen the bags considerably. At that altitude, with such low temperatures, they would never dry out. Sleep proved difficult due to the high winds buffeting the tent walls and everyone was experiencing an acute lack of appetite. By the evening of May 30, Bill Hackett would write, "Every movement requires effort—we all pray that good weather will release us from this existence by morning."[30]

Until his trial on K2 in 1960, one of the darkest days for Bill Hackett personally was May 31, 1954. He awoke at 3:15 AM to discover forty-mile winds and blowing snow sweeping over the ice outside. It was freezing though clear—the first time in days. With careful yet sluggish effort, the team began to rally to make their attempt on the true summit. McLean, exhausted from weeks of hard work, opted to remain behind while Beckey, Meybohm, Wilson and Hackett made preparations for the assault. While eating their breakfast the men attempted to dry their clothing as best they could over the expedition's two burning stoves. It would take them an astonishing five and-a-half hours to make their preparations: chores that had they occurred at sea level, would have taken but an hour![31]

Their attempt to reach the South Summit was doomed from the start, but at first the men refused to retreat. The weather had worsened since Bill had first checked it earlier in the morning. Tied into a single rope, they had to lean forward into the wind and ascend cautiously, carefully placing each foot before the other and trying their best to maintain their balance. Frost grew on their exposed beards and Bill found himself knocking a chunk of ice off here and there merely because it annoyed him to no end. He would record in his diary later that night that, "…movement was all but impossible as we were facing into it—all complaining of cold hands, feet and faces. We went for about as far as we could take it." In all, Beckey, Meybohm, Wilson and Hackett had been outside their shelter for only an hour when they all agreed upon an immediate and hasty retreat. Back inside their tent in Camp VI, Hackett experienced a type of depression that he would grow all too familiar with throughout the early 1960s—a sensation he hated above all others—failure!

The following morning, Hackett was itching to make another attempt, anything to rid himself of the sinking sensation that had kept him up most of the night. But the day would bring Bill only frustration and pain. Hour after hour, the weather seemed to toy with him. When he first popped his head out the tent flaps he did not like what he saw. Conditions closely resembled those of the previous day. He couldn't even *see* the South Peak, as it was completely socked-in. A secondary check roughly an hour later showed the summit clear and that the winds had died down. Time to move!

As the team began their preparations to depart, the clouds rolled back in and Bill cussed up a storm of his own. McLean, who had asked to be left behind the day earlier, was now in worse condition. He would note in his diary, "We waited…days for better weather, but the wind continued to blow and the south peak was almost constantly shrouded in clouds. It had been extremely uncomfortable living for five men in a small, frost-coated tent for almost a week at so high an elevation. When the fuel ran out and we were forced to descend, we left without regret." Hackett did not share McLean's opinion.[32]

The five-man party was able to descend 3,000 vertical feet to a lower camp that day despite the fact that one of their party (McLean) had to take each step with extreme caution. They then divided into two teams: Wilson, Meybohm and McLean and Hackett and Beckey. The first team left Camp VI around 1:00 PM, with Meybohm and Wilson ensuring McLean made a safe descent. Beckey, who was nearly recuperated by now, and Hackett were left behind to pack up the supplies and equipment. They took down the Logan tent, packed all of the gear up and still descended at such a speed as to overtake the first party. Beckey and Hackett then continued their descent to 15,600 feet where they set up the Logan tent, stocked the camp and started melting snow for drinking water. In this way McLean could be placed in immediate shelter and given fluids upon stopping for the day.[33] This leap-frog descent was a strategy the team would employ over the following few days to ensure the safety of each man and in addition, provide work for Beckey and Hackett—the power-horses who were now gaining strength the further they descended.

McLean writes:

> "The actual descent took four days to Peter's Basin. We went down the rock pitches using long rappels with a double length of rope. We needed a series of ten continuous rappels to descend the Abruzzi Ridge, which proved rather bad because of recent snow. The great cirque over which we had strolled in our ascent was now covered with six feet of new snow. Fortunately, we had a small aluminum shovel which could be attached to an ice-axe, so we were able to dig a path until we finally came to the ridge where the winds had blown much of the snow away."

Beckey, who rigged most of the rappels, would note that the team made five 200-foot rappels and even tied all of their rope together in order to descend a full 440 feet in one sequence. The men additionally had to knock the balling ice off of the bottom of their crampons from time to time as sticky snow continually adhered to their surfaces.

Today's mountaineers who descend the West Buttress Route find themselves on the Kahiltna Glacier with only a radio call needed to bring their aircraft up and retrieve them. They are then sipping hot beverages back in Talkeetna before nightfall. In 1954 however, on the north side of Mount McKinley, Meybohm, Beckey, Hackett, Wilson and McLean would have no such luxury. After assisting two downed pilots to safety, after seeing to the security of their aircraft, after pioneering a brand new route on the highest mountain in North America, after enduring some of the harshest weather ever recorded on the mountain, and after taking four days to retreat to lower ground, they were now faced with a seventy-five mile march out to civilization!

In order to re-group and focus on the new task at hand, the team took the time to take a full inventory of their gear and supplies and map out a plan of action for the days to follow. Snowshoes were doffed at a moraine at Peter's Pass and mosquito repellent and head nets were soon donned. Due to the fact that Beckey had undertaken a sizeable filming project during the expedition, team members now had to pack out a heavy movie camera and seemingly countless rolls of sixteen-millimeter film. Bearing seventy-pound loads and a wide range of aching muscles, the five men started their lengthy march from Crosson Corner to Bar Cabin.

The seventy-five mile march, though exhausting to be sure, nevertheless provided the team with some of their fondest memories of the trip. As there was no mosquito netting to cover the tents or sleeping bags, sleep was nearly impossible and on more than one occasion Bill would erupt in a tirade about the 'stupid, mosquito infested country!' If seeing Bill run around swatting swarms of bugs wasn't enough to provide laughs, then Beckey's near encounter with a grizzly bear surely was. Beckey, whose feet were suffering slightly from frostbite, had slowed up to the point where the rest of the team waited for him on one of many moraines the region offered. Meybohm, Wilson, McLean and Hackett were enjoying some fresh water and beef jerky, while looking back down the trail towards their companion. Eventually, from around the corner, Beckey came into view but he was not alone. Unbeknownst to him, he was being followed by a sizeable grizzly! Wilson and the others jumped to their feet and cried out loud for Beckey to turn around. He did so but at that same moment, the loud sounds of their pleas caused the bear to rise up on his hind legs and stand upright. Beckey turned around and what a sight! For the moment, Fred forgot all about tired leg muscles and both he and the bear departed rather quickly in opposite directions! [34]

The laughs were not to end there. When the team reached the banks of the Muddy River it became evident that someone was going to be taking a serious swim. The river, which drains Peters Glacier and merges with the McKinley fork of the Kantishna, was naturally as cold as ice. Even the ice from Wickersham Wall made its way to this river. Wilson was acknowledged as the best swimmer and he had, in fact, made the swim two years earlier on a previous expedition. He stripped down till he was 'in all his nakedness,' tied a rope around his waist, and took the inevitable plunge. Bill, curious as to just how cold the water was, stuck his exposed foot in the river. "Oh! For the love of—!" He couldn't believe Wilson was faring as well as he was. Partway across the rushing water, Wilson struck his knee on a rock and would have been swept downstream had he not been able to grasp onto a submerged root. He was able to extricate himself from the water and drag his shivering body right up the bank into a swarm of mosquitoes. He would later write that his friends seemed more interested in laughing at him than in throwing him his trousers. Wilson was then able to rig a belay rope from a tree and a hand line for the others to cross.[35]

When the expedition reached Bar Cabin, three days after leaving the mountain proper, they noticed an odd set of signatures in the cabin register. Les Viereck and Morton Wood had placed their sobriquet but in the comments section, they would write, "In memory of Elton Thayer." When the team hired a local man to drive them all to McKinley Park Hotel, the driver informed them of what had happened. Elton Thayer, Morton Wood, Les Viereck and George Argus were making an attempt to traverse the mountain from south to north and were climbing at the same time Hackett and the others had. During their attempt, the four were all roped into one line when Thayer slipped on the ice. One by one he pulled them all down until the party had slid over 900 feet! Though Viereck had checked the slide by falling into a crevasse, Thayer had been killed. With this news, Beckey, Wilson, Hackett, Meybohm and McLean forgot all about their missed chance to reach the south summit and set aside the fact that their legs were sore from over a month's work. They were alive, they had achieved a first ascent and all had returned unscathed with the exception of minor bumps and bruises.

CHAPTER X

The
Journeyman

*"Great numbers of flies, smaller than the common housefly,
inhabit the bush and swarm over one's body and clothing in the same
manner as the mosquitoes of Alaska."*[1]

—Bill Hackett

A year after Bill's success on McKinley's Northwest Buttress, he received orders from the Army to assume duties as the Intelligence Officer for the 17th Regiment, 7th Infantry Division just north of Seoul, Korea. The regiment was severely undermanned and Bill performed double duty as their Operations Officer. He spent the first month in Korea getting his bearings. During the second month, once he had the office running smoothly, he submitted a request for a leave of absence in order to climb Mount Fujiyama in Japan. The consummate politician, Bill was somehow able to open the doors that were necessary to grant him, once again, paid time off to pursue his passion.

Though many people feel they would be unable to serve in the military since the Government has the right to dispatch you anywhere in the world, Bill openly embraced the opportunity. A review of his climbing record shows a man who never sat in his stateroom for long. He climbed fifteen peaks in the Canadian Rockies and Columbia Ice Field when he was stationed in the valleys below them.

He climbed an additional fifteen peaks in the Rockies while stationed in Colorado during the war. Wherever the Army placed him, be it the Julian Alps, the Zillerthal Mountains or the Dolomites, Bill took full advantage of the opportunity. When he received word that he would be stationed in the Far East, Bill immediately set about making plans to climb as often as his position would allow.

In late summer, 1955, Hackett juggled both his duties at the office and his preparations for climbing in Japan and Australia. His diary entries reveal a man whose idea of every day life was far different from most. In just nine days in August for instance, Bill caught his houseboy stealing, was tasked with the destruction of thousands of classified documents, got in contact with representatives of the Japanese Alpine Club, met with authorities to discuss an uprising in Pusan, and he even grabbed the base interpreter to meet with a village police chief to discuss methods to rid the area of prostitution.[2] Bill sent a letter to the Military Attaché in Melbourne, Australia[3] and even worked with Army air pilots, based in Japan, on how best to fly to Australia for free.[4] All of these arrangements for climbing in Australia were made before he even left Korea to go climbing in Japan. He was always thinking about future climbing ventures and breaking down the obstacles that stood in his way of achieving them.

On August 25, Bill flew to Japan and landed at Tachigawa Air Force Base. He checked into the Yuraku Hotel and soon contacted Yuko Make, President of the Japanese Alpine Club. Make was able to provide Bill with maps of the region and tips on how to relate with other climbers along the way. Bill was grateful for the assistance and thrilled to meet with Make who would go on to lead the first ascent of Manaslu in Nepal, the world's ninth highest mountain.

Joining Bill on Mount Fuji was Mr. Andrew Headland, feature editor for the *Pacific Stars and Stripes*. On August 27, 1955, they took a bus to Umagaeshi, where the road terminated at the base of the mountain. They emerged from the bus in a torrential downpour and with winds quite high, they were soon soaked to the bone. Seeking shelter, they jogged to the nearby village of Tanai. There, Bill bought an alpenstock from a friendly shop owner.

Hackett had a very good reason for purchasing a new alpenstock. He was aware that there were ten established stations along the path to the summit. Within these stations climbers or pilgrims could retreat from the elements, rest their limbs or receive refreshments. At each of these stations you could receive a colored flag to affix to your alpenstock. As you want to return with all ten flags, their presence can be a positive motivator to reach the summit. Those who think they can cheat and purchase similar flags in the lowlands are in for a shock. Each station additionally keeps a red-hot branding iron that burns a particular emblem into the climber's alpenstock.[5]

This journey to the summit had been undertaken by hundreds of thousands of pilgrims for centuries. Though there is no clear documentation that reveals the identity of the first climber to reach the summit, the first ascent is attributed to En-no-Shokaku in the year 700 A.D. During the 12th Century, a Buddhist monk erected a stone temple on the summit to honor Sengen Dainichi, the deity of Mount Fujiyama. In the 14th Century, a sect known as the Shugendo began to formally worship the great peak. Followers believed that the mountain had perfect form and achieved the state of Zenho, perfect concentration. The Shugendo were the first to build huts along the mountain to help the *true believers* during their journey.

Hackett and Headland began their ascent of the Yoshida Trail on the northeast side of the mountain. They reached the fifth station just past timberline around noon. Still climbing through the rain, they opted to continue their ascent. By the time they reached the seventh station however, they decided they had had enough of foul weather. They wrung their clothes out and supported their coats on poles to dry. After a supper of fish and tea they discovered they could spend the night. They were given blankets and *ki makura*, wooden pillows. Lying on a wooden floor with a wooden pillow, Bill knew he wouldn't be getting the best night's sleep.[6]

Up before dawn, they emerged from the hut into the same awful weather conditions they had fled from the night before. Hiking up the well-worn trail, they passed stations eight and nine. At Station 10 however, they decided to rest for a meal and dry out to the best of their ability. Station 10 was not only larger than its predecessors it was more structurally sound. Constructed below the crater rim, it provided climbers with a dry place to enjoy an afternoon meal.

When they reached the 12,397-foot summit, they were met with winds in excess of 70 miles per hour. The rain and sleet were so thick that they were unable to see the steel siding of the summit weather station until they nearly ran into it. The employees within were shocked to see that tourists had even braved the weather to make a summit bid. They welcomed Hackett and Headland, offering them oranges and warm tea.[7]

When they departed the weather station, Bill chose the wrong trail and began a lengthy descent of the mountain. When he reached a position below the majority of clouds and realized he was lost, he didn't seem to care.

"Hell, we took a cab here!" he shouted to Headland. "We can take a cab back!" When all was said and done, they had made a full traverse of Fuji in less than two days. When asked what he thought of the trip, he replied simply, "We reached the top!" There was no view visible from the summit, no idyllic walk along a summit ridge, and the men were soaked to the bone. But Bill Hackett had added another of the world's great peaks to his growing collection.

When Bill returned to duty in Korea, a mound of mail was waiting for him on his desk. Among the correspondence were letters from Peter J. Cameron, honorable secretary for the New South Wales Federation of Bush walking clubs and Don Richardson of the Ski Council of New South Wales. Hackett had written to Cameron and Richardson in an attempt to solicit their assistance in finding a climbing companion for him on his proposed trip to Australia. Similar to his experience on Aconcagua, Bill's charm and people skills had secured him a climbing partner, food supplies and a host of information concerning the Australian Alps.[8]

Hackett used military cargo flights and civilian aircraft to transport himself to Sydney, Australia on February 4, 1956. Here, he telephoned his climbing contacts and made arrangements to travel by rail to the town of Cooma, some 270 miles south south-east of Sydney.

A few years earlier, the Australian government had embarked on a twenty-five year program, the *Snowy Mountains Scheme*, designed to harness the waters in the region to develop watersheds and hydroelectric generation of power. Bill was forced to purchase a visitor's pass from this organization in order to continue his journey over fifty-three miles of dirt roads. He arrived in Island Bend, a small community comprised mostly of employees of the hydroelectric company. In this remote outpost, Bill was introduced to the climbing partner Cameron and Richardson had pre-arranged to accompany him.[9]

Mr. Reinhold "Olda" Schaefer was born to a Czechoslovakian mother and an Austrian father. At age eighteen, he had been drafted into the German Army and was captured by American soldiers in 1945. Three years later he emigrated from Czechoslovakia to Australia, and since 1951, had been in the employ of the Investigative Division of the Hydrology Branch of the Snowy Mountains Hydro-Electric Authority. His work kept him in the field most of the time.[10]

On the morning of February 7, Hackett and Schaefer drove a jeep up the Mungyang Valley. At the Guthega Power Station they switched to horseback and rode out to the White River Hut. At this point they hobbled their horses with leather straps to prevent their straying while the men were off climbing the nearby crags.

Bill recorded his observations of the terrain and its inhabitants:

> "Most of the trees fall within the more than 300 vari-
> eties of gum: a few pines exist; the mountain ash
> grows at higher elevations. Mountain streams hold
> rainbow trout. The wombat is a nocturnal pig-like,
> short-legged animal of 150-180 pounds; it lives in
> holes; we saw much evidence of rooting around on
> the Geehi River. Other animals include hares, foxes,
> and the dingos, which are wild dogs a third larger
> than a fox. Great numbers of flies, smaller than the
> common housefly, inhabit the bush and swarm over
> one's body and clothing in the same manner as the
> mosquitoes of Alaska. The March fly, similar to an
> oversize housefly, abound in quantity and inflict a
> painful sting."[11]

Between February 7 and 13, Hackett and Schaefer climbed all throughout the Australian Alps. They would awaken early, eat a hasty meal and see to the care of the horses. Schaefer would use a rod and reel to catch rainbow trout for food and for water; the Crakenback River was but a stone's throw away. While their horses grazed on rolling meadows, the men would climb to the top of every peak within range: Gungatarn, Twynam, and the Ghost! Caruthers Peak, Rams Head and the Big Bogong! Their seven-day trip would take them a total distance of ninety miles on horseback and fifty miles on foot. They would climb twenty-two mountains, which included every major peak in the Australian Alps and the fourteen highest mountains on the continent.

For Bill Hackett however, all of these peaks were only minor amusements; he was in the region for one purpose and one purpose only—Mount Kosciuszko.[12] At 7,310 feet, Kosciuszko was the highest moorland summit in Australia, and therefore, another continental summit. A mere hike when compared to the other massive peaks comprising the Seven Summits, the small Australian peak was still needed in order to achieve his goal.

After lunch, on the afternoon of February 11, 1956, Bill Hackett achieved his fourth continental summit, the first person in history to do so. He and Schaefer had enjoyed a leisurely hike over the treeless expanse that is the Kosciuszko plateau. Bill would stumble on occasion, along the thorny vegetation, but Schaefer seemed at ease among the terrain he called his 'office.'[13] Bill enjoyed the view the simple summit afforded. He could see the Abbott and Mueller Ranges to the northwest and the Ramshead Range to the south. An obelisk, several feet high, stood nearby. Its plaque revealed a quote from its first western visitor, Paul Edmund Strzelecki:

> "The particular configuration of this eminence struck me so forcibly by the similarity it bears to a tumulus elevated in Krakow over the tomb of the patriot Kosciusko, that, although in a foreign country, on foreign ground, but amongst a free people, who appreciate freedom and its votaries, could not refrain from giving it the name of Mount Kosciusko."[14]

There was no euphoric sense of accomplishment for Bill as he began his descent of Kosciuszko. McKinley's summit in 1947 was truly memorable and the top of Aconcagua was a hard-earned reward. Bill's thoughts while descending Kosciuszko were simple and two-fold; fourth continental summit achieved, time to write to the French Alpine Club.

Bill Hackett never dreamed that he would live to see the fall of the Soviet Empire. When he set out to achieve his fifth continental summit he ran headfirst into a barrier that even his charm and military connections could not overcome—a line on a map! The highest mountain in Europe was, and remains, Mount Elbrus in the Kabardino-Balkaria Caucasus. Unfortunately, this 18,510-foot mountain was hidden for decades behind the southern borders of the USSR. Due to the fact that it was situated between the Black and Caspian Seas, Bill wondered if there was some way he could sneak over the border to make the attempt. He certainly wouldn't have been the first mountaineer to disguise himself and sneak across a closed border. Such feats had been performed in forbidden lands like Tibet for a hundred years. If Bill had been a civilian he might have pursued this path but he was a serving officer in the United States Army. Had he been captured behind Soviet borders and identified, he might have been declared a spy. Bill simply could not allow that to happen. Elbrus was out.

What do you do when a necessary step in achieving your goal is off limits merely because of political or geographical concerns? Bill Hackett would answer this question the only way he knew how, by selecting the *accepted* highest mountain in Europe for his time. For nearly eighty years Mont Blanc was considered the highest peak throughout Europe and few climbers even understood there were rivals for supremacy. Straddling the border between France and Italy, Mont Blanc stood at an impressive 15,767 feet and scores of mountaineers had scaled her heights by the time Bill Hackett arrived in the town of Chamonix. If you asked these climbers if they had scaled the highest mountain in Europe, they would have responded, "Certainly. Blanc was spectacular!" Had Bill completed the Seven Summits during the 1950s or 1960s, with Blanc as his representative for Europe, his record would have stood, and he would have received the laurels and attention such an achievement warrants.

One thing Bill knew for certain was that he would be pressed for time, and he wanted to ensure his attempt would meet with success on the first try. He had been fortunate with weather and route conditions on McKinley, Aconcagua and Kilimanjaro, and Kosciuszko had naturally been a mere hike in comparison. Mont Blanc however, could prove just as technically difficult and unpredictable as any great mountain. Bill would be transferring duty stations and making the first of two around-the-world trips during his lifetime; stopping in France to make an attempt on Mont Blanc in the process. He wanted to secure the companionship of a handful of climbers who were well familiar with the peak and who could accompany him to the summit. This would provide a better safety margin, cut down on the time needed for the ascent, and of course, expose him to fellow mountain climbers from another country. With these factors in mind, he dispatched a letter to Maurice Herzog in Paris. In this communiqué Bill basically introduced himself as an Army officer, outlined his continental summits record to date, and respectfully requested Herzog's assistance in arranging climbing companions for him when he arrived in La Roche.[15]

The United States has never accorded her high-altitude mountaineers the respect and admiration they so richly deserve. Europe however, has historically treated their famous alpinists as heroes, going so far as to have photographs of their houses made into picture postcards that are sold over the counter at the corner markets. It is difficult for the average American citizen to comprehend the level of respect France held, and continues to hold, for Maurice Herzog. It was he who, in 1950, inaugurated the Golden Age of Himalayan Mountaineering by leading the first ascent of an 8,000-meter peak! Tasked with a mere reconnaissance trip and an ascent only if *possible*, Herzog nevertheless led a French team to the summit of Annapurna in Nepal. This achievement did not come without a price. Herzog and his companions suffered massive frostbite injuries that necessitated several amputations. Herzog brought France honor and they loved him for it.[16] So when Herzog wrote to the *Club Alpin Francais*, requesting that companions be selected for a Mr. Hackett of the USA, club members practically stumbled over themselves to fulfill the request.[17] Monsieur Jean Morin sent a letter to Hackett indicating that he and others would be pleased to accompany him to Mont Blanc "if the condition of the mountain is proper."[18]

While en route to France, Hackett kept himself occupied by reading Edward Whymper's *Chamonix and the Range of Mont Blanc*. In this book he would read of the adventures of Michel Paccard and Jacques Balmat who, in 1786, had made the first ascent of the mountain. For centuries the Alps were avoided as often as possible and few people had been to any significant elevation. The Mont Blanc Massif was rumored to be the prison cell for the devil himself. Apparently, Satan had lost a battle with Saint Bernard, and the latter confined him to a site with such incredible boundaries that escape would be impossible. For years there were stories circulating through the villages that men who ventured too high were swallowed up by 'cracks' in the mountain, only to reappear years later in nearly perfect preservation. It is perfectly understandable why the local inhabitants were fearful of the alpine environment.

In 1761, however, a determined naturalist by the name of Horace Benedict de Saussure arrived in the Chamonix Valley. After several failed bids for the summit, he offered twenty gold thalers to anyone who could reach the summit of 'the Great White Mountain.' As early as 1775, villagers from the surrounding valleys took up the challenge in earnest. Several attempts were made from the *Glaciers des Bossons* on the northern side of Mont Blanc. Another attempt on the northwest ridge also fell short of the mark but the reason for these initial failures is clear. In the late eighteenth century, men simply refused to be caught out high on the mountain at nightfall. It was almost a forgone conclusion that to remain at such heights, exposed to such conditions, would mean death itself. This fear would be dispelled, in part, through the accidental efforts of a crystal hunter named Jacques Balmat.

Balmat had made an attempt on the mountain's northwest ridge as a member of a sizeable party. They had reached an elevation estimated around 14,000 feet when they decided to turn back. Balmat however, was certain he had spotted a path to the summit. While his companions descended Balmat continued the pursuit and made a fateful decision. He would spend the night in a snow cave, stomping his feet to stay warm as the hours slowly passed. In the morning he departed and continued his push for the summit. He spent the majority of the day cutting steps in the ice to make his advance. An incredibly time-consuming chore, his progression nearly drained him of all of his reserve energies. In the late afternoon, he felt he could see the way to the summit but being thoroughly exhausted, he retreated back to the valley and to the safety of his home. After assuring his wife that he was all right, he ate a hasty meal and then slept in the barn for a full twenty-four hours. When he awoke, Balmat felt ill but well enough to begin walking through the village to see Dr. Michel Paccard. Though Balmat had kept his stories from everyone else, he confided in the good doctor that he had accomplished two goals; he had proved a man could survive a night on the great mountain, and that he had found a practical route to the summit. It is unclear precisely why Balmat made this announcement but perhaps he was in search of a companion who could witness *his* achievement and ensure the prize money would be his without a significant investigation. Dr. Paccard had responded that he too had made some initial forays onto the glaciers and was curious to see the higher slopes. The pair agreed to join forces. On August 8, 1786, they reached the summit of Mont Blanc, a quarter-century after de Saussure's initial attempts. De Saussure, still alive and quite active, paid the men the money he had promised and Balmat even led him to the summit in 1787.[19]

After checking with his schedule, Hackett knew he could only spare two or three days for his own ascent, and this severely curtailed the number of possible routes he could attempt. With the fact that he was pressed for time, coupled with the knowledge that he was being extended a courtesy by having companions supplied to him by Herzog, Bill made the decision to ascend the mountain by way of the *Aiguille du Gouter*. This route, pioneered in 1861 by Leslie Stephens and the Swiss guide Melchior Anderegg, had become the standard route. Bill wasn't fooling himself. He knew more climbers had perished on Mont Blanc than any other mountain in the world. A technically free route was still exposed to the environmental and geologic hazards that are so prevalent among the great peaks. This particular route is normally completed in two days given fair weather and good ice conditions. Bill was also aware that from this route, some of the most beautiful alpine vistas could be had. His paltry black and white camera could never adequately capture the views he would be afforded.

When Bill arrived by train in La Roche on September 28, 1956, Mons. Jean Morin and the Chamonix guide, Jean Bozonnet, met him at the station. Alfred Four later joined them, and they all sat down for some beers and discussed their plans for the ascent.[20] Neither of the Frenchmen spoke much English, but Bill was able to discern that ice and snow conditions on the mountain were poor. They all agreed on a meeting time and place for the following morning and then sat down to enjoy an evening meal.[21]

In the morning the party departed La Roche and drove to Les Houches, a village below Chamonix. After parking their car, they shouldered packs and began their approach march towards the Hotel Bellevue. Here they took a break for lunch and admired the alpine scenery surrounding them. They then followed the cog rail line to Mont Lachal and the Hotel Pierre Ronde at the end of the line. From here they would rope up and begin climbing the mountain proper. They followed left of the *Glacier de Tete Rousse* and traversed a steep snow couloir to the right and up a rock arête. Bozonnet advised Bill that this rock rib would be the only true technical portion of the route and to be vigilant for rock fall. Verglass ice and deep snow were encountered throughout this early stage of the ascent. The party reached the *Refuge Aiguille du Gouter* near 7:00 PM and bedded down for the night.[22]

Bill was awakened at 4:30 the following morning to groans and pleas for Army coffee. He would recall that though he was extremely tired, he was grateful that his companions were *true* mountaineers and able to awaken early. He had never forgotten how much trouble he had motivating his Aconcagua teammates in 1949. After consuming a hasty meal and strapping on crampons, the party departed the hut and immediately encountered poor snow conditions. A breakable crust sent their feet anywhere from two inches below the surface to two feet. They had a quick meal while seated on the ice at *Le Grande Plateau*. Only five hours after awakening, Bill Hackett reached the summit of Mont Blanc and obtained his fifth continental summit.[23]

"The weather was very cold and windy but completely clear," Bill recalled, "The view was magnificent with all the peaks shrouded with a blanket of new snow—such classic peaks as the Matterhorn, Monte Rosa, Grandes Jorasses, and all of the Aiguilles."[24] The team only stayed on the summit for twenty minutes and then began their long descent to the lower huts and the valley.

In the months to come Hackett would correspond with all of his companions on the mountain. In response to Bill's first letter of thanks, Alfred Four would write, "(Gaston) Rebuffat has written somewhere 'The luxury of our sport is friendship.' He is right and I hope this friendship will last in spite of time and distance, by exchanging some news now and then. And you never can tell...the world is small...The God of Alpinists will perhaps make us meet, one day, on a mountain, somewhere."[25]

Hackett also expressed his thanks to Maurice Herzog:

> "It was through your kind effort, and that of those with whom you put me in touch, that I was able to accomplish the ascent of your highest mountain. Mr. Morin was most kind in his hospitality and personally saw that I did not want for a thing during my stay in La Roche. I could not have been with finer companions and mountaineers than Jean Bozonnet and Alfred Four as they are exceptional men in every respect. My only regret is that I did not have the opportunity to make your acquaintance. I am certain this will occur in the future and that I shall then be able to personally express my appreciation for your assistance in permitting me to achieve a fifth continental summit."[26]

When Bill returned to North America he made a quick ascent of Mount Whitney in California, the highest peak in the continental United States. After this uneventful climb however, something would happen that rarely occurred to him—nothing! The entire year of 1957 would pass without Bill making so much as a rock-climbing venture. Not until the summer of 1958 would he again pick up the ice axe and head into the hills.

—❖—

CHAPTER XI

The Veteran

"Of Major William D. Hackett's formal letter, I remember only the phrase: '...thirty days, thirty-five dollars, phone immediately.'"[1]

—Smoke Blanchard

On June 7, 1958, Bill Hackett was aboard an L-23 airplane, flying over Alaska's Mount McKinley. Jack Matteson was also aboard while Captain Johnson manned the controls. They were on a reconnaissance flight around the southeast spur of the mountain, inspecting the Muldrow Glacier and Pioneer Ridge. Hackett was checking out route conditions for his fifth McKinley expedition, an astounding number of ascents given the fact that it had only been a decade since the mountain was climbed on a regular basis. This was the peak where Dr. Washburn had given Bill his big break in 1947. With *Operation White Tower*, Bill was introduced to high altitude mountaineering and found his calling. Four years later he would accompany Washburn and others on the first ascent of the West Buttress, which remains the most popular path to the summit. In 1952, he led a small team up the Muldrow Glacier Route, and in 1954, he was in the party that made the first ascent of the Northwest Buttress. He was the new kid on the block in 1947, but a decade later he was a well-respected McKinley veteran with years of experience.[2]

David Dingman, of Ann Arbor, Michigan, organized the 1958 expedition that Bill would later join. Dingman had recruited fellow Teton buddies, Jake Breitenbach and Dave Dornan to accompany him. Breitenbach, at twenty-two, was a mountain guide from Seattle, Washington. He also guided in Wyoming's Teton Range and was a graduate of Oregon State University, holding a degree in mathematics. He started climbing in 1949 at the age of thirteen and quickly amassed an impressive resume. By the time Dingman asked him to join the '58 trip to Alaska, Breitenbach had experience in the Olympics, the Cascades, and the Central Rockies. It was in the Tetons though, that he really excelled. He made first ascents of Jensen Ridge on Teewinot and the Fourteen Hour Pinnacle. He additionally scaled the South Buttress of Mt. Moran and the North Face of the Grand Teton. The trip to McKinley would mark his first full-scale expedition and he was eagerly awaiting his chance to climb on what Fred Beckey would call, "The Icy Crown of North America."[3] Dave Dornan, of Moose, Wyoming, brought not only his climbing resume but also his quick wit and an endearing sense of humor. Bill would recall that Dornan always had a joke up his sleeve or a humorous story to tell.

Dingman invited Captain Hackett and Ross Kennedy to join the expedition. Hackett was invited for his obvious familiarity with the great peak and for his many military and mountaineering contacts in Alaska. Ross Kennedy was an apprentice guide on Washington State's Mount Rainier. Dingman still felt he needed one more climber to complete the roster and Bill said he knew just the man.

Smoke Blanchard, a diesel truck driver from Bishop, California, was an old climbing buddy of Bill's going back to the late 1930s on Mount Hood. Hackett dispatched a letter to Blanchard who was off on a skiing trip. Blanchard's wife, Vi, met him on a ski hill waving the letter in the air. Smoke read the letter knowing such a trip would take place in the early summer. He realized that propane hauling would slack off in June so, with the blessing of his wife, he agreed to head north. "Of Major William D. Hackett's formal letter," Blanchard recalled, "I remember only the phrase: '...thirty days, thirty- five dollars, phone immediately."[4] Smoke was scheduled to be picked up by Jake Breitenbach in Seattle, but they encountered some initial confusion.

Blanchard explains:

"When I called Jake, he said the Chrysler deal fell through, but a friend had given him a second-hand Buick for the nineteen-dollar license fee. Jake picked me up on his second pass by the Seattle Greyhound Station. He didn't expect an older man, he explained. Let's see, 1958, only forty-three years old. That's okay, I saw Jake slow down the first time but figured a guy that young couldn't be Breitenbach."[5]

The odd pair of climbers made their way north along the Alcan Highway. The spring thaw had only recently occurred, exposing every pot hole imaginable. The sedan was shaken violently and Smoke seemed to be hugging the driving lane on the left-hand side, a fact that did not please his companion. Over the course of the following four days, Breitenbach and Blanchard would exchange a multitude of climbing stories and bring one another up to speed on their family backgrounds and history. This minor trip helped form a fast friendship with one of the oldest and one of the youngest members of the climbing party.

The original objective of the expedition was to make a first ascent of Pioneer Ridge, on McKinley's northeast side. Hackett was able to retrieve aerial photographs of the Muldrow Glacier that had been taken by the Alaskan Air Command a year earlier. After reviewing the data, the group decided that the "current chaotic icefall conditions rendered this approach impractical."[6] There was some serious debate over the next objective but the group of climbers eventually determined to take their chances with another virgin route, the Southeast Spur of the South Buttress! Blanchard, who avoided the route-selection meetings, secretly hoped for an easier path, but the Teton guides were just itching to put their skills to the test on a mammoth peak, and Bill was never one to pass up on a chance for a first ascent.

With their objective defined, the big day came on Wednesday, June 11, 1958. Hackett awoke at 6:00 AM and awakened his old friend, Don Sheldon. Now one of the most recognizable pilots in southern Alaska, Sheldon had refused to make earlier flights to the mountain as he felt the weather was too poor and unpredictable. He had managed to deposit Dingman on the mountain's Ruth Glacier the day before but clouds soon enveloped the area and Dingman was forced to bivouac on the ice. The following morning Bill was the next member to be flown to the site, followed by Breitenbach, Kennedy, Dornan and then Blanchard.[7] Smoke was dutifully impressed with the view the flight afforded, writing, "The sudden transition from Talkeetna to the mountainside by air is only a little less mind-jarring than the reverse journey. When the engine sound fades and the thin speck of the Super Cub vanishes down the canyon, the world contracts to white silence."[8] Blanchard was even fortunate enough to spy a sizeable avalanche roaring down the western wall of The Moose's Tooth. Mounts Huntington, Barrille and Dickey were all visible and higher up the mountain itself, the gateway to the Ruth Amphitheatre could be seen.

The day was filled with a flurry of movement. Since Sheldon could only fly one climber at a time, work at base camp grew exponentially. Dingman had erected a single tent by the time Bill arrived and both men decided to move Base Camp a half-mile down the glacier. They wanted to have a better launching point for their attack on the Southeast Spur. Pop tents and Bill's old Logan tent were soon visible at the 7,500-foot level of the West Fork of Ruth Glacier. After Breitenbach had been delivered, the three climbers spied an Army L-20 flying overhead. Hackett had pre-arranged to have seven bundles dropped near camp. Only 100 feet off the ice, the plane made two passes, dropping 508 pounds of provisions to the appreciative expedition. Dingman and Breitenbach then made a reconnaissance foray up to 9,000 feet on what Bill would call 'the Southeast Prong'. [9]

Establishing Camp I would prove far easier than anyone expected. Up early, the entire team stepped outside their tents and geared up for the march. Bill shouldered his pack under pink cloud cover and a light snowfall. It was a perfect morning and it looked as if the weather would hold. Everyone bore seventy-pound packs and Bill was very impressed with Jake Breitenbach. Though the Teton guide only weighed 155 pounds, he was carrying a pack half as heavy as himself, and apparently showing no signs of slowing down!

Dornan and Hackett led that morning, breaking out the previous day's steps. They bypassed the high point reached by Dingman and Breitenbach and continued to press on up to the 9,500-foot level. There, on the lower edge of a crevasse they erected the Logan tent. Supplies were cached and as everyone agreed the ascent was not too taxing, they returned to bring the balance of their provisions up to Camp I.[10]

During the descent, Bill got ahead of himself a little bit and grew careless. He swung his ice axe too close to his own leg and the blade stuck him directly in his kneecap. Bill was pretty upset that his wound was on a 'hinge' instead of a more fleshy area such as the thigh or calf. When he reached Base Camp he had Dingman sew him up.[11] Bill thanked him for the job while the rest of the team continued to pack their gear.

A second carry that afternoon may not have been the wisest choice, but it did enable the party to transport all of their supplies a full 2,000 vertical feet in a single day. When the team reached Camp I, they were definitely spent. The air temperature had dropped considerably and, as they were climbing in wet clothes, they began to freeze. It would take a full three hours for the men to make dinner, erect the balance of the tents and thaw out.

Camp II, though fixed in a large bergschrund, was harder to reach. On June 14, Blanchard and Hackett roped up and re-cut the steps that Dornan and Kennedy had made on a reconnaissance trip a day earlier. Bill found himself on hard ice on a fifty-degree slope. They carried nothing but their climbing hardware, food and water, as this was merely another recon trip, pushing the route higher in order to locate a suitable location for another camp. "About 400 feet above Friday's highpoint," Bill recorded in his diary, "we found a good campsite. We descended to Camp I and carried up heavy loads to establish Camp II in a tremendous Bergschrund at 10,500 feet. Breitenbach, Dornan, and Kennedy went down to clean out Camp I, while we set up tents and put the camp in order."[12] They did encounter some small avalanches that concerned them. The snow was dry and had recently fallen. A climber would take a step and trigger a small slide and the climbing partner below would have to dart to one side or brace for the possibility of an avalanche.[13]

When Bill awoke the following morning his leg was stiff and sore. He pulled back the sleeping bag and thought the cut on his knee looked infected. Other members of the team agreed and Dingman recommended taking Achromycin every four hours. Bill thought it best to stay off the leg for a day while the younger climbers continued the route.

Breitenbach and Dingman took the lead on the attempt to reach a proposed Camp III. Again, due to the fact that they were performing recon duties, they carried only the essentials in order to work fast for a longer period of time. Only 500 feet above Camp II, they were stopped in their tracks by an overhanging wall of ice. It was clear that reinforcements and additional gear would be needed. Dornan and Dingman gave Breitenbach double rope tension, but rotten ice prevented his surmounting the wall. Dingman then scouted another possible route and went up 120 feet to set pitons and a fixed rope. They were forced to abandon the attempt, however, and established Camp III at the base of the ice wall.[14]

Life in camp, as always, was a combination of hard work and good times. Bill got upset when Breitenbach, wearing his crampons, accidentally walked across the plastic plates! After a day or two, Bill could at last see the humor in the mistake. They played poker, bridge, and Bill had even brought a miniature pegboard chess set. On the top of the case he would write, "Watch your queen, stupid!" The men talked for hours and held trivia contents to see who would have to suit up and clear the tent of snow that had accumulated.

On June 17, the team was ready for action. They had been cooped up in their tent for two days and were aching to get climbing again. From their experience gained on the 15th, the team knew the ice wall would be their sole objective for the day. Dingman and Breitenbach therefore left camp with every available piton. In order to get the best ice conditions, they departed at 4:30 in the morning and soon set up positions at the base of the wall. Breitenbach took the lead with Dingman belaying. For a time, it appeared as if the young Teton guide might be successful, but with one misstep, he fell and the rope came under tension. Instantly, the pitons ripped clean out of the ice, one after another! Ping...ping...ping...out they came and Breitenbach tumbled farther with each release! It was a wonder he wasn't seriously injured but he landed in a heap at the base of the wall, none the worse for the wear. Breitenbach would try again but every time he went up, down he would come. Of these repeated attempts to surmount this ice wall, Bill would write:

"Piton failures caused Breitenbach to suffer a leader fall. The rest of us came up at 6 AM. Dornan, Breitenbach, and I all tried in vain to climb this tension pitch. Dingman tried a route to the right, which was not successful. Breitenbach and I tried a route to the left. I chopped steps for several hours, until they called me down at 2:30 PM. We were all cold and out of pitons. We returned to Camp III for a much-needed meal, and then Dornan, Kennedy, and Dingman went back up at 4:30 to finish the pitch. First they had to recover the pitons from the other pitches, and Dornan fell as he went up on tension on a retrieval. Weakened pitons zippered out, but Dingman held him on dynamic belay on the anchor pitons, which held. They were then able to attack the route on which I had worked earlier in the day. With Kennedy and Dingman belaying, Dornan was finally able to get his head and shoulders over the crest about 8:30 PM. He wanted to go on, but was not sure how he would be able to get back after climbing the next pitch."[15]

At long last, the expedition had reached the knife-edged ridge of McKinley's Southeast Spur. It seemed strange that after so much work the expedition was only nearing the 11,000-foot mark, some 9,320 feet shy of the summit! The key now was continual advancement as several days worth of valuable supplies had been exhausted. The trip thus far was taking longer than expected. There had been a few days of down time due to storms and the complexities of the rotten ice wall had kept the team at bay for over two days.

The morning after their initial success, Dornan and Breitenbach departed camp to recon the area just above the ice wall, assuming of course that they could re-climb the original obstacle. They were blessed with fair weather all day with only fog enveloping the lower peaks. A lenticular cloud cap settled around the mountain's summit in the late afternoon, a probable indication of foul weather to come.

Dornan and Breitenbach returned to Camp III with bad news. They had managed to pass the crest but what they saw farther up concerned them. The ridge was dangerous and considered 'unfeasible' by both men. Heavy cornices significantly increased the chance of avalanche and continuing on would entail climbing on wet snow perched on rotten, nearly vertical ice. A conference was held and—ever the optimists—they elected to make one last attempt on the Southeast Spur. They would try to cut steps for 200 feet on sixty-degree ice. Dornan and Breitenbach were tasked with removing ice pitons so that Dingman and Kennedy could employ them during the attempt. The poor quality of ice would simply not hold pitons in place during a fall and given this fact, the climbers returned to Camp III unsuccessful.[16]

The expedition fared no better the following day, June 19. Hackett stuck his head out of the tent first thing in the morning and was disgusted with what he saw. "Checked weather early," he would write, "and found the same damn thing again—in clouds and snowing...a miserable day ensued."[17] Over breakfast, the men discussed the possibilities of safely surmounting the obstacles overhead. None of the plans seemed attractive and the matter was a popular topic of conversation throughout the day.

On the 20th, Hackett again poked his head outside and was greeted by a foot of fresh, wet snow. It was quiet in the tent though everyone was clearly awake. Bill mentally took stock of their provisions and progress. The team had landed on Ruth Glacier eight days earlier and in that time, had only reached 11,000', an elevation gain of only 3,500'. For a peak in excess of 20,000 feet, this was slow progress indeed. True, some of the most technical climbing to occur on McKinley had been undertaken, but there was still an incredible amount of terrain to cover if they were to gain the summit. Provisions were running low. Morale was taking a down turn. It was time to retreat.

Smoke Blanchard was more than happy to hear of the decision. In regards to the ice wall that had given the team so much trouble, he would write, "I heaved a sigh of relief, for I dreaded climbing that exposed pitch even protected by a belay from above."[18]

During the descent, an event would occur that Blanchard would recall with a smile for years afterwards. Dingman was protecting Dornan with an ice axe, ankle boot belay, as Dornan was crossing a snow bridge over a bergschrund. The bridge collapsed without warning and Dornan fell forty feet into the abyss before his partner caught him on belay. Dornan yelled up to his friends that he was unhurt and Dingman lowered him a few more feet onto an ice ledge. After anchoring the rope, Dingman went for help.[19] Blanchard, unaware of the incident above him, thought he heard someone calling his name. He anchored, looked up, and saw Dingman all by himself.[20]

"Smoke?" Dingman calmly said from above, "We've got a little trouble up here. Dornan's in a crevasse." When Blanchard and Breitenbach reached the lip of the trap and peered down, they were surprised to find Dornan so far down. The situation, though not life-threatening at the moment, was still more critical than Dingman's voice implied.

"I've heard many crevasse-associated sounds here and there in the mountains," Smoke would write years later, "including my own call of the Yukon, 'I'm *in*, Jack!'—But I best remember Dingman's cool, matter-of-fact, 'We've got a little trouble...'" Together, Breitenbach, Blanchard and Dingman were able to give Dornan tension, who was then able to climb out under his own power.

During this time frame, Hackett was farther below, chopping steps across an ice traverse above Camp I. Kennedy was belaying him and together, they lowered backpacks by rope and continued to descend. The trail had been marked with wands during the ascent so there was no trouble locating the route back to Ruth Glacier. When Hackett and Kennedy reached Camp I, they found that the site had been swept by an avalanche.[21] Unsettling news to be sure. By suppertime, the entire expedition had returned to Base Camp and settled in for the night.

After being stuck in camp for a day due to inclement weather, the team assembled on the morning of June 22. Bill presented the possibility of having Don Sheldon fly the group one by one over to the Kahiltna Glacier, which would place them in a position to make an attempt on the West Buttress. Most in the party approved of the plan so Base Camp was moved back to the original landing strip. There, Blanchard and Hackett donned snowshoes in order to tramp out a suitable landing area for Sheldon.[22]

It would take a few more days before Don Sheldon would have the time and weather in his favor. On Wednesday, June 25, his 'taxi service' went into overdrive. Bill writes:

> "Sheldon came in at 9 AM, and I went out on the first flight, a spectacular ride past Mount Huntington and Mount Hunter. We landed on the Kahiltna Glacier near Mount Hunter, a mile outside the park boundary, due to clouds higher up on the glacier. With a USAF plane flying cover, (Sheldon) brought Blanchard over on the second trip, and receding clouds permitted a landing higher on the glacier about two miles inside the park boundary. Sheldon flew down and brought me up to Blanchard, then returned to ferry Dingman across from Ruth Glacier. Digging the plane out of the soft snow became a problem with every flight. It took forty-five minutes to free the aircraft after Breitenbach landed on the fourth trip."[23]

Blanchard would also recall his flight with a chuckle. "I hadn't taken that many mountain flights. Everywhere I looked the clouds had rocks in them. I saw Sheldon scrunched down in his seat, apparently doing something desperate to save us. Scary! I figured I should see what he was doing, even if it was to be my last experience. I loosened my seat belt and reared up to look in the front. Sheldon was leaning over sideways, using the reflecting glass of his instrument panel as he combed his hair."[24]

With everyone assembled on the Kahiltna Glacier, attention turned to tackling the West Buttress. As Hackett had been in the party that made the first ascent seven years earlier, he knew the route well enough to shave off valuable time that would otherwise have been spent route finding. When Bill and Smoke took an inventory of their supplies they were shocked to discover that they had more provisions

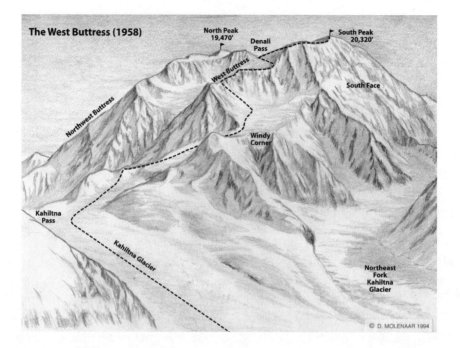

The West Buttress (1958)

North Peak 19,470'

Denali Pass

South Peak 20,320'

West Buttress

South Face

Northwest Buttress

Windy Corner

Kahiltna Pass

Kahiltna Glacier

Northeast Fork Kahiltna Glacier

© D. MOLENAAR 1994

than previously believed. The team still had 175 man-days of food and seven gallons of fuel for the stoves. Bill was at a loss to explain the oversight.

It soon became evident that Hackett had assumed more of the leadership roles and responsibilities, based upon his experiences with Washburn and the route itself. This caused some initial tension in the group, but everyone was eager to gain the summit since they had worked so hard during the proceeding weeks.

The climb itself was uneventful and in many ways mirrored the adventures Bill experienced during the first ascent in 1951. Both Hackett and Blanchard were impressed with the skills and stamina of the younger climbers, Breitenbach in particular. The Teton guide had carved a daylong, blue ice staircase straight up the Buttress Wall! Near 17,000 feet, they encountered another party under the leadership of Ed Cooper, preparing to give up and retreat down the mountain. A discussion was held as to their reasons for abandoning the attempt and Hackett discovered Cooper's men were running out of food. They had also encountered the same foul weather that had plagued the Southeast Spur team. Some of Cooper's men had actually made a summit bid earlier on and *believed* they had reached the top, but due to low visibility they could not swear to the fact. Dingman, Dornan and the rest of the men agreed to share supplies, information and chores. The following morning several of Cooper's men accompanied Hackett's party to the summit.[25]

The original Southeast Spur team had climbed from Base Camp on the Kahiltna up to striking distance from the summit so fast that they were now suffering from the effects of altitude. Blanchard recalls that he was dragging along when he encountered Breitenbach lying face down in the snow. Smoke was pleased to see that it wasn't just the older climbers who were suffering.

"Come on, Jake!" Smoke yelled as he tried to rouse his friend, "Don't give up, we started from Seattle together, and we'll finish together."

On July 2, 1958, Bill Hackett stood on top of the North American continent for the fourth time in his life, the only man up to that time who had made so many ascents. He had taken part in five expeditions to the great peak but his 1954 Northwest Buttress party failed to reach the South Summit, the higher of McKinley's two summits. The Northwest Buttress expedition was still a success however, as they succeeded in making the first ascent. This 1958 summit marked the second ascent of the West Buttress and Cooper's party registered in as the third.[26]

"The descent went rapidly." Blanchard would note, "We chose a different route down the steep part between 16,000 and 15,000 feet. I found it easy enough but was upset by something red in the snow of the bergschrund. Jam? *Ed Cooper's party descending below us had jam!* And I was so hungry. It wasn't jam—it was blood. Marty Mushkin had been beaned by a rock, and when I reached them at 14,000 feet, Dave Dingman, a doctor, had just finished sewing him up."

This wouldn't be the only incident during their retreat down the West Buttress. One of the rope teams consisted of Hackett in the lead, followed by Blanchard and Kennedy. Hackett passed over a crevasse bridge without trouble but Blanchard fell right through! This immediately pulled Kennedy off his feet and sent him into a somersault. He landed directly on his Trapper Nelson pack board, breaking it into several pieces.[27]

When it came time for expedition members to return home, Blanchard and Breitenbach didn't trust the old Buick to stand another 3,000 mile trip over the Alcan Highway. They opted to sell the car and fly home, figuring this was the wiser and certainly safer option. They flew home aboard a DC-6 but when one of its inboard engines caught fire, Smoke couldn't help but laugh. He was glad he had selected the *safer* method of travel!

◄─ ═◆═ ─►

Five years after the completion of the expedition, Hackett received word that Jake Breitenbach had been killed on Everest. On March 23, 1963, Breitenbach had been the last member of a rope team consisting of Dick Pownall and Sherpa, Ang Pema. They were navigating through the Khumbu Ice Fall along Everest's South Col route. Surrounded by towers of ice known as seracs, one moved and toppled over onto the climbers. This thirty-foot wall of ice and snow was two railroad cars high and Pownall recalled thinking, "So this is death." Pownall and Ang Pema survived but Breitenbach was lost, a crippling blow to the first American expedition to ascend Mount Everest. It also did not escape Bill's attention that Norman G. Dyhrenfurth was leading the expedition, the same man who Bill had worked with a few years earlier when Bill had received the first permit to make such an attempt.

◄─ ═◆═ ─►

CHAPTER XII

The Logan Massif

*"Bill seemed to feel neither altitude nor cold, but when he realized
how long and late the day had become, and how very far back to camp it was,
he turned to me with just a hint of fear in his voice and said,
"I've never been this far out on the hook before!"[1]*

—Smoke Blanchard

Mount Logan was a peak that had several aspects that appealed to Bill Hackett. First and foremost, Logan was the highest mountain in Canada and second highest on the North American continent. For a man who loved the feeling of standing on top of the world, Bill could have used this justification alone to make a pilgrimage north. At 19,850 feet, Mount Logan was additionally one of the largest single mountain masses in the world. The fact that Logan was located in the Yukon Territory was certainly beneficial as well. With the peak only fifty air miles from the coast of Alaska, Hackett could count on the many personal contacts he had made in the region over the years.

Before Bill could make the determination to proceed with an attempt, he would have to check the history of mountaineering on this remote peak. He was not disappointed by his research. The first ascent of Mount Logan occurred thirty-four years earlier, in the summer of 1925. A.H. MacCarthy led a party of eight to the summit on

June 23.[2] The second and third ascents of the peak occurred nearly simultaneously. Andre Roch and Norman Read reached the summit slopes in 1950 and were promptly followed by a team from the University of Alaska less than two weeks later. Hackett knew a fourth ascent, with slight route modifications, could be a historic, challenging and worthwhile undertaking.

Hackett was convinced he would need a strong team and most especially a *Lead Dog*, or Deputy Leader. Bill again enlisted the services of Smoke Blanchard. Hackett knew he could rely on Smoke to fulfill such a position. The two had been climbing partners on Mount Hood and the Central Cascades during the late 1930s and on up through the outbreak of the Second World War. They had additionally made the second ascent of McKinley's West Buttress Route, certainly fair training for an attempt on Logan. Blanchard had been dreaming of making an attempt on the Logan Massif since he was a teenager. He had placed it beside the North and South Poles as goals he wished to obtain during his lifetime. He would train for Logan by wading up sand hills at the base of Buttermilk pinnacles, just west of Bishop, California.[3]

Once Smoke's presence on the team had been secured, Hackett turned his attention to the rest of the expedition members: Dr. Norton Benner of Hillsborough, California, would act as Expedition Physician. David Bohn was a climber familiar to both Hackett and Blanchard. A Portland-based social worker, Bohn was also a fellow member of the Mazamas climbing club. Hackett was aware of Bohn's ascents throughout the Pacific Northwest and welcomed his participation in the expedition.[4] Richard N. Kaufman, a printing firm executive, was an accomplished photographer and would act in that capacity during the venture.[5] Kaufman's extensive rock climbing experience in the Alps was an additional bonus. Clarence LeBell, a jet engine designer from Peabody, Massachusetts, was an admired member of the Appalachian Mountain Club. He had made a successful ascent of Mount McKinley the year previously, though not as a member of Bill's party. The last member of the expedition was Jules Eichorn, a Sierra Club member from Atherton, California. He had made the first ascent of Mount Whitney's East Face and, in the process, helped usher in the modern age of rock climbing in the Sierras. In addition to his climbing resume, Eichorn brought his organizational skills to bear on the lengthy supply lists. Under his direction, miscellaneous materials were dropped from the roster and replaced with more practical alternatives. Eichorn's cooking skills were also a highlight of the expedition. Blanchard found it interesting that Eichorn, a piano teacher, had studied under Ansel Adams, the pianist who went on to become the renowned mountain photographer.[6] Though Eichorn and Hackett had their differences in climbing technique and philosophy, Bill nevertheless respected the man and his abilities.

After so many expeditions to Alaska, Hackett had a great number of sponsors, supporters and connections in Alaska. Dr. Bradford Washburn, the man who had opened the door for Bill's high-altitude career, provided him with copies of his splendid 8x10" aerial photographs of the Logan Massif. L.R. Younger of the Department of National Revenue in Ottawa, and F.H. Collins handled most of the documentation and red tape connected with the expedition. Bill was also very grateful for those who donated supplies and equipment to his expedition. He took the time to record every name, item, and their usefulness to the team. "Mr. John V. Underhill," he would note, "Vice President of Duofeld, Inc., provided each member of the party with one set each of the standard Duofeld underwear, and the latest quilted Scottfoam insulated two-piece underwear. Eddie Bauer down insulated parkas and sleeping bags were made available to us by Bill Niemi of the William F. Niemi Company. A 3x5' forty-nine-star US flag was presented to the expedition by Mr. William C. Spangler, sales manager of the Dettra Flag Company. Mr. Michael C. Marsden, Acting Director of the Montreal Office of the Arctic Institute of North America, presented the expedition with a 3x5 Canadian flag. Insulated rubber boots were made available to the members of the expedition through the assistance of Mr. Robert L. Woodbury in the Textile, Clothing and Footwear Division of the US Army Quartermaster Research and Engineering Command. Major Clifford H. Reynolds, Research and development Coordinator for the US Army Quartermaster Food and Container Institute for the Armed Forces, assisted in providing the expedition with dehydrated food items. Several US Army, Alaska (and military) officers helped in making many items of Army equipment available to the expedition."[7]

Team members agreed to meet in Chitina on Alaska's Copper River, just northwest of Valdez. Bohn and LeBell arrived on the afternoon of June 9 via commercial airlines. They looked the place over and were made to feel welcome. Though the village had only twenty or so permanent residents, Chitina nevertheless held Cordova and Wilson Air Service as well as several bed and breakfast establishments. Bohn and LeBell pitched their bright orange high-altitude tent on the shore of the Cooper River that evening. They spent a relatively comfortable night with the only disturbances being mosquitoes the size of bumblebees and the occasional tramping of animals nearby.

Near 2:00 in the morning, Chitina residents were awakened by the sound of a backfiring automobile entering town. The *Sierrans* had arrived: Dr. Benner, Blanchard, Eichorn and Kaufmann. They had traveled nearly non-stop from San Francisco, pulling a trailer over what even they acknowledged was some *rough* terrain. They awakened Bohn and LeBell, attempting to enlist their services packing food. After several attempts, the *Sierrans* were finally able to calm down and agree to sleep in for an additional five hours.[8]

In the morning, Blanchard relayed an entertaining story as to how they managed to bring the provisions over the Canadian border:

> "Immigration inspectors were shocked at our careless stretching of their rule about importing food. To protect the interests of their countrymen's grocery stores, they permitted only two days of food for each person entering Canada. Two times four equals eight, but we had 280-man-days of food aboard! After two hours spent haggling, I smartened up enough to produce from our files a manifest of our food supplies, which showed much of the bulk of our food to be from the U.S. Army for testing on the mountain. This meant little to the officers, but they were able to find in the long list one lone can of biscuit mix from the Canadian Army. That did it. Our papers were stamped 'NATO Supplies,' and we passed through."[9]

Later that afternoon, Hackett arrived in town with bush pilot, Don Sheldon. They had flown from Anchorage in the latter's Super

Cub.[10] Sheldon additionally brought two other planes to assist in ferrying supplies and equipment. Jack Wilson and Howard Knutson piloted these additional aircraft. Once in Chitina, Hackett linked up with Blanchard and discussed matters pertaining to the expedition. They met with the balance of the team and reviewed the route ahead. Plans were set, time schedules agreed upon, and orders given to depart camp at 3:30 the following morning.

On Thursday, June 11, Sheldon took Hackett on a reconnaissance flight around the Logan Massif. Clouds below obscured the Chitina River, but Sheldon was able to point out the Logan Glacier as they approached. "To avoid this obstacle," Bill would recall, "we turned right which took us up the Tana River Valley. After gaining more elevation, a left turn was made over the Granite Range and we found ourselves above the upper Logan Glacier basin beyond the cloudbank that was filled in further down the glacier. A banking turn was made to the right when the relatively short Ogilvie Glacier was reached, and our journey continued toward the main icefall where we had thought to land at or near the site of the Cascade Camp of the 1925 expedition." Hackett and Sheldon both agreed that the heavily crevassed strip below should not be used and as a result, they were forced to look elsewhere for a practical alternative. They flew past the Ogilvie Glacier and over Quartz Ridge yet were still unable to fix an appropriate landing strip. Only once they had descended to the 9,300-foot level above the Quintino Sella Glacier were they able to agree upon a site. Sheldon banked the plane, dramatically decreased their elevation and then skimmed the surface of the glacier, clearing the highest seracs with only a few yards of clearance! This was no stunt, the pilot merely wanted to get a better look at the consistency of the snow and gain a better appreciation for the glacier's unique terrain. During a second pass, Sheldon dropped tree branches onto the ice that he had brought specifically for the purpose of gauging the distance between the bottom of the plane and the field below. They landed at 6:00 AM and immediately began unloading the aircraft.[11]

Hackett remained on the glacier while Sheldon took off again, bound for Chitina and the waiting expedition members. Once the aircraft was out of view Bill donned his snowshoes and started tramping out a makeshift landing area. He then marked the area with bamboo trail markers tipped with bright pennants in order to assist Sheldon and his pilots in locating the strip. Each round trip Sheldon and his pilots made took two hours and Bill was just erecting the first tent when he heard the whine of the aircraft in the distance.[12]

Dr. Benner was the first to arrive and he and Hackett continued to erect Base Camp while the supply trips continued. Bill writes:

> "By the time Blanchard had arrived our Base Camp was firmly established with the erection of two more tents. Benner, Kaufmann and I roped together and with pack board loads put in a trail through a crevassed area to about 10,500 feet on the King Glacier. A supply cache was established near the site of the 1925 party's Observation Camp. Sometime after our return to Base Camp, the last man was delivered to us and our party was all together at 10:30 PM. The weather had remained good for us and the daylight, which permits working around the clock at this time of the year in the North Country, had made this happy accomplishment possible."[13]

Situated on the Quintana Sella Glacier, their base camp was an ideal setting for those who loved alpine beauty. Bill and others took the time to admire their surroundings. Bill, who enjoyed the sense of isolation, was happy to see the wing lights on Sheldon's retreating aircraft.

During the following day, the expedition moved north and onto King Glacier. An extensive trench in the ice had to be crossed before the team could establish Camp I at 12,000 feet. Over dinner that evening the men checked each other's blisters and bandaged minor cuts and bruises, all the while savoring Eichorn's soup and potatoes. In the distance, the sun dipped quite low and the temperature dropped to ten-degrees. When their evening chores were complete the team hastily entered their sleeping bags.[14]

"To ensure that everyone had an equal chance at reconnaissance trips," Hackett would note, "and a respite from the laborious grind of relaying seventy-pound pack board loads, two different men were selected daily by the alphabetical order of their last names to form the day's reconnaissance team. These teams moved forward, normally with light loads, beyond the latest established camp, while the other hands toiled with heavy freighting loads from the camp below. In this way, we worked in two different directions concurrently without the complications of splitting the party and maintaining more than one camp at a time."[15]

On June 13, Dave Bohn awoke refreshed, writing, "The sun has just touched the tiny tent—this is always a happy moment in the early morning—the inside becomes toasty and one can shed part of the sleeping bag—lay here and think.... But time for me to get up, take some pictures, and eat some breakfast."[16]

Later that same morning Blanchard and Dr. Benner pushed the route forward, climbing up the ice trench, intent on establishing a secondary camp near King Col. During this outing, Blanchard fell victim to one of the oldest mountaineering tricks in the book. Distances can be quite deceiving at such altitudes. It would take him an additional day to erect Camp II, a full eight miles from the rest of the team! This camp was situated in the col between King Peak and the Logan Massif, enabling its occupants to get a better view of their proposed ascent route.[17]

While Blanchard and Dr. Benner were making headway higher up, the remaining personnel returned to Base Camp to make additional carries. Bohn, Eichorn, LeBell, Hackett and Kaufmann, bearing packs weighing in excess of eighty pounds, climbed up to Camp II in a single, exhaustive day's march. They arrived near sunset. "There was Alpenglow on King Peak," Bill would recall, "and the savage magnificence of Logan's icefalls to our north helped buoy our spirits, but did little to remove the ache of weary shoulders."

The following morning, it was Bohn and Eichorn's time to shine. They worked their way up an ever-steepening slope above King Col, fixing bamboo wands along the way. Roughly 500 feet above Camp II, Bohn suddenly dropped through a hidden crevasse! He hung suspended by the snowshoes that were lashed to the back of his pack. Though Eichorn was roped to his partner, Bohn was carrying a sixty-pound pack and it was unclear whether Eichorn could hold the line if Bohn slipped into the crevasse any further. Fortunately for both men, Bohn was able to stem his way out of the trap under his own power and after a brief rest, continue unassisted.[18]

Once past King Col, the route turned sharply to the left and the recon team encountered a 45-degree slope extending for 800 feet. This obstacle was overcome with the assistance of crampons. Snowshoeing then resumed once they reached the upper King Glacier. Over the next couple of hours, Eichorn began to suffer from the effects of working at higher altitude. Bohn, seemingly unaffected and ready to continue the ascent, pushed the route forward to the 16,000-foot level. Alone and on snowshoes, he leaned forward to rest while taking in his new surroundings. Below him lay the entire Saint Elias Massif in all its grandeur some thirty air miles to the south. He had additionally reached the position of the "Icy Cliff Camp" used by the first ascent party in 1925.

Meanwhile, far below, the balance of the team descended in order to continue the weary task of supplying the higher camps. LeBell, Dr. Benner and others continually made relay marches with some of the heaviest packs they had ever shouldered. A thankless yet necessary chore, they patiently waited their turns to take the lead.

Hackett and Blanchard held a private conference on the morning of the 16th. They hadn't expected such fair weather and the team was advancing faster than originally planned. Though Bill hated being cooped up in tents during storms, such periods of inactivity at least provided some valuable acclimatization time. Kaufman would later acknowledge that he wished for a brief spell of bad weather in order to rest from their tiring schedule. Eichorn, clearly the most skilled climber in the group, was still showing the effects of working at higher altitudes. Hackett was torn between acclimatizing properly and making a dash for the summit. This issue was debated between them but they were unable to reach any decision other than to agree to keep the dialogue open.

Over the following two days, the expedition proceeded to stock Camp III near 16,000 feet. During their final carry to camp on the second day, cloud cover finally descended on the team. There was no wind present and under their heavy packs, the men began to sweat and get chilled. They counted the bamboo trail wands when they passed them, not out of any particular reason; they just wanted something to occupy their minds. The team was reminded of the importance of such wands by remembering the story of Macarthy's party in 1925. Forced to endure an open bivouac in a storm at 19,000 feet, they were saved the following day when they stumbled onto a wand in a whiteout. Expedition members could also see why the 1925 party named their current location Windy Camp. The sastrugi ice they encountered was clear evidence of the heavy winds that whipped over the ice field.

Hackett recalled his impressions of the challenges ahead once the expedition was firmly established in Camp III: "Toward our summit lay a gigantic crevasse, sixty feet wide. There was only one bridge across it, and great cascades of ice stood above it. King Peak, 17,130', which had reared so impressively above us at Camp II, was now dwarfed by higher summits, its crest standing little higher than our own elevation. The stark silhouette of Mount Saint Elias stood on the southern horizon, barely twenty miles distant. A pass on its east side revealed a glimpse of the vast Malaspina Glacier which spills into the Pacific Ocean on the Alaska Coast." Bill wasn't the only one impressed with the scenery. Dick Kaufman would initially forgo the warmth of his sleeping bag and tent in order to capture the awesome terrain on film. The temperature outside was 0-degrees Fahrenheit and yet Kaufmann risked frostbite in order to take his photographs.[19]

June 18 dawned and after a breakfast of cereal and hot cocoa, Dave Bohn shouldered his pack and joined Hackett, LeBell and Dr. Benner outside. They divided into two rope teams: Bohn and Hackett on one, Le Bell and Brenner on the other. The teams crossed the ice bridge with little difficulty but after a time, LeBell and Benner began to show signs of fatigue. They cached their packs near 16,700 feet while Bohn and Hackett continued to climb higher. There, on an expanse sloping plateau, they established Camp IV.[20]

Friday, June 19 brought the eighth day of consecutive fair weather. The men discussed the issue of acclimatization at great length but decided to move to Camp IV en masse. During the journey, several members of the team continued to suffer from a variety of altitude related ailments. Eichorn's condition appeared to deteriorate even more. Dr. Benner believed his patient was developing a streptococcal throat and administered penicillin injections to counter the infection. As there were more days of sunshine than originally planned, there were more sunburns and blisters on the faces of expedition members. LeBell, Blanchard and Kaufman encountered sores on their lips and foreheads. Bohn suffered a bout of snow

blindness just after passing the 17,000-foot mark. This condition lasted periodically between 17 and 18,500 feet.[21] At this point during the
ascent however, only Eichorn's condition concerned Hackett and
Blanchard. The other ailments were foreseen and had been experienced countless times before on a multitude of outings.

The only other concern for expedition members was the loss
of appetite and many felt the pangs of thirst for the majority of the
day. They drank water they had melted from snow the previous
evening but when carried in plastic bottles, their contents often froze
solid. Kaufman would later report that water was so scarce he neither
shaved, washed or even brushed his teeth during the entire course of
the expedition.

It would take a full two days to establish Camp V at 18,000 feet.
Team members were required to traverse a small mountain pass on
Logan's West Ridge towards the north side of the peak in order to reach
their tents. "Our camp that night was another world," Bill would write
years later, "The familiar landmark, King Peak, was out of sight, and we
were perched on the enormous Logan Plateau, an east-west mass which
runs about seventeen miles. Any problems at this point would mean
climbing up to the pass, before we could begin descent."

Forty-one years after the expedition, Bohn would acknowledge that Bill Hackett "was a mountain of energy. One who possessed
tremendous endurance and was extremely motivated."[22] Bohn felt
however, that Bill's leadership style was too autocratic...to militaristic for his taste. This difference in climbing styles was a source of
several arguments during the course of the expedition.

Following the conclusion of the expedition, Bill typed up a
small, unpublished article concerning the trip, and mentions his
movements on the afternoon of June 20:

> "Since we were unroped, I climbed ahead to the top of
> "False Double Peak," removed my pack, and sat down
> to eat some dried fruit and await the arrival of the
> others who were perhaps 500 feet below. As I watched,
> it became apparent that some of the men were not
> taking the elevation well, and were suffering from the
> effects of the cold wind. Since there was a doctor pres-
> ent (Brenner), and it appeared the others would be

along as soon as they had rested and prepared warm drinks, I climbed back up (indicating he had descended to the scene) "False Double Peak", shouldered my pack board and descended into the Logan Plateau."[23]

Bohn felt Hackett was pushing the men too fast.[24] In his 1985 memoirs, *Walking Up and Down in the World,* Blanchard recalls the same incident: "Dave Bohn accused Bill of risking the safety of the party from misguided machismo, and Bill countered by accusing his party of being under motivated. The next year the two principal disputants locked arms and marched off to K2 together, so I guess they were able to call it a normal anoxia problem."

—— ◄◆► ——

On the morning of June 21, Hackett and Blanchard crossed the Logan Plateau, climbed a short snow ridge and then to the summit of North Peak. The air temperature dropped to negative twelve degrees Fahrenheit, prompting the men to stick to the tasks at hand and keep moving.[25] From their vantage point, the climbers could see the many sub peaks that made up the lengthy summit ridge. Just which of these summits was higher than the others was difficult to ascertain. They made their best educated guess and chose a location for a future high camp.

When Blanchard and Hackett returned to camp they held a special meeting in their largest tent. Over the evening meal they discussed Eichorn's medical condition. Dr. Benner recommended that Eichorn remain at Camp V to rest. Benner then initiated plans to have his patient removed to Camp IV the following day. The remainder of the party agreed to continue the ascent as fair weather still prevailed.

Hackett felt himself fortunate that he and Blanchard had studied the terrain ahead. They were quickly able to climb around 'False Double Peak' and past the location of the 1925 expedition's high camp. They continued climbing and were able to establish Camp VI in a single day, ferrying loads five miles to the 18,500-foot level. This was the highest campsite established on the North American Continent up to that time.[26]

The following morning Bill stuck his head through the tent flaps and couldn't help but laugh. He then tied the flaps back in order to let some of the sunshine of the twelfth consecutive dawn shine inside. He couldn't even recall reading about such fair weather this far north! The team couldn't believe their good fortune and hurriedly set about packing for a summit assault. After roping up, they donned snowshoes and began their exhaustive hike towards the top.

The slopes became steeper and as a result, crampons were substituted for snowshoes. Hackett and Blanchard pulled ahead of Bohn, LeBell and Kaufmann. Bill even carried a six-foot bamboo pole with which he hoped to plant on the summit and raise the National Ensign. As they continued to climb, Hackett and Blanchard became enveloped in clouds. They reached the summit of the peak they had earlier guessed was the highest along the summit ridge. As they stood there congratulating one another on their accomplishment, the clouds above parted suddenly, revealing a peak even higher in the distance.

"Uh, did you see that, Smoke?" Bill asked.

"Yes, but I'm willing to ignore it if you will." Smoke replied.

"You know we can't do that."[27]

Unbelievable! They were on the summit of West Peak and still had a four to five hour ascent ahead of them![28] After shaking their heads and sharing a laugh, they proceeded to continue the ascent. "Since our further work was cut out for us," Bill would write, "nothing remained but to depart for the higher peak. Over 1,000 feet was descended on good crampon snow into a large saddle, and a direct line was taken toward the top of the Central Peak on steep snow. By 4:00 PM we were better than halfway up, at which time I turned to look back at the West Peak and saw two tiny figures on its summit. We were to learn later that our companions had followed us at a slower pace, and by the time they had reached the West Peak, their desire to continue on was diminished by the lateness of the hour. By this time the clouds that had enveloped the mountain had dissipated to the point where only scattered clouds remained at lower elevation."

An example of how tired Hackett and Blanchard had become can best be illustrated by an action they took later in the afternoon. They encountered crumbling ice several hundred feet below the true summit but instead of using proper crampon technique or cutting steps in the ice, they opted to make horizontal traverses or switchbacks at alarming speeds, all the while carrying their six-foot bamboo flagpole. This step was the reaction of tired men to a long and tedious day of climbing. They made their way up the knife-edge summit ridge to its highest point and finally reached their goal near 5:00 PM June 23, 1959.

When they had reached the crest, they were struck by gale force winds. Hackett and Blanchard had been climbing on the leeward side of the summit ridge until that point. There was just enough room on the summit to comfortably accommodate eight to ten men. The air temperature was negative twenty degrees but both men were elated with their achievement. Bill planted the bamboo pole and raised the American and Canadian Flags. The fourth ascent of Mount Logan had been accomplished and only once he returned to civilization did Bill realize that their ascent had taken place on the anniversary of the first ascent in 1925.[29]

Of the day's events, Blanchard would write:

> "Crossing and recrossing the deep gap separating the two summits was a big job. It was a fitting final examination for mountaineers involved with a lifetime mountain. Not only did we have to lose and regain the devil knows how much altitude, but we had to do it twice, because the way home lay back over the West Summit. And we did it with conditions icy enough to require step cutting in poor visibility against a strong wind. In spite of, or maybe because of, these conditions, it remains the one-day of the whole expedition burned into my memory. I remember the small crevasse I fell into, the clouds blowing and snowing on us, the tremor of the ax shaft as I sliced steps, the crunch of the crampons as I footed into the steps; most of all I remember the spot of sun that showed us the final steepening rise to the satisfactorily small summit, and, glory of glories, a hole in the cloud permitting a view of the Pacific Ocean!"[30]

After half an hour spent on the summit, Bill and Smoke faced each other and simultaneously cried out above the wind, "Let's get the hell out of here!" They then turned and made a more cautious descent of the summit pyramid. This trip was uneventful but a traverse of West Peak needed to be performed before they could return to Camp VI. This traverse used up the last of their energy resources and both climbers stumbled into camp around 9:30 PM. Blanchard said, "Bill seemed to feel neither altitude nor cold, but when he realized how long and late the day had become, and how very far back to camp it was, he turned to me with just a hint of fear in his voice and said, "I've never been this far out on the hook before!"

Over the course of the next two days, the team descended to 16,000 feet where Dr. Benner was still attending to Eichorn's needs. The expedition, now reunited, would make their way to Base Camp as a single group. The team encountered some sizeable crevasses during the descent and instead of enjoying them as he usually did; Smoke became ticked off at his rope mate. Hackett, on the other end, was apparently descending too fast.

"You son of a bitch!," Smoke yelled, " I've told you over and over I can't go that fast; the next time you speed up I'm going to yank you off your feet." Hackett nodded his head in understanding and slackened his pace. After a time however, he unknowingly sped up and Smoke had had enough. He wrapped the rope around his ice axe and then sank it deep into the snow, causing Bill to flip over and fall. The jerk was so sudden it ripped the snowshoes right off of Bill's feet!

— ◄═◆═► —

Kaufman wasn't too impressed with the expedition other than the fine photographs he was able to take of the region. He felt the trip was "uneventful, involving more work than excitement." He flew home to California, armed with his fine photographs but little else. Eichorn nearly recovered from his infection, accompanied Dr. Benner down the Alcan Highway. This would be a more scenic if time-consuming alternative to flying.

The 1959 American Mount Logan Expedition achieved several firsts: they established the highest climbing camp on the North American continent and made the first ascent of Logan's North Peak. Beautiful photographs of the region were taken by Bohn and Kauffman and Blanchard would look back on the experience as one of the most rewarding he had ever known.

━━━━

For Bill Hackett, the expedition was an ideal training ground for his ultimate goal—an 8,000 meter peak. He had submitted a request for a permit to climb either Gasherbrum or K2, the world's second-highest mountain. It is not clear exactly when Bill decided to invite Dave Bohn to the Karakoram. On Logan however, both men had spent in excess of twenty-four days on the ice, endured temperatures that dipped below -24 degrees at night, and made serious load carries at higher elevations. These experiences would be similar to those they would encounter in the Karakoram, home to what several generations of climbers have called *The Savage Mountain*!

━━━━

CHAPTER XIII

The Black
Pyramid

*"Today is the first day that I really have come to terms
that we're doomed to failure."*[1]

—Bill Hackett

On the afternoon of May 6, 1960, Major William Hackett boarded a C-121 Super Constellation cargo plane on the tarmac of Wheelus Air force Base in Tripoli, Libya. He ensured that his personal gear, weighing over 160 pounds, was properly handled and stowed. As he was about to depart on what he hoped would be the crowning achievement of his mountaineering career, he believed he was leaving nothing to chance. He had received every inoculation foreign travel required, had properly secured the necessary leave of absence from his military duties in Bad Tolz, Germany, and was now slowly checking off the series of plane flights it would take to bring him to Pakistan. A man capable of attending to every detail of a serious mountaineering expedition, he nevertheless forgot to obtain a Saudi-Arabian Visa. This oversight would become only one of many obstacles he would need to overcome if he were to succeed in reaching his goal—the summit of K2, the world's second-highest mountain.

In 1959, while returning from Mount Logan, Hackett had received word that his application to the Government of Pakistan had been approved. The Pakistani authorities had granted him authorization to travel up the Baltoro and Godwin-Austen Glaciers for an attempt on K2's Abruzzi Ridge. If successful, Hackett and his team would become the first Americans to reach the summit of what three generations of climbers had called *a mountaineer's mountain,* or *The Savage Mountain.*

In the late 1950s, Hackett had found himself in a quandary. He had military and family responsibilities that limited the amount of time he could spend away from Naydene and home. He had reached the highest summits on five of the seven continents and keenly felt the pull of the remaining two: Vinson Massif in Antarctica and Mt. Everest in Asia. No American expedition had been mounted to attempt Everest and Bill certainly wanted the chance to stand on the highest summit in the world. At the same time, thoughts of K2 began to enter his mind. Quite naturally, he wanted both.[2]

There were similarities as well as differences between the two objectives. Mount Everest, located in the Central Himalayas, had been a focal point for Western mountaineers ever since the first British expeditions were undertaken in the early 1920s. Merely *because* it was the highest in the world, mountaineers craved her summit like no other. K2, in the Karakoram Range of the Western Himalayas, initially failed to capture the public's imagination. Second highest surely meant second best. Most of the high altitude climbers of the time however, understood that K2 was the more isolated, more technical and therefore more rewarding peak to attempt. Bill was torn between both peaks so he submitted permit requests to the governments of Nepal for Everest and Pakistan for K2 or Gasherbrum and left the choice to fate. When he received word that it would be K2, he characteristically threw himself headlong into the necessary preparations. As always, he thoroughly researched the challenges that lie ahead; interviewing, corresponding and reviewing the documentation presented by his predecessors. His findings only inflamed his desire for an American conquest of K2.

In 1856, Colonel T.G. Montgomerie of the Survey of India located several large peaks in the central Karakoram Range. His initial responsibility was to accurately fix their positions and attempt to track down their local names if any existed. During his initial work, Montgomerie used a generic system to name these massive peaks.

Every mountain was listed with the letter K to denote their presence in the Karakoram Range. A number in progressive order (K1, K2, etc.) followed this letter, indicating the order in which they were surveyed. In this simple way, the name of the most dangerous mountain in the world came into being. There were several attempts to affix new titles and name it after prominent explorers but these names never seemed to stick for very long. The 'K2' listing remained on the maps for so long that over time, it retained a sense of permanence and even the local Balti porters began to call her *Kee-Tu*.

In 1861, H.H. Godwin Austen made the first 1:500,000-scale map of the region and in the process described the initial approaches to the base of K2. Between the late 1880s and the turn of the century several accomplished explorers brought more information out of the Karakoram to the attention of European mountaineers. Men like William Conway and Francis Younghusband set the stage for the more experienced alpinists to follow.[3]

In 1902, Oscar Eckenstein led a joint British-Austrian expedition, whose sole purpose was to make an attempt for the summit. One of his chief climbing companions on this venture was the infamous Aleister Crowley. Magician, poet, and 'the wickedest man on earth,' Crowley was nevertheless a mountaineer after Eckenstein's own heart. Both were climbers ahead of their time, using ice axes and ten-point crampons when most of Europe was still preaching the gospel of the alpenstock. Their combined efforts, though impressive for their time, were thwarted at the 6,000-meter level.[4]

Seven years later the Italians made their first attempt. Led by Luigi Amedeo di Savoia, The Duke of the Abruzzi, this team attempted the most practical route up the mountain. Though they were unable to reach the elevation mark set by their British predecessors, the Italians had at least pursued the route that four subsequent expeditions would employ in their attempts to reach the elusive summit.[5]

In 1938, the first of three American expeditions arrived on the Baltoro Glacier, the ice field leading to the base of K2. Led by Dr. Charles Houston, they were able to perform a proper reconnaissance of the southern routes and pioneer the Abruzzi Ridge Route clear up to the mountain's shoulder. This team was additionally able to solve the crux of the route, a rock chimney they named *House's Chimney* after the first man to successfully negotiate it. Foul weather and a shortage of matches forced their retreat but they had made the largest advance on the mountain to date.[6]

The second American attempt occurred the following year, led by one of the most accomplished yet controversial mountaineers in alpine history. Fritz Wiessner was a German ex-patriot who steadily built up one of the most impressive rock climbing resumes in the United States. Accompanied by Pasang Dawa Lama, he reached a point only several hundred feet below the summit of! They had set a new altitude record, proved man could survive at high altitudes for extended periods of time without supplemental oxygen and yet, still failed to reach the summit. The 1939 Second American Karakoram Expedition additionally incurred the first casualties on the mountain. Four lives were lost during the retreat from the mountain's upper slopes.[7]

In 1953, only weeks after Hillary and Norgay's first ascent of Everest, Charles Houston returned to lead the Third American Karakoram Expedition to K2. Though they came within striking distance of the summit, they encountered an emergency situation that halted any chance of an advance. Expedition member, Art Gilkey, suffered blood clots in his legs. Houston, a physician, knew his teammate would perish but he refused to simply leave him to his fate high on the mountain. Houston's team began a cautious descent of the Abruzzi Ridge, transporting Gilkey in a makeshift litter. One of the climbers slipped on the ice, causing an uncontrolled slide involving several different rope teams. At this point, Pete Schoening arguably performed the most famous ice axe belay in history. He had been belaying Gilkey's litter but somehow managed to save five lives when the rope teams became entangled during the fall. Gilkey would later perish but the rest of the expedition survived and safely retreated to base camp.[8]

The first ascent of the peak occurred the following year, 1954, when Ardito Desio led an impressive Italian team. Following the route that Houston and his men had pioneered, the Italians were able to place two climbers on top through the use of supplemental oxygen. As a public acknowledgement of Houston's efforts, Desio invited him to Europe to celebrate the achievement.

With all of this impressive history behind him, Bill Hackett desperately wanted to add his own chapter to the annals of American exploration on K2.

—— ⚞✦⚟ ——

At Base Camp on K2's Godwin-Austen Glacier, Hackett thanked his team for their efforts thus far. With him were fellow Americans Dave Bohn and Lynn Pease; Germans Dr. Wolfgang Deubzer, Lüdwig Greissl, Günter Jahr and Herbert Wünsche; Hayat Ali Shah, a Pakistani interpreter. Also present were Captain Sharif Ghasur, a liaison officer, and high altitude porters Asad, Makhmal, Longino, Taqi and Sirdar. Hayat Ali Shah would prove to be a valuable asset to the team. A mountaineer and interpreter, his knowledge of the region, its people and their dialects would be a continual benefit to the expedition.[9]

The trek to the mountain had been both memorable and historic. In regards to the terrain, American Dave Bohn remarked, "May I never see a more desolate, inhospitable spot on this earth."[10] Over a hundred Balti porters had been employed to carry supplies from Skardu to the base of K2 on the Godwin-Austen Glacier. Bohn and Hackett found it humorous that they needed to hire so many men. A hundred and fifty porters carried equipment and provisions for expedition members. An additional twenty-five men were employed to carry food for the porters carrying food for the bulk of the expedition. The sheer scope of the venture was impressive and it marked one of the few occasions an American expedition to K2 received a strike-free approach march. Hackett attributed their lack of a porter strike to their multi-talented liaison officer, Captain Sharif Ghasur. Hackett had also played a part in keeping the morale of the group up. He had Deubzer, their physician, attend to the needs of the porters. Dr. Deubzer had even pulled an abscessed tooth from a Balti man, earning himself a fair reputation among the troops.[11]

Base Camp, at 16,400 feet, was established on June 14, merely 300 yards above the site used by the successful Italian team six years earlier. Hackett had agreed with Bohn that the location was desolate and wind-swept. There were advantages to the site however. The ground was relatively level and free from the danger of rock fall. It also proved to be an adequate location from which to launch the assault on Abruzzi Ridge.[12]

On Wednesday, the morning after establishing base camp, the entire party opted to sleep late. A leisurely breakfast was shared and initial discussions among the men led Hackett to believe that the day should be spent resting and organizing camp. Over the following hours however, several of his men convinced him that an attempt to establish Camp I should be made. Dave Bohn, Wolfgang Deubzer and the porter, Taqi, volunteered to begin the ascent.

This trio of climbers roped up near the top of a nearby moraine. Nine other porters accompanied them on the first leg of the ascent. Ali, Asad, Longino and Muhammed collectively carried 585 pounds of food and equipment.[13] This team hadn't even managed twenty-five yards before Dr. Deubzer fell through a hidden crevasse! Fortunately, he outstretched his arms as soon as he felt he was losing his balance. As a result, he caught himself before falling further into the ice. Deubzer had been in the lead, followed by Bohn, Longino and then the others. Bohn was so shocked by what he saw he was momentarily paralyzed and froze in his tracks. Longino immediately recognized the seriousness of the situation but was not educated in the art of crevasse rescue. His enthusiasm and eagerness to rescue a friend overcame his sensibilities. Without thinking, he darted forward and passed Bohn. Longino could just as easily have fallen into a crevasse so Bohn quickly cried out for him to stop. He then signaled for Longino to back up in his original footprints until he reached safety. Wolfgang was able to extricate himself, but the incident unnerved the porters and caused the regular climbers to take a slower, more deliberate pace.

Later in the afternoon, Deubzer had Taqi and the other porters drop their loads in a cache behind some rocks. This position was just below that of the proposed site for Camp I. Bohn and Deubzer had every reason to celebrate. They had survived a hidden crevasse, encountered fair weather throughout the day, and had brought a substantial amount of supplies, ahead of schedule, to the very base of Abruzzi Ridge. While the two men conversed over the day's achievements, they noticed Taqi and the others had scattered in an attempt to locate and pilfer any remaining supplies left over from the Italian's first ascent of 1954. Bohn yelled at Taqi to cease this scavenging and return to base camp with the remaining porters.[14]

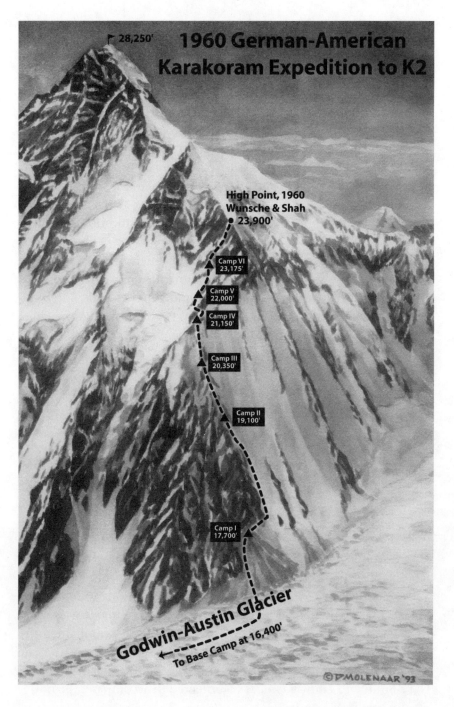

28,250'

1960 German-American Karakoram Expedition to K2

High Point, 1960
Wunsche & Shah
● 23,900'

Camp VI
23,175'

Camp V
22,000'

Camp IV
21,150'

Camp III
20,350'

Camp II
19,100'

Camp I
17,700'

Godwin-Austin Glacier

To Base Camp at 16,400'

©D.MOLENAAR '93

　　　The following morning Bill awoke from an uncomfortable night's sleep. He had been pleased with Bohn and Deubzer's success the previous day and desperately wanted to establish Camp I before foul weather returned. The entire expedition, with the exception of Bohn and Ghasur, left camp and started up the icefall. Impressive seracs, large crevasses and pressure ridges are only a few of the barriers they had to overcome in order to reach the region of the Abruzzi Ridge. Once off of the glacier itself, they had to climb up a detritus rock pyramid in order to reach a suitable location on which to establish Camp I.[15]

　　　During the following few days, Hackett ensured that the men had Camp I fully stocked before continuing forward with the ascent. There were 765 pounds of equipment and supplies and nearly 200 pounds at the first cache, established by Deubzer and Bohn. There were over twenty liters of gasoline and enough rations to sustain four men on the mountain for eighty-four days.

　　　Faulty radio communications between Ghasur at Base Camp and the climbers on the ridge would consistently plague the expedition. Bohn would later write, "We were having trouble with the small two-way radios, and contact with Base Camp was always questionable. I remember dragging out of the tent one morning and crossing to the ridge east of Camp I. There I stood for twenty minutes in the biting wind trying to get through to Lynn Pease, and when I finally did, I could hear about every fourth word."[16] During the early stages of the assault on the Abruzzi Ridge, radio communications would be their only concern. This would change in the weeks to come.

　　　Sunday, June 19 would prove to be one of the most memorable days of the expedition. A beautifully clear morning with only a few clouds on the horizon, Bill thought conditions were ideal to push the route higher to Camp II. He would be relying heavily upon the memory of Taqi, one of his porters who had accompanied the Italian team six years earlier. Taqi had assured his Sahib that he remembered the route to Camp II and Bill took the man at his word. Dave Bohn and Lüdwig Greissl volunteered to accompany the porter on this reconnoiter trip.[17]

Initially, Taqi appeared to know where he was going. He pointed towards an ice couloir, which began just above camp and led upwards through a multitude of rock bands. For over four hours, Bohn and Greissl struggled through hip-deep powder. On occasion, they crossed over rock slabs covered in ice and an outer coating of fresh powder. The necessary ingredients for an accident were present, and Bohn and Greissl began to have serious reservations about continuing the ascent. They eventually became convinced that the Italians would never have taken their current route and as a result, they confronted Taqi. The porter eventually conceded that he was lost. Not sure whether they would ever return to such a precarious position, they nevertheless cached their packs and began a treacherous descent back to camp.[18]

That same day, Asad, Jahr, Wünsche and Makhmal departed base camp. Their timing could not have been more ideal. At 11:20 AM, a booming sound echoed from above. A massive slab avalanche broke away from the southeast face of K2 and sent tons of snow, ice and rock debris down the mountain. This wall of snow swept completely over base camp on the Godwin-Austen Glacier and up the lower slopes of nearby Broad Peak. The mass of air moving swiftly in front of the slide blew the climbers completely off their feet and forced them to the ground. Though spared from enduring the full force of the avalanche, they nevertheless caught its outer fringe. Snow was forced through their layers of clothing and Asad suffered a slight blow to the head. If these men had enjoyed a longer breakfast, they might have been lost in the slide.[19] Hackett and Longino were higher up on the route and witnessed the entire affair. They were just about to head down in order to lend whatever assistance they could, when Bill suddenly stopped in his tracks. He looked down at the edge of the debris field, where his men were last seen. He grinned as he saw figures far below, seemingly popping out of the snow. Bill quickly counted four heads and watched them move about the ice. Everyone appeared to be counted for, there were no obvious external injuries and the men below were not signaling for assistance. Tragedy had been averted.

The expedition had endured several close calls that particular Sunday morning. In addition to the avalanche, Bill would later learn that Taqi had nearly broken his neck! Accompanied by Bohn, he had been climbing near Camp II when he suddenly slipped and entered an uncontrolled slide. Taqi barrel-rolled for roughly twenty yards before Bohn saved him on belay. Bill was very troubled by these occurrences but was able to rationalize them in his head. The avalanche from the southeast face of the mountain would have been very difficult to predict but Taqi's actions that Sunday seemed inexcusable. Bill would have understood had his porter come to him and confessed that he had forgotten the way to Camp II, but to risk his own life and that of his colleagues seriously jeopardized the expedition. Bill would be more leery of Taqi's advice in the months to come.

The team fared better the following day. Bohn and three porters left to retrieve supplies from the cache at the base of Abruzzi Ridge. Jahr, Wünsche and Deubzer were sent up the mountain in order to locate a more practical route to Camp II. It was Bill's hope that the men could reach the objective while avoiding the dangerous couloir the team had encountered the day previously. Hackett, Longino and Greissl followed in their footsteps an hour behind Bohn. Halfway between Camp I and the hopeful site of Camp II, Deubzer came upon the Italian route. Several pitons had been left in the rock at key belay points. When Bill received news of this discovery he was overcome with joy. Baring any unforeseen emergencies, Camp II could be established before nightfall![20]

Expedition members continually thanked Hackett for his careful planning regarding food. It was evident that his many years in the mountains had prepared him for organizing such fare. Bohn would note:

> "There was at first total agreement that the food we were eating on the mountain—for the most part Army dehydrated—constituted a fine diet. Later on, some opinions changed, and there were discussions over the merit of our rations. I myself do not see how it would have been humanely possible to have obtained a better balanced diet, nor do I know of any way to avoid repetitious meals when in the field for three months. Certainly Bill Hackett deserves great credit for the menu he worked out. I *will* admit that occasionally a dish did not turn out to be as savory as anticipated,

and I remember creating a magnificent casserole of hamburger, string beans, cheese, and red cabbage, which concoction was so salty it went begging. Some days later I discovered the red cabbage was in reality Malwa Tea leaves! Porter rice on the mountain became for some of us a delicacy. Taqi and Asad, huddled in their tent, would prepare it in the pressure cooker, then pass to us a steaming bowl. With the addition of maple syrup (at Lynn's suggestion) we had what I felt was the taste sensation for K2, 1960."[21]

——— ⋯⋯ ———

At 19,000 feet, Hackett and his companions came upon the Italian's Camp II. Signs of the earlier campaign were clearly evident. The metal skeleton of a two-man tent was still standing after enduring six years of storms. Other man-made debris littered the site. Tins of food were scattered about a rocky platform that constituted the extent of living space. Most of the seals on these containers had been broken or were otherwise compromised. Several however were still in fair condition, much to the surprise of Bill and the team. A few stoves and cooking utensils were also found, evidence of a hasty retreat on the part of the Italians. Hackett and Greissl were particularly pleased when they discovered a cache of pitons. No ropes were discovered but this was not surprising, as the men knew porters from Askole had retrieved several of the lines shortly after the first ascent.[22]

The rock shelf that comprised Camp II was extremely inhospitable. On a steep incline, exposed to high winds and the natural elements, one felt their tent would be blown clean off the mountain! Another inherent danger was rock fall. Camp II would prove to be the most hazardous station on the Abruzzi Ridge. On several occasions, men reported seeing sizeable rocks flying by their heads. Bill made a conscious decision to limit their time at this site.

On Wednesday, June 22, Bohn, Greissl and Hackett enjoyed a hearty breakfast while discussing strategies for the coming week. The weather was improving though high winds were still a concern. Although the expedition was technically proceeding on schedule, it was in Bill's nature to always push forward. He wanted Camp III to be established for two main reasons. He was concerned for the safety of his men and the rock fall danger at Camp II was still on his mind. He wanted to keep his men occupied and knew morale could only be improved with the occupation of a higher camp.[23]

Bohn, accompanied by Hackett and Greissl, carefully led the way towards the proposed site of Camp III. Initially the path seemed clear, as Bohn was able to follow fixed lines left behind by the Italians. Around noon, the team ran out of fixed rope and began to climb unassisted. For reasons unspecified in his diaries, Bill gave the order to retreat to Camp II. Even Bohn's account in the *American Alpine Journal* is silent in regards to this decision. Perhaps the powder snow along the traverse to Camp III was too thick, delaying the party and forcing their retreat. Perhaps the powder presented an avalanche danger that the team was unwilling to accept.

There were other issues that Bill was forced to contend with. Makhmal, a porter with previous high-altitude experience, had complained of a knee injury that Bill was unable to verify. Lynn Pease informed the team that he had caught Makhmal removing fixed ropes between Camps I and II. Expedition members might have to cling to such lines for their very lives in the event of future storms. Upon hearing this revelation, Bill naturally became furious. Knowing he would still require the services of the porters, he restrained himself and merely gave a stern lecture that evening that put an end to such pilfering. Whatever the reason for temporarily turning back, the men would return in two days to complete the traverse and establish Camp III.[24]

A small rock shelf at 20,650 feet, Camp III had been difficult to reach. The powder snow that covered rock slabs were oftentimes hidden from view. The pitches were steeper, requiring more time and effort to cross. A particularly treacherous pitch was an ice traverse just below the camp. Only after successfully crossing these barriers could the men take a break from their labors. A hasty meal was prepared and Greissl, Jahr and Hackett all shared their provisions. Somewhere along the Abruzzi, Bill had found a can of Canadian Apricot Jam that had been a leftover of Dr. Houston's 1953 attempt. This jam made a perfect topping to the German bread Greissl had brought from Camp II. Butter and cheese were also consumed before they began erecting the tents.[25]

Creating suitable shelter at Camp III proved nearly as difficult as the traverse to reach the site. Hackett discovered that his eyes had deceived him, that the rock platform was even smaller than he origi-nally anticipated. The Gerry tent could only have one of its vestibules used and even the Pioneer tent was perched on a narrow snow spur! The men didn't want to sleep in the tents, so certain were they that they would end up on the Godwin-Austen Glacier far below. There seemed to be no means of support and the men feared that if they rolled over in the night, they would take the tent with them.

On June 28, Bill received news that boosted his spirits even fur-ther. He had descended to Camp II in order to retrieve supplies while simultaneously dispatching Jahr and Greissl on a reconnaissance to Camp IV. Later in the afternoon, once his chores were complete, Bill heard someone shouting down from farther up the mountain. He leaned out and craned his neck in order to discover what was amiss. Greissl was calling down to him from Camp III, gleefully informing him that he and Jahr had reached Camp IV earlier in the day.[26]

For the next two days, Hackett and Dave Bohn were bed-ridden, stuck in Camp II with a variety of medical ailments. Bohn was dealing with some gastrointestinal issues while Bill was nursing his right ankle. For nearly two weeks his boots had been irritating his right Achilles tendon. Bill had used a variety of padding, insoles and different types of socks but nothing seemed to work. His ankle grew inflamed and infection set in. Lynn Pease, hearing of the problem, brought six units of sigmamycin up with him from the lower camps. Bill religiously took his medication but in the days to follow, no improvement could be seen. It was clear that further steps needed to be taken. On July 2, the expedition doctor, Deubzer, arrived in Camp III to have a look at the infected ankle. As soon as he saw the wound, the doctor grabbed some scissors and set about surgically removing a nodule. Once completed, he administered a shot of penicillin.[27]

Flushed with the success of the establishment of Camps III and IV, Bill grew concerned once again over a mishap in an ice couloir below Camp III. On June 30, the day Bill's heel forced him to remain in camp, several team members were returning from the higher camp. At 11:30 AM, Lynn Pease and porters, Asad, Hayat and Taqi, were carefully descending over powder snow and ice-covered rocks. When they reached the ice couloir, Hayat took the lead. When it was Pease's turn, he clipped into a fixed line in case he should slip during the descent. This action undoubtedly saved his life as his iced-over

crampon snagged on his pant leg and caused him to enter an uncontrolled slide. His sure descent to the Godwin-Austen Glacier was only
checked by the carabineer hooked to his waist harness and the fixed
line. The incident was yet another close call for one of the expedition's chief climbers.

Such incidents, unfortunately common on high-altitude
expeditions, infuriated Bill. He was never upset at the men in particular, he just seemed to believe that accidents could be quelled or at
least curtailed by his very presence. He believed that in the presence
of their leader, the men would take extra precautions and safety
measures. Bill was used to leading military men, not seasoned
climbers with free-thinking, independent, and democrat leanings. At
elevations exceeding 20,000 feet, on extremely steep terrain, no fig-
urehead was needed to tell you to watch your step. Hackett was
known as a safe climber but his mere *presence* would not have
deterred an accident. With each man taking thousands of steps a day
on the ice, it was only a matter of time before someone slipped.

On July 2, Taqi and Asad poked their heads in Hackett's tent.
Between excited utterances from both porters, Bill learned that Hayat
and Bohn had reached Camp IV at 21,540 feet. Soon after the porters
brought this news, Lynn Pease returned and delivered his own report.
Greissl and Jahr, preceding Pease's team, had successfully ascended
House's Chimney and reached a position only fifty meters below
Camp V! Bill was ecstatic, but no sooner had the porters departed
than his eyes fixed on what appeared to be an approaching storm.[28]

The snowstorm that struck on the Third of July forced the
entire expedition to remain in their shelters. Pease and Hackett, holed
up in Camp II, spent most of the day reading and talking amongst
themselves. Dr. Deubzer and Herbert Wünsche did likewise in a nearby tent. Though only three feet separated their tents, these two parties
were unable to hear each other's conversation over the roaring of the
wind. During a break in the weather, which is to say, a man could actually stick his head out of the tent, Bill tried to rouse his troops to work.
It was his hope that one or two of his men would make the descent to
Camp I for supplies or make a carry to Camp III. Deubzer and Wunsche
stuck their heads out of their tent and surveyed their surroundings.

"Bill, you're nuts!" one of the climbers shouted. With that
said they returned to the relative comfort and warmth of their

sleeping bags. For Bill's part, he just laughed and then prepared a meal. He was certain that his pleas for work would go unanswered but he was equally convinced that should a true break in the weather present itself, the team would rise and eagerly continue the ascent. It was common knowledge that House's Chimney was perhaps the most technically difficult section along the Abruzzi Ridge. The fact that Greissl and Jahr had already surmounted it renewed unit morale. There was clearly no more motivating event during the expedition than the successful ascent of House's Chimney. Team members now waited impatiently to capitalize on this success.[29]

Life in Camp IV wasn't always so bad. Bohn recalls patches of better weather. He and Hayak were then afforded a clear view of the Karakoram. "At Camp IV, " Bohn writes, "we began to get the perspective of height, for Broad Peak was gradually sinking, and we could see more of the vast Karakoram. I well remember the day Hayak and I sat at the top of House's Chimney for a lunch break, before heading for Camp V with the fixed rope. There was hardly a cloud in the sky, and prominent to the southwest was Masherbrum, which for many days had been plagued with bad weather. Hayak claimed he could see the pyramidal tents of Base Camp on the moraine 5,000 feet below, but I accused him of telephoto vision because even with the binoculars I could see nothing."[30]

On July 4, clearer skies were visible and a dramatic drop in wind velocity was perceived. The men didn't need Bill's prodding to begin work. Asad and Longino began a descent to Camp I in order to clean it out and take a secondary inventory of everything it contained in the event of an emergency. After the tragic results of the Second American K2 Expedition, Bill was taking no chances. He needed to know exactly what provisions were housed in each camp, depot and cache. Wünsche, Pease, Taqi and Deubzer departed Camp II soon after Asad and Longino had made their exit. Jahr had awoken early and made a swift carry to Camp III. With his load secured, he joined Hayak and Dave Bohn on an ascent of House's Chimney. These three climbers reached the Italian Camp V in the early afternoon, the culmination of the day's work.[31]

Camp V, at 21,930 feet, was in poor condition. All along the Abruzzi Ridge, Bill and his team had been able to use food, equipment and supplies left behind not only by the Italians, but three previous American expeditions. At Camp V however, Bohn, Jahr and Hayak found only scraps of metal and a few tins of food. Nevertheless, they were well pleased with progress and looked forward to continuing the advance.

On July 10, the expedition took a calculated risk that fortunately paid off. Hackett arose after having spent a miserable night tossing and turning. The higher altitudes and burden of leadership were beginning to take effect. Taqi stuck his head into the tent and stated he had just seen two climbers departing Camp I and start up the mountain. Bill nodded and ordered Taqi and Asad to the head of House's Chimney. Once there, as instructed, they were to assist Pease and Deubzer in their advance to Camp V. Bill then looked outside to inspect the sky. What he saw was not comforting. Winds had picked up and it looked as if the mountain would be plagued with periodic snowfall throughout the day. Convinced that it wasn't an actual storm brewing, he began to suit up for another day's work.[32]

Hackett conferred with several of his companions and all agreed to make a major push and hopefully establish Camp VI in a single day. They discussed the loads they would need to carry and the deteriorating weather conditions but all agreed that the attempt should be made. They started after breakfast with Bill leading Hayak, Wünsche, Jahr and Greissl on the ascent.

There were several reasons why Bill was in good spirits that morning. Primarily, he was happy to be out of his tent after such a miserable evening and glad to be back on the slopes, directly contributing to the expedition's advance. He was also tired of waiting for his ankle to heal and was anxious to give it a 'proper test.' These feelings were public knowledge but Bill kept other feelings to himself. He knew that should he be able to make the ascent to Camp VI that day, he would break his previous personal altitude record of 22,835 feet. His ascent of Aconcagua occurred eleven years earlier and Bill had eagerly awaited the opportunity to break this personal record.

When the team reached Dr. Houston's old Camp VI, foul weather descended. In high winds and snowfall, Hackett inspected the site. Remnants of Charlie Houston's green canvas tent were visible and Bill was unsure whether this was from the doctor's 1938 or 1953 effort. A tin of apricot jam was also found, half-frozen in the ice. At such an elevation, over 300 miles from the nearest civilization, such a find was a treasure to be relished no matter what the weather conditions. Hayak and Bill eagerly devoured the jam without the benefit of bread or chapattis.

After a brief respite at the American site, the men advanced to the Italian's Camp VI at 23,175 feet. Bill had only broken his personal altitude record by 340 feet but it cheered him up nevertheless. The group congratulated themselves, cached their loads and sat down for a welcome pot of tea. This simple celebration was unfortunately cut short when the skies grew thick with storm clouds, seemingly appearing out of nowhere.

There were several contributing factors to their safe descent to Camp V. First and foremost, they were free of their heavy packs, having deposited their loads in a cache at Camp VI. Visibility had dropped to only a few yards, but the men fortunately had the assistance of the fixed lines to guide them down. They also had psychological reasons for expedient departure. The knowledge that they must descend or die had an uncanny ability to strengthen and focus their efforts.

When they reached Camp V, Bill was presented with a problem. Pease and Deubzer had spent the day retrieving provisions from below and had been trapped in Camp V for hours. The small tents in Camp V would have to hold Hackett, Jahr, Hayak, Wünsche, Greissl, Pease and the doctor. The quarters were cramped, but the men were grateful to be out of the elements. No sooner had they settled in for the remainder of the day, then the storm increased in intensity and all agreed that they would be stuck in camp for several days.

At 2:00 AM, on July 11, one of the two main poles in Lynn Pease's tent collapsed. Pease suited up and went out into the storm to make repairs. He additionally took the opportunity to clear some of the accumulating snow from around the tents in Camp V. Hackett, in another tent at the time, could barely hear a commotion outside and decided to investigate. He stuck his head out of the tent flaps and was violently accosted by icy winds that struck with such force, he would later label it 'sand blasting!' Even stepping outside, unprotected from the elements, would have exposed oneself to the risk of frostbite. Through the snowstorm Bill was able to see Pease making repairs and he was very grateful to have such a man on his team.[33]

Between July 11 and August 1, the 1960 German-American expedition endured some of the worst weather ever recorded in K2's history. These storms would come and go but there would only be short periods of time between each when expedition members could move from camp to camp. Further progress seemed impossible. Wind gusts, predominately from the south, were in excess of eighty miles per hour. Bohn would write that it was too cold and windy outside the tents to relieve themselves and that the men had to use plastic bags to store the urine.[34] The porters refused all attempts to make them work. They pointed to the extreme weather, shook their heads and chanted to their gods for deliverance. Hackett would write of restless nights and "seemingly endless periods of weather tantrums, punctuated by the noise of tortured tent flaps. The incessant rattle to the tent surfaces had begun to work on our minds." Every hour or so, men would need to abandon the warmth and comfort of their sleeping bags in order to clear away snow that had accumulated around the tent. Rime ice coated the tent guy lines and frost feathers covered their food cache.

The expedition was seeing shortages in nearly every field. They needed more rope for fixed lines and more pitons to hold them down. By inspecting his records, Hackett discovered they would not have enough emergency rations to sustain them in a crisis situation. Bill was forced to reduce rations as a result.

The men were also dealing with medical conditions. Lynn Pease was coping with gastrointestinal problems. Taqi and Longino were also ill. Hayak was having eye trouble and vomiting profusely. Greissl was so taken with fever that he had to descend one camp at a time until he reached Base Camp. Once there he suffered kidney problems. Bill had written him a note stating that he had granted authorization for the porters to carry Greissl out to the village of Askole. Bill himself was nursing not only his ankle, but two injuries sustained by rock fall. On July 23, he was climbing with Hayak when tension on the rope dislodged two sizeable rocks. One clipped the tip of Bill's cap while the other struck him square above his left knee.[35]

Saturday, July 30, would be a day Bill Hackett would remember for decades to come. He awoke near 7:00 in the morning, feeling rested and ready for another day's work on the Abruzzi Ridge. He was unaware that the highest elevation mark achieved by the expedition would occur later that afternoon. Bill emerged from his tent and had to shield his eyes from the sun. The frost had been melted off his tent, winds were moderate, and the skies appeared to be clearing. A beautiful morning in the Karakoram. After suiting up, he began a difficult descent to Camp V. He had to clear ice, six inches in diameter, from the fixed lines. When he arrived in Camp V, he greeted Jahr and Taqi and remarked on the fair weather. Jahr shared his breakfast with Bill and informed him he planned on ascending to Camp VI. Taqi had also expressed an interest in carrying loads farther up the ridge. Bill was pleased and agreed to join them. All three shouldered heavy packs and departed camp.[36]

Before they even reached Camp VI, yet another storm descended. Hackett, Jahr and Taqi hurriedly erected an additional Gerry tent. Hayak and Wunsche then entered Camp VI. They had returned from higher up, setting fixed ropes to the top of rock formations known as *The Black Pyramid*. Bill was excited to hear the news but ushered his men into the tents and out of the wind. Hayak and Wunsche were spent, exhausted from their efforts. Taqi and Hackett set about making them comfortable while they all discussed their foul luck with the weather. Even as late as 7:00 PM, Bill was scribbling down summit team strategies in his notebook, unaware that there would be no further progress for him or his team.

The following morning, Bill awoke with a groan. At first he thought a water bottle might have broken its seal inside his sleeping bag but upon closer examination, he realized he was mistaken. New snowdrifts on the outside of the tent were pressing in and his own body heat had caused the snow to melt. The waterproof capabilities of the shelter had seen better days and as a result, the water leaked through onto his bag.[37]

Hackett had other concerns that morning as well. A scheduled radio contact with Sharif Ghasur at Base Camp met with static or silence. Bill couldn't remember if Sharif had gone to the village of Askole to hire porters for the expedition's eventual retreat or made carries to the lower camps. Longino was unaccounted for and this also concerned the men higher up.

Hackett prided himself on knowing where his men were and what tasks they had been assigned to each day, a habit adopted even before his career in the Army. At the moment, his men were spread out all along the Abruzzi Ridge. Taqi refused to do even simple cooking duties. Bill was convinced the man feigned illness every time a storm appeared. Dave Bohn had descended to Base Camp in order to "get his perspective straightened out." He and Wolfgang had several arguments during the previous week and Bohn simply needed some time alone.[38] The windless in House's Chimney was broken and supplies could only be carried up the chute on the backs of the men. This was no easy feat as it was the most technical pitch on the route. It was a trip few volunteered to make.

Bill cursed the bad luck that seemed to plague the expedition. No party on K2 had ever suffered such a dramatic shift in the weather. There were moments when expedition members felt they would surely reach their goal. At other times, it appeared as if they were miles from their objective. It was the weather however, that prevented Bill Hackett from accomplishing his goal. Such weather few can imagine, storms lasting days with intensity seldom seen at lower elevations. Though there had been no loss of life and incredible obstacles had been overcome, Bill nevertheless laid in his sleeping bag and muttered to himself. In his eyes, he had failed. He had had a taste of defeat during his involvement with the Northwest Buttress expedition to McKinley in 1954. Though that team had successfully completed the route to the summit of North Peak, they were stormed off the mountain, unable to reach the south, and true summit of the mountain. Though his companions on that journey had nothing but good memories after that trip, Bill nevertheless felt the bitter taste of failure. His anger over the weather soon turned to a depression that would keep him up at night. While his tent mates were fast asleep, Bill reached over and grabbed his K2 diary. He pulled a pencil from his breast pocket and wrote, "This can't be anything but the monsoon...today is the first day that I really have come to terms that we're doomed to failure."[39]

The following morning, August 1, 1960, Hackett had the sad task of outlining their evacuation plan. He shared his findings with the men and was finally able to make radio contact with Base Camp. It would take nearly a week just to descend to the glacier. Once there, they cleaned the site up for the unknown expeditions that would surely follow. During this cleaning, the men came across an August 6, 1938, copy of *The Statesman*. Bill instantly recognized it as a scrap left behind by Dr. Houston's earliest attempt. Like Houston's efforts in 1938 and 1953, Bill Hackett would be departing the Karakoram without the prize—the summit of *The Savage Mountain*. The American mountaineering community would need to wait an additional eighteen years for the summit.

It would take the expedition another twenty days to reach the village of Skardu and some semblance of civilization. During that time Bill contemplated the outcome of the expedition and the future of his own climbing career. In the months to come he would continually analyze his own performance on the mountain and those of his colleagues, desperately searching for the reason or reasons for the team's failure to reach the summit. Only with time did he come to realize that it was simply the weather, a force of nature completely out of his hands. There was no doubt that Bill had enjoyed a long series of successful ascents. He had been climbing for decades in relative safety and reached the summits of some of the most fascinating mountains in the world. And yet, Bill had also been *extremely* fortunate with the weather. Nothing could have prepared him or his men for the punishing storms sweeping through the Karakoram that summer.

⊷ ⋈⊹⊠ ⊷⊶

For nearly forty years, Hackett would occasionally endure a spell of depression whenever he thought of the 1960 German-American Expedition to K2. In the fall of 1998 however, an event opened his own eyes to the contribution he made to the history of K2. The Portland-based Mazamas had organized a reunion for American expeditions that had been sent to K2. Charles Houston and Bob Bates of the 1938 and 1953 attempts were present, as were Pete Schoening, Dee Molenaar, and others from the '53 team. Jim Whittaker and members of both his 1975 and successful 1978 expeditions were also in attendance. Between the Italian ascent of 1954 and Jim Whittaker's 1975 attempt, only Bill Hackett and his team had visited the slopes of K2. Bill was therefore one of the few American climbers for a twenty year period to have explored the great peak. Through slide shows, presentations and speeches from all, Bill gradually began to realize that his efforts and those of his team *had* been appreciated and respected all along. That evening of camaraderie and shared stories would be one of his fondest memories during his remaining months.

⊷ ⋈⊹⊠ ⊷⊶

CHAPTER XIV

New Year's Eve

"Alone in my room with my thoughts...so ends another year."[1]

—Bill Hackett

When Bill Hackett returned to Bad Tolz, Germany on September 7, 1960, he was already in a deeply depressive state.[2] For weeks his sole thoughts centered around his defeat on K2. His first train of thought focused solely on his team. Had the language barriers and cultural differences been a factor in their failure? Had there been any critical miscommunication that resulted in a serious time delay? He reviewed his K2 diary thoroughly, attempting to pinpoint locations and times where the team had failed in some way or delayed progress. After studying these pages he had to admit that not only had his team taken advantage of every available opportunity, they had had some good fortune during the early portion of their journey. Hayat Ali Shah's knowledge of the region, its people and their different dialects had been a key to the team's continued progress during the approach march. Numerous logistical concerns were overcome through his efforts and those of Captain Sharif Ghasur, their Pakistani liaison officer. Bill read diary entry after entry where his fellow Americans, Dave Bohn and Lynn Pease, had demonstrated initiative and determination in the face of incredibly harsh weather. Bohn's technical climbing skills were employed time and time again. The Germans: Lüdwig Greissl, Günter Jahr and Herbert Wünsche were hard working, contributing members of the expedition who rarely complained of anything. Bill did however, have several reservations about their expedition physician, Dr. Wolfgang Deubzer. According to Bill, he seemed to be uncooperative and negative most of the time. Bill felt however, that none of these personality differences directly contributed to any delay or problem during the course of the venture. High altitude porters: Asad, Makhmal, Longino, Taqi and Sirdar were carefully scrutinized. A few of them had been caught pilfering provisions left behind by previous expeditions. This, in and of itself, did not cause Bill much alarm but he could never forget, nor forgive Makhmal's attempts to steal fixed lines that the team might have had to rely on during an emergency descent. In addition, Taqi had endangered the lives of Dave Bohn and Ludwig Greissl during the reconnaissance trip to locate Camp II. Taqi, who had accompanied the successful Italian team in 1954, had told Bill that he knew the way to the proposed site and this was not an accurate statement. As a result the trio of climbers had to endure a difficult day of climbing on steep pitches that were not only unnecessary but exposed them to hazards they would not have had to face had the porter simply owned up to the fact that he had forgotten the route. Bill had climbed with Argentine mountain troops who were often times sluggish and hard to motivate, he had climbed with people he considered out of shape, and he had climbed with people he had felt were not pulling their own weight. None of these could be said of his 1960 K2 team and Bill could find no evidence to indicate that his team had let him down in anyway. The reason for their failure must lie elsewhere.

Bill naturally looked within himself. Could I have done something different? Was there a moment or day where I hesitated when I should have forged ahead? Had I selected the appropriate positions for the camps? Did I do enough to ensure that they were stocked appropriately? Numerous questions filled his mind, far more than he could dream up for his team. As a military man he knew that the leader assumed sole responsibility for failure, and this expedition was no different. There must have been something he had done to cause this failure. He knew it but simply could not put his finger on it. Rather than seek advice from Naydene, the one individual who knew him better than anyone, he quietly began seeking counsel from some of his fellow Army officers. These men that knew him on a professional level were certainly aware that Bill rarely, if ever, discussed his personal feelings and misgivings. Because of this fact, they took the time to sit down with him in the officer's club and try to cheer him up. They advised him that he had clearly taken a blow to his sense of self-confidence. As a military officer, in a clear leadership role, such confidence could make or break you, and Bill's colleagues did not want to see him slip into an even darker state of affairs.

There were several issues that even these fellow soldiers were not aware of. First and foremost was the fact that Bill Hackett had encountered favorable weather during the majority of his high-altitude ascents. It is true that he had endured incredible storms on McKinley in 1947, and even worse weather on the same peak in 1954. Nothing, simply nothing could have prepared him for the severity and duration of storms encountered on the second-highest mountain in the world. The 1953 K2 team had dubbed the peak, *The Savage Mountain*, and this was primarily due to the inclement weather encountered on her slopes. Charles Houston and Bob Bates were well aware of the impact the weather would have when they returned to the Karakoram for their 1953 attempt. Bill was not prepared for such a challenge.

Another fact that these Army officers were unaware of was that the thought of returning to K2 hadn't even entered Bill's mind. When Houston and Bates returned to the United States after their pioneering efforts in 1938, they provided the American Alpine Club with their findings and route descriptions. Fritz Wiessner, who would lead the 1939 effort, would use this information to come within 800 feet of the summit! When the Second World War put recreational matters as *climbing* on temporary hold, Houston and Bates began to ponder the idea of returning to the Karakoram. They worked for years after the cessation of hostilities to secure the necessary permission and paperwork to have another go at the still virgin peak. They did their best to employ the lessons they learned from 1938 and their other experiences on Nanda Devi and Alaska to their advantage. Hackett on the other hand didn't consider mounting another attempt and during his hesitation and depression, the curtain of opportunity closed behind him—the Karakoram became off-limits to western climbers. When it would open again in 1975 through the efforts of Jim Whittaker and US Senator Edward Kennedy, Bill was fifty-seven years old. He was still young enough to have *led* an attempt from Base Camp, but such a scenario would never stay in his mind for very long. If he couldn't be in the summit party...why go?

For Bill Hackett, his experiences on K2 could not have come at a worse time in his life. Had the expedition taken place earlier on in his career, he could have shrugged it off and perhaps mounted another attempt. He was forty-two years old, a time when many men are pondering their future and more importantly, reviewing their past. It is at this point that a man realizes he will never be able to accomplish all of the goals he has set forth for himself. He'll never climb all of the mountains he wants to climb, never visit as many countries as he desires, and probably never achieve something substantial enough (in his own eyes) to warrant public acclaim and attention. In 1960, Bill was clearly battling a severe mid-life crisis. He knew that a high-altitude mountaineer peaked in his career during his thirties and few were still attempting the higher slopes in their forties. Not until the late twentieth century would high altitude climbers in their fifties be considered *normal*. Bill knew his climbing days amongst the *Big Ones* were numbered and this fact alone contributed heavily to his depression.

In today's high-altitude mountaineering community, with more information concerning the dangers of working at such heights available, a mountaineer can better project their climbing career. The baseline of experience on lower peaks needs to occur in their youth or as soon as possible. Initial forays at higher altitudes can then be undertaken: the volcanoes of Mexico or the standard Northwest Ridge of Aconcagua for example. Most climbers would agree that their thirties and forties are the prime time to be climbing at even higher altitudes. The inherent risk to oneself and to others only increases with age. There are naturally climbers in their fifties demonstrating incredible skill and experience amongst the 8,000-meter peaks but the number of high altitude climbers in their sixties is incredibly small. Hackett had already been climbing for twenty-seven years and K2 had been his *first* experience on one of the Himalayan giants. In another twenty-seven years Bill would be sixty-nine and surely unable to work in the environment that he loved so much. These facts weighed heavily on his mind.

→ ≍✦≍ ←

Hackett additionally took stock of his military career. He had served over three years in the 10th Mountain Division during World War II, winning the Silver Star in the process; he had been a combat infantry unit commander in the Apennines and Julian Alps of Italy, he had served a year and-a-half in Korea's Chorwon Valley as Intelligence Officer for the 7th Infantry Division and he had been Chief of Training for the Mountain and Cold Weather Training Command at Fort Carson, Colorado. Only a year before the expedition in the Karakoram, Bill had received his bachelor's degree in Business Administration from George Washington University. He had spent eighteen years in military service so far and had a wide variety of combat and civilian experience to his credit. But the Army was placing a freeze on promotions for a multitude of reasons and Bill felt like he was stuck with nowhere to go.

When all else fails in a man's life, he can at least turn to his family for solace. Hackett however, did not turn to his family for support. Naydene, who had waited patiently for him during his expeditions, was unaware of the true depth of Bill's depression, simply because the 'Major' refused to confide in her. For Bill, his marriage, though functional, was somehow no longer spiritually fulfilling for him. Naydene had stood by his side for over fifteen years, supporting his efforts to build not only a military career but a mountaineering one as well. It was she who would cook up some of Bill's crazier ideas for high altitude food and use their kids as guineas pigs. It was she who would oftentimes inventory Bill's equipment prior to his departure on a lengthy trip, freeing him up to handle the logistical side of the venture. She would use her language skills to translate foreign climbing publications, she would perform research at the Mazamas library, and she would be Bill's most ardent fan when 'the boys came home from the hills.' In addition, she was busy raising the children, a full-time job in itself. It wasn't that Bill wasn't appreciative of her many sacrifices, it was simply that he no longer felt that family life fulfilled him.

Bill had decided that radical change was needed and only three weeks after returning from the Karakoram, he had a lengthy discussion with Naydene. He advised her that he was giving serious consideration to a legal separation and the couple talked for hours into the night. They came to some sort of an agreement that would, for a time, forestall any legal action.[3] What this step would do to the children was of primary concern to both parents. They were still so young, would they understand or even be able grasp the fact that their father's need to leave their mother had nothing to do with anything they or their siblings had done? Toni Naydene Hackett had been born in the Fitzsimone Hospital in Denver, Colorado on July 30, 1947, only a month after her father had returned from *Operation White Tower*. Pati Lenna Hackett was born on December 10, 1950 in the same hospital. Peter Alcanzy Hackett, Bill's only son, was born on November 22, 1952 at the Army hospital in Fort Richardson, Alaska. Mari Dickson Hackett, the youngest of the clan, made her appearance on September 30, 1958 in Fort Monroe, Virginia. What Bill's decision would mean to his children then, and in the future, was uncertain.

Another contributing factor to Bill's depression was a proposed expedition to Mount Everest. When Bill returned from K2 he discovered a mound of correspondence requiring his attendance. He had been away from Bad Tolz for over four months and all kinds of important documentation were intermingled with commercial advertisements and miscellaneous statements. It would take him two days to sort through this mail but one letter stood out among the others, a cable from Nepal. Bill Hackett had been granted a permit to lead the first American expedition to the highest mountain in the world—Everest![4] There was a moment of euphoria and Bill couldn't believe his good fortune. It seemed as if providence would deliver him from his defeat on K2 and provide him not only with another continental summit, but with a leadership role that would surely be challenging and rewarding. On October 10, he received a letter from Norman Dyhrenfurth, which included a brochure outlining a proposed schedule for an expedition to Everest. Dyhrenfurth had led the 1952 Swiss attempt on the great peak and was in a position of great authority on the subject. Bill admired the man greatly. Dyhrenfurth proposed that they join forces and co-lead the 1961 expedition to which Bill readily agreed.[5] Shortly thereafter, Hackett dispatched a letter to Bob Bates in New England.[6] Bill apparently wanted to enlist the assistance of Bates in the Everest endeavor but by December 13, Dyhrenfurth had cabled that even with their combined forces and the backing of the American Alpine Club, there would simply not be enough time to procure adequate funding for the expedition.[7] Americans would have to wait until 1963 for the opportunity to try again, and this time, Dyhrenfurth alone would be at the helm.[8] Hackett had lost out on the greatest opportunity in his climbing career merely because he was 'on' K2 when his Everest permit arrived in Germany. Had he known it was buried under a box filled with correspondence for three months, he might have turned leadership of the K2 expedition over to Dave Bohn and returned to Europe to mount the Everest effort.[9] We will never know.

During the fall of 1960 and throughout the early 1960s, whenever Bill found a moment's peace, something would occur to pull him back into a deeper depression. Some of these factors were internal, some external, some caused by himself while others were out of his sphere of influence. November 5, 1960 was just such an occasion. Bill received a telephone call from his K2 buddy, Lüdwig Greissl. Lüdwig informed him that Günter Jahr had just died in a tragic motorcycle accident in downtown Munich.[10] Bill was stunned and dropped the telephone receiver. He had managed to lead a team through some of the worst storms ever recorded on K2 without losing a single man and here, less than two months after returning to Europe, Günter was gone! The news was unbelievable and sent Bill over the edge. He was angry, upset that he was unable to control the events in his life. Everything seemed to be turning upside down and nothing was making sense to him anymore. Naydene was able to console him somewhat and the two made it to Jahr's funeral in Munich five days later. Lynn Pease, Lüdwig Greissl, Herbert Wünsche and Dr. Deubzer were also in attendance, a melancholy first and last reunion of the 1960 German-American Karakoram team.[11]

⊷ ⊷ ⊷

On October 8, 1961, Bill's father passed away due to natural causes. Though Bill had been adopted, he would always recognize Fred Alcanzy Hackett as his father, his "Dad" and naturally, "The man who encouraged me to climb Mount Hood." It was only natural that at such a time, he reflected on what his family had meant to him.

Bill had actually been abandoned when he was only five years old! His biological mother, Ada, took him by the hand one day and walked him over to her sister's house. Bill was old enough to remember his own mother saying, "Here! You take him." Lena and Fred Hackett began to raise young Bill as their own son when suddenly, after three years, Ada returned to claim the boy. The Hacketts protested and the matter eventually ended up in court. The judge turned to Bill and asked where he wanted to stay. "With my family," he quickly responded, "the Hacketts." Ada left alone and bitter.

Bill took the passing of his father very hard and the loss only added to his ever-growing depression. It didn't help that he had to attend his father's funeral on the day of his own forty-third birthday![12]

On New Years Eve, 1961, Bill sat alone in his room. Beside his chair were two empty bottles of French Beaujolais. There he would scrawl, "Alone in my room with my thoughts...so ends another year." He thought about the myriad of changes that had occurred in that brief but incredibly frustrating year: Naydene, his separation from his children, the loss of his father and his recent disappointment with Army life. He believed, that with the exception of the ascent of the Matterhorn with Compagnoni, the year was a total loss. His ascent of the Matterhorn, in a way, became the "Eye of the Hurricane" in a year of depression and unfulfilled hopes.[13]

CHAPTER XV

Eye of the Hurricane

"You stop, you listen, you sense a certain quality in things: the taste of the air, the sun enveloping the mountain, the undulation of the meadows, the camber of the moraine, the curves of the glaciers. The other peaks are beautiful—the Matterhorn is a presence."[1]

—Gaston Rebuffat

Bill Hackett had dealt with a deep depression for over a year and desperately needed to regain some of his self-confidence. Though his defeat on K2 was the primary factor contributing to his depression, he nevertheless thought a climbing venture might help break him out of his melancholy mood. He wanted some type of 'grand slam' however, an experience that would surely be memorable. He wanted a singular peak that would be challenging enough and yet hold a great value to him personally.

Bill wanted the Matterhorn like no other peak in the Alps. His choice of route however, would not be the standard Hornli Ridge that Edward Whymper had made famous, but the Italian Ridge; the other side. Though Hackett was clearly qualified to make the attempt himself, he wanted a guide in order to ensure there would be no wasted time in route finding. Bill knew that at least one night would need to be spent on the mountain, but he hoped it could be spent in the relative comfort of one of the Alpine huts. There would have been several highly skilled guides to choose from in Italy, but Bill would take the venture a step further by requesting Achille Compagnoni to accompany him.[2]

Hackett took to Compagnoni immediately. The men were only four years apart in age, were nearly identical in height, were both lovers of fine spirits, and naturally had shared memories of K2's Abruzzi Ridge. Compagnoni was born at Valfurba (Lombardy) and ran an inn on the outskirts of the town of Breuil, at the base of the Matterhorn. An alpine guide and skiing instructor, he had climbed extensively throughout the Alps and was well familiar with the *Dent d'Herens* and the Matterhorn. He was a natural choice to accompany Ardito Desio to the Karakoram in 1954. After Walter Bonatti and other members of the Italian expedition helped supply the higher camps, Lino Lacedelli and Achille Compagnoni were the first to stand atop K2.[3]

Bill arrived at the Compagnoni inn and was greeted by Achille's wife, Gattlin. She showed her guest to a comfortable room and allowed him some time to freshen up before coming downstairs for an afternoon meal. This lunch was served in the dining room where climbers, skiers and general tourists were gathered to fuel-up before re-entering the mountains and valleys nearby. During the course of this meal, Compagnoni walked into the room and the place seemed to come alive. He was a celebrity like few others. He had been skiing all morning but merely stated he would need a few minutes to pack his rucksack and he would be ready to begin the climb. Bill was taken aback. He hadn't expected to begin the ascent until the following morning. He had just finished a heavy meal and had consumed his fair share of wine. He was hoping to recline in the sofa by the fireplace and share stories with his host.[4]

Bill ran upstairs to pack his equipment and supplies. He packed lightly as he knew they would only be gone for two or three days at the most. Camera, water, and military rations were all hastily stuffed into a small rucksack. When Bill reappeared in the dining room, he had found that Compagnoni already had the car started and was awaiting his arrival. After bidding Mrs. Compagnoni farewell, Achille and Bill departed for the mountain.

The approach to the Italian Ridge of the Matterhorn was pretty straightforward, a path Compagnoni could probably have done in his sleep. The pair of climbers would travel via automobile up the picturesque *Vallee de Valtournanche*, which contained the Cervino River. Bill tried to take photos of this valley but Achille was driving so fast that the opportunity was lost. At a trailhead near a small mountain tarn, the car was parked and the climbing would begin. After strapping on their small backpacks, Achille motioned him to follow him up the trail. Bill needed no such prodding. Since they hadn't left the hotel until 3:15 in the afternoon, they both wanted to ensure that they climbed high enough to spend the night in a hut.

As Bill hiked up the grassy lowlands towards the *Glacier du Lion*, he was alone with his thoughts. He knew he was entering the arena where Edward Whymper and Jean-Antoine Carrel had vied for the honor of making the first ascent. The history of how this first ascent occurred, and resulting tragedy were some of the primary factors in Bill's selection of the peak.

The Alpine Club, founded in England in 1857, launched the first serious attempts to conquer the Matterhorn. Members of this organization hadn't actually singled out the monolith, but rather sought the virgin summits of some of her less technically challenging neighbors. As time progressed however, and the easier peaks had been tackled, a new breed of climber was required to assault the harder routes. One peak after another fell and yet the Matterhorn seemingly towered above all others. Viewed head-on from outside Zermatt, the east face of the mountain seemed impregnable and indeed, many prominent alpinists of the day declared it 'unclimbable.' John Tyndall had made several attempts along the Italian Ridge, most notably in August of 1860 and July of 1862. During this latter attempt he had reached a position less than a thousand feet from the 14,780-foot summit. Cesar Carrel, Luc Meynet and others made similar attempts, all along the Italian Ridge and it was for this reason that Bill selected the Italian side of the mountain.[5]

Edward Whymper and Jean-Antoine Carrel, contemporaries of Tyndall, had initially pooled their resources on several occasions. Whymper had first seen the Matterhorn when he was only twenty years old. He had been commissioned by a London publishing firm to travel to the Alps and make sketches of the region. Being paid for his time, the *artist* soon became a climber. He climbed Mont Pelvoux, the *Aiguille de Trelatete*, and the *Aiguille Verte* in order to build his skills. It was the Matterhorn that he truly craved. "The Matterhorn," he would write, "looks equally imposing from whatever side it is seen. It never seems commonplace; and in this respect, and in regard to the impression it makes upon spectators, it stands almost alone amongst mountains. It has no rivals in the Alps, and but few in the world."[6] Whymper made attempts from a variety of routes in 1861 and several attempts the following year. He was organized and able to work with a wide range of personalities. On the debit side however, he could be impatient, impulsive, and worst of all; he would agree to climb with virtually anyone. This impatience was to have dire consequences in the future.

Jean-Antoine Carrel, eleven years Whymper's senior, was born within view of the great peak. After eight years in the military, Carrel returned to Northern Italy and offered his services as a guide though he had little experience in the field. Whymper would become one of his chief clients and the two would make several of the first attempts along the Italian Ridge.

1865 would be the year. Whymper had switched his attention from the Italian Ridge to the Hornli Ridge on the Swiss side of the mountain. Lord Francis Douglas, Rev. Charles Hudson, Michel-Auguste Croz, Peter Taugwalder, his father 'Old' Peter Taugwalder and Robert Hadow, would accompany him. This party of eight would attempt the Hornli Ridge and hope to push the route above 12,000 feet; the elevation record set on that particular route. Carrel decided to stick with the *Col du Lion* and the Italian Ridge, taking a few companions along for what he hoped would be his final assault. Both parties would be climbing the peak on opposing sides, at the same time.

When Whymper and his companions reached the summit on July 15, 1865, they were still unsure whether they had beaten Carrel to the prize. Whymper would write:

> "...we were tormented with anxiety lest they should arrive on the top before us. All the way up we had talked of them, and many false alarms of 'men on the summit' had been raised. The higher we rose, the more intense became the excitement. What if we should be beaten at the last moment? The slope eased off, at length we could be detached, and Croz and I, dashing away, ran a neck-and-neck race, which ended

in a dead heat. At 1:40 PM the world was at our feet, and the Matterhorn was conquered. Hurrah! Not a footstep could be seen."[7]

Whymper and Croz eventually spied Carrel and his team farther below, down the Italian side. The victors yelled down to Carrel until they were hoarse. They wanted to ensure that Carrel recognized he had been beaten, not out of malice but rather to ensure their place in history would be secured. Whymper couldn't be sure that Carrel had seen him on top so he and Croz rolled boulders down the Italian side in order to catch their attention! It worked. Carrel was so dejected he retreated without even attempting to push his route any further.

━━◆━━

Bill and Achille were now following the very route Carrel had taken. Their passage over the *Glacier du Lion* was uneventful but Bill marveled at the series of deep, yawning crevasses. From here, they climbed up a lengthy snow couloir that deposited the climbers on an adequate snow saddle called the *Col du Lion*. This saddle divided the mountain proper from a smaller peak known as *Tete du Lion*. Carrel and other early explorers had used this smaller summit as a point to study the higher walls of the Matterhorn while remaining out of range of the rock fall that continually rained down from above. On the other side of the saddle lay their goal—the Southwest Ridge, or Italian Arête. Others would call this line the Lion Arête or even Carrel's Route. The sun was setting and darkness was enveloping the mountain walls. With flashlights in hand, Achille led the way up the lower section of the arête, and headed towards a small hut that their he hoped would have space available.[8]

"Will there be room?" Bill inquired, cupping his hand near his mouth in order to direct the sound of his voice up to Achille.

"Probably!" the Italian responded, "we shall see!"

When they reached the *Luigi Amedeo Refugio*, Bill could barely make out the hut in the darkness. He shined his flashlight on the structure and could see that it was constructed out of long wooden planking with wood protection covers for the windows. When they entered the hut they discovered that it was packed with fellow alpinists and as a result, they were forced to occupy the floor. Bedding down for the night, Bill thanked Achille for the journey thus far.

Bill had regained a happiness that he hadn't felt in quite some time. He was experiencing sensations he hadn't felt since the early stages of the K2 expedition; the smell of the damp timber forming the hut, the sound of climbers snoring and the wind howling just outside, and the feel of his dependable down sleeping bag. He looked over into a corner of the hut and saw a climber's face illuminated only by the faint orange glow emanating from the cigarette that was dangling from his lips. In another corner, a man was stretching his limbs, preparing to depart the hut for the higher slopes. There were so many climbers packed into this small cabin that Bill was instantly reminded of his early days with the 10th Mountain Division. On their off time while stationed in Colorado, a handful of the soldiers would occupy a similar cabin in the hills before departing the next day for their rock scrambling adventures.

⊷⊶ ⩴⬩⊟⬩ ⊷⊶

Achille awoke Bill at 4:30 the following morning. Sitting up in their sleeping bags, they ate a small breakfast while talking quietly with several climbers who were also readying themselves for the ascent. Compagnoni was naturally a celebrity amongst them and the occupants paid him every respect. For his part, Achille would introduce Bill as 'that great American who tried very hard on K2.'

When the pair emerged from the cabin an hour after breakfast and looked up towards their proposed route, Bill was amazed at what he saw. The cabin was situated on a small platform directly beneath the *Grande Tour*, an immense rock formation that towered above them. It had not escaped his attention that any sizeable boulder crashing down the face was sure to hit the roof of the cabin. While Achille untangled the climbing rope, Bill was free to enjoy the view. The *Tete du Lion*, *Dent d' Herens* and the Tiefenmatten Glacier were visible to the west and the shadow of the Matterhorn was stretching out over the Central Pennine Alps.

Climbing from the hut to the summit involved climbing skills that Achille and Bill had in spades. Bill would write that they "...encountered a few steep stretches where fixed ropes and ladders were installed."[9] They made surprisingly good time considering they were forced to wait, on occasion, for other climbers to complete one of the more difficult pitches. They reached the summit just as Bill's watch read 8:30 AM, only three hours after departing the hut. Their first objective was to stand beside the Matterhorn Cross, an iron fixture located on the Italian summit. The Matterhorn has twin summits, the Italian to the south, and the lower Swiss summit to the north, both joined by a ridge spanning 350 feet. Bill asked a climber who had reached the Italian summit before them to take a few snapshots of the triumphant pair. These photographs reveal a Bill Hackett clearly happy to be standing on the summit of the historic peak with his new friend, Achille Compagnoni. In the decades to come, Bill would look back on this ascent with pride and believe that it was the only highpoint amidst a year of depression—the eye of a hurricane.

When Bill and his companion reached the Swiss summit, they peered over the edge and down the famous East Face of the Matterhorn. Bill was dutifully impressed and had the urge to make a full traverse of the peak by descending down the Hornli Ridge, the route Whymper had used in 1865. Achille would naturally have to tend to his duties in Italy so Bill knew a descent back down the Italian Arête would be in order. Bill was also impressed with the view the summit afforded. The valleys below were shrouded in a sea of clouds but the Alps themselves rose above and the early morning sunshine bathed the region in beautiful colors. Bill would later read Whymper's remarks regarding his view from the same position ninety-six years earlier:

> "Mountains fifty-nay a hundred-miles off, looked sharp and near. All their details—ridge and crag, snow and glacier—stood out with faultless definition. Pleasant thoughts of happy days in bygone years came up unbidden, as we recognized the old, familiar forms. All were revealed—not one of the principal peaks of the Alps was hidden. I see them clearly now—the great inner circles of giants, backed by the ranges, chains, and *massifs*. First came the Dent Blanche, hoary and grand; the Gabelhorn and pointed Rothhorn; and then the peerless Weisshorn: the towering Mischabelhorner,

flanked by the Allaleinhorn, Strahlhorn, and
Rimpfischhorn; then Monte Rosa—with its many
Spitzes—the Lyskamm and the Breithorn. Behind were
the Bernese Oberland, governed by the Finsteraarhorn;
the Simplon and St. Gothard groups; the Disgrazia and
the Orteler. Ten thousand feet beneath us were the
green fields of Zermatt, dotted with chalets, from
which blue smoke rose lazily. Eight thousand feet
below, on the other side, were the pastures of Breuil.
There were forests black and gloomy and meadows
bright and lively; bounding waterfalls and tranquil
lakes; fertile lands and savage wastes; sunny plains and
frigid *plateaux*. There were the most rugged forms, and
the most graceful outlines—bold, perpendicular cliffs,
and gentle, undulating slopes; rocky mountains and
snowy mountains, somber and solemn, or glittering
and white, with walls—turrets—pinnacles—pyramids—
domes—cones— and spires! There was every combination that the world can give, and every contrast that
the heart could desire."[10]

When Bill had performed his initial research on the
Matterhorn he was pleased to discover that three days after
Whymper's ascent, Jean-Antoine Carrel had led Ame Gorret, Jean-
Augustin Meynet, and Jean-Baptiste to the summit via the more chal-
lenging Italian Arête. News of a tragedy that had occurred to
Whymper's party during their descent had not yet reached the Italian
side of the Alps. When Carrel finally heard the news he was devas-
tated. He learned that near a formation known as *The Shoulder* high
on the Hornli Ridge, Douglas Hadow slipped and knocked Michael
Croz off his feet. The two entered a fall that immediately ripped Lord
Francis Douglas and Charles Hudson from their positions. The rope
above Hudson snapped, saving the lives of Whymper and the
Taugwalders. The four unfortunate climbers fell over 4,000 feet to
their deaths. The historic first ascent and resulting tragedy have
entered mountaineering legend.

As Carrel and Whymper eventually teamed up again for an
ascent of the Matterhorn and several first ascents in South America,

Bill hoped that he and Compagnoni might have the opportunity to climb together again.

Throughout the course of 1962, Bill's life was filled with one meeting after another and mounds of paperwork that completely bored him. He was a man of action and to be a 'desk jockey' was simply something he was not cut out to do. His diary entries have repeated entries of "In office to face another week," and "Back to the office as usual, with little enthusiasm." He missed his children and missed the type of duty that challenged him physically. At some point in late 1962, he had made the determination to leave the Army and resume some form of civilian life. He knew this would be a monumental task as the last time he was a full-time civilian, he was a young man working at the Gilbert Brothers store in Portland.

When Bill officially retired from the US Army on January 31, 1963, he could look back on a twenty-one-year career filled with many exciting positions in some fascinating locations. Drafted in January of 1942, he had reported for Army Basic Training at Fort Riley, Kansas. As he and Russ McJury were first serving in the 115th Cavalry their old climbing partner, John Carter sent Letters of Recommendation to the Army; a gesture that helped Bill and Russ get into the 87th Mountain Infantry Regiment in late May of 1942.[11] Bill's first duty station was Ft. Lewis, Washington but he would not remain there for long. In June of 1942, he became a member of a seventy-five-man detachment being sent on detached service with the Columbia Ice Field Expedition to Athabaska Pass. This team would test various vehicles that could transport mountain troops over snow and glaciated surfaces. One of these vehicles would go on to become the *M29 Weasel*.

In December of 1942, the men of the Tenth were moved to Camp Hale, Colorado, just north of Leadville. Here they would receive the training needed to perform in Northern Italy. Bill was made a ski instructor and enjoyed the work thoroughly. He would serve in this capacity for three months and was then made a climbing instructor.

On September 10, 1943, Bill couldn't believe his luck when he was selected to accompany four officers and fourteen other enlisted men on detached training to Washington State's Mount Rainier. The soldiers traveled by rail to Tacoma where trucks were waiting to transport them to Paradise Inn on the mountain's southern slopes. When they arrived, Bill thought it hilarious that none of the officers had the key to the dormitories so the men were forced to bivouac under a full moon in a nearby meadow. On the following morning the entire group roped-up and made a serious reconnaissance of the Nisqually Glacier. Bill would recall that the ice was "cut up badly which made it very interesting." From September 16 to October 8, Bill Hackett, Ken Spangenberg and a man named Hindermann instructed the rest of the men in mountaineering essentials.[12] Their subjects were varied and most interesting to the group, as Bill would fondly recall. "(We) practiced step cutting," he would write, "in snow and ice, rope management and discipline, party climbing, self arrest techniques, belaying, ice piton placement, overhang climbing, crevasse rescue, prussicking, pulley work, proper crampon techniques, knot tying, glissading, rappelling, and even Tyrolean traverses."[13] Not once did the group make the ascent to the 14,410-foot summit but this was never their intention. Their task was to gain the skills that they would need in order to fight amidst such alpine terrain. Along with his fellow instructors, Bill performed admirably and the period of duty was one of his fondest memories of his early service.

Bill was promoted to Private First Class in mid-April, 1944 and two months later, was ordered to Camp Swift, Texas in Company A of the 85th Mountain Infantry Regiment. He then attended Officer Candidate School in Ft. Benning, Georgia under the command of Captain Sam Kroschel. After graduation he was commissioned as a Second Lieutenant.[14]

On January 3, 1945, Bill boarded the *USS West Point* in Newport News, bound for the European theatre of war. He served over three years in 10th Mountain Division. He would win the Silver Star for "Gallantry in Action" and two Bronze Stars for "heroism in ground combat and meritorious achievement in ground operations against the enemy." Elevated through conventional and combat promotions, Bill would become a Combat infantry unit commander in the Apennines and Julian Alps of Italy. While in Europe, he was elevated to First Lieutenant of Infantry.

Shortly after the war he left the Army and tried to find civilian employment that would provide him with the same level of excitement. After only a year, Bill returned to the service and was assigned to Camp Carson, Colorado, to teach mountaineering and skiing to the 38th Regimental Combat Team. He would additionally serve for three years as Chief of Training for their Cold Weather Training Command.

While at Camp Carson, Bill was able to finally get paid to climb. As a member of Dr. Bradford Washburn's 1947 *Operation White Tower* expedition to Mount McKinley, Bill was able to experiment with new cold weather clothing, food and equipment. He was additionally able to assist Washburn during the survey portion of the expedition. All elevation figures were officially adopted by the US Coast and Geodetic Survey, along with official acceptance by the Department's Board on Geographic Names.

While stationed in Alaska, Bill spent four years as a research and development test officer in the field of cold weather clothing and related equipment. He spent a good deal of time working in the Climatic Research Hangar at Elgin Air Force Base. When he was a staff officer at the US Continental Army Command at Fort Monroe, Virginia, Bill was responsible for environmental combat training. For three years he trained NATO and US troops in how to fight under the most unusual and severe weather conditions. Mountain warfare, cold weather survival and jungle tactics were just a few of the subjects on his training roster and he even helped form the new desert warfare command.

Bill would spend a year and-a-half in Korea with the 7th Infantry. He would serve as their intelligence officer in the Chorwon Valley. At this time he was on the staff of the 17th Infantry Regimental Combat team. He was soon transferred to Division Headquarters as a General Staff intelligence officer.

In Bad Tolz, Germany, Bill would serve in several capacities. He initially was charged with instructor duties at the Seventh Army Non-Commissioned Officer's Academy. Though he hated paperwork, the Army clearly recognized his organizational skills and had him oversee serious audits. Budgetary concerns and organization charts during this period helped contribute to his dissatisfaction with the service near the end of his career. To offset this tedious portion of

military life, Bill volunteered his time and talent as Chairman of the
European Division of the National Ski Patrol at Garmisch in the
Bavarian Alps. In August of 1961, Bill was transferred to Mannheim
to instruct students at the 3rd Armored Rifle Battalion, 51st Infantry.
Bill's organizational skills were also put to use at Frankfurt am Main,
the Headquarters for 4th Armor Group. Bill tired of the routine and
endless paperwork however, naturally missing such duty as he had
seen on Mount Rainier or on his endless periods of detached service
while on one expedition after another.

On the afternoon of November 28, 1962, Bill flew to New
York City, en route to Madigan General Hospital at Fort Lewis,
Washington.[16] At the hospital, Bill would receive his last physical and
retire from active service on January 31, 1963. Bill actually signed his
final paperwork at Fort Lewis. He had ended his career where it had
all began.

It was a decision he would regret for the remainder of his life.

Chapter XVI

Vinson Massif

"Even with my reduced load, the shoulder and neck pain soon crowded my tolerance level. A decision was imperative!"[1]

—Bill Hackett

On November 19, 1984, June O'Rourke was awaiting the arrival of her blind date. She had been a widow for a number of years and had never dated a military man, let alone a mountaineer. An interior decorator and artist, she had only recently started dating again. She had received a call earlier from a man who identified himself as Bill Hackett. He said they had mutual friends and perhaps they should get together for a drink or dinner. With a little research June learned that Hackett owned a successful sporting goods company, loved to travel and had been a bachelor for many years. June agreed to have dinner with him at his house in the West Hills of Portland, Oregon. When she thought of the sporting goods aspect of her potential date, June envisioned a house filled with fishing rods and a Sears plaid sofa. She was surprised when Bill showed up in a Lincoln Towne car, dressed in a German tweed jacket and slacks. When they arrived at his house, June expected to see a typical bachelor pad but here again, she was pleasantly surprised.

The contents of Bill Hackett's house reflected a lifetime of collecting. His pride and joy was a fully stocked, 180-case wine cellar packed with rare French and German wines. Lining the walls of his living room was shelf after shelf of rare mountaineering books. He had first editions of historic works dating back to the mid-nineteenth century, many signed by the authors. June was dutifully impressed as she loved antiques, interior decorating and was quite the bookworm herself. She would always be fascinated by the fact that Bill knew all of these books from cover to cover. "His books were never for show," she says, "He used them for his research and always kept his library open for writers and scholars to use. Fred Beckey, a frequent houseguest, would stay up late into the evening hours with Bill, rummaging through the shelves. Fred would ask Bill a question regarding some rare ascent that occurred decades earlier and Bill would be able to go to a particular shelf, pull out a volume and turn to the exact page that listed the ascent. Those fellas would stay up late and discuss how many pitons were used on a given pitch on some remote peak on the other side of the world! I had never known a mountaineer before, nor a military man. Bill opened up both of these fascinating worlds to me."

"Bill introduced me to a lifestyle I had never known," June continues, "and that first date was the beginning of fifteen years of books, travel, and shared adventure. He was a sentimental man and when we decided to get married, he wanted it to be on the fifth anniversary of our first date!"

Bill promised to show her the world and he certainly delivered. He took her up to Alaska and the two chartered a small plane to deposit them on the Kahiltna Glacier. Here, Bill was able to show her the terrain that Brad Washburn had first spotted from the air and their 1951 efforts that led to the first ascent of the West Buttress. As a well-respected McKinley veteran, Bill was granted official access to locations in Denali National Park that were off limits to tourists. He'd pitch his tent out in the middle of nowhere and when a passing ranger would approach their site, Bill would merely produce documentation from inside his jacket that proved they were allowed to camp there. He brought June with him on a grand tour around the world, visiting countries as varied and interesting as Bill could find: Mongolia, Tibet, China, Chili, etc. They toured Europe, South America, Asia and many of the historic sites in their own United States. It was during these years of travel that Bill began to get the 'itch' to climb again. He had climbed on six of the world's seven continents and had the urge to add that last elusive land to his resume—Antarctica!

⊷⊶ ▰◆▰ ⊷⊶

Bill was as comfortable as a man could be while strapped into an overcrowded Twin Otter aircraft. Looking around, he had to chuckle while confronted with his surroundings. He had temporarily given up the comfort of his West Hills home in Portland for the cramped quarters of an aircraft cabin. Eight men were forced to share limited space with an auxiliary fuel tank and over 1,000 pounds of mountaineering equipment. Occasional turbulence caused Bill to firmly grip his seat but he was certainly no stranger to extraordinary plane flights. Leveling off at over 10,000 feet, he crossed the Antarctic Circle, bound for the world's southernmost continent. Looking out of his nearby window, he could clearly see the ice-strewn waters of the Bellingshaven Sea below. To the east, off in the distance, he could see the great Antarctic Peninsula leading inland towards Ellsworth Land.

Bill turned to view Pat Morrow, co-leader of the 1985 Canadian-American Antarctic Expedition to Vinson Massif. A commercial photographer from British Columbia, Morrow was the type of climber Bill greatly admired. He was certainly ambitious, determined, technically skilled and highly organized, but above all, he was patient. Bill would be continually amazed at Morrow's patience and tolerance during the course of the Antarctic expedition. No stranger to the role of leader, Bill found Morrow to be quick at solving problems both logistical and technical, understanding with his companions, and 'cautiously direct.' Morrow would hit an obstacle head on and immediately begin to work the issue and not the person.

Born in 1952 and raised in Kimberely, British Columbia, Morrow was introduced to mountaineering while still in his teens. After moving to Alberta he joined the Calgary Mountain Club and first walked on to the Canadian mountaineering stage with a winter traverse of Mount Assiniboine in 1971. Two years later, he put up a new route on the east face of Gibraltar Mountain with Jack Firth and John Lauchlan. Though not pursing the Seven Summits dream at the time, he nevertheless collected his first continental summit as a member of the 1977 CLODD Expedition to Mount McKinley. With Bernard Ehmann, Morrow made the first ascent of a 1,200-meter rib rising from the Northeast Fork of the Kahiltna Glacier to the West Buttress. In 1981, he climbed Muztagata in the Xinjiang region of Western China. That same year he collected his second continental summit by ascending the Polish Glacier Route on Aconcagua in South America. On October 7, 1982, Morrow reached the summit of Mount Everest with Pema Dorje and Lhakpa Tsering. Morrow achieved this third continental summit as a member of the first Canadian expedition to Everest. It was after his success on Everest that Morrow began to realize that he had already climbed three of the *Seven Summits*. Quietly, with initial financing from *Equinox Magazine*, Morrow set about pursuing the others. In 1983, Morrow actively pursued three of the continental summits. He reached the summit of Kilimanjaro in Africa, considering it one of the most interesting and ascetically beautiful ascents of his career. He hiked to the top of Kosciuszko in Australia and made his first attempt on Vinson Massif in Antarctica. On four separate occasions during this venture, he tried to reach the top but was forced to retreat by foul weather. In 1984 he had returned to make his second attempt on Vinson but his plane sustained serious damage when it was ripped from its moorings by extreme winds. Now, in 1985, he was back for a third attempt and he was more determined than ever.[2]

Morrow would recall that Bill Hackett "was a good team player. Perhaps it was because of all the expeditions he had taken part in during his youth." Morrow didn't have much time to spend with Bill however, as their schedule was extremely tight. "We were rushed on Vinson," says Morrow, "as two other teams were climbing close behind us. A Korean expedition and an American team were scheduled to land precisely when our team was supposed to be wrapping things up. With the incredible financial expenses involved with the trip it was simply a matter of getting in and getting out!"[3]

Bill took to Pat Morrow immediately and would call him "quiet and gracious. An experienced and safety-conscious mountaineer."[4] They were men who shared similar ambitions. Bill had five continental summits under his belt with only Everest and Vinson remaining. In early 1985, Bill heard through the mountaineering grapevine that Morrow was planning on returning to Antarctica. At the age of sixty-seven, Bill was well aware that the summit of Everest was a slice of real estate he would never reach. It had been nearly thirty years since he had even added a peak to his Seven Summits resume. Nevertheless, he chose to make the attempt on Vinson for two reasons. He naturally wanted to pursue his sixth continental summit but more importantly, he wanted to climb in Antarctica itself.[5] Even if he failed to reach the summit, he would have expanded his mountaineering resume to include all seven continents. Within days of hearing of Morrow's third expedition, Bill hurriedly contacted him in Canada to discuss the venture.

After joining the expedition, Bill learned he would be climbing with several Canadians. Along with Morrow, there was co-leader, Marty Williams of the Yukon Territory. A mountain guide and ski instructor, Williams had been with Morrow on the unsuccessful attempt in 1984. Dr. Roger Mitchell, also from the Yukon, would act as expedition physician. Rumor had it that Doc Mitchell was just jumping at the chance to perform field surgery with a Swiss Army Knife![6]

The remaining members of the expedition were three Americans: Pat Caffrey, a logging supervisor from Seely Lake, Montana who was also in pursuit of the Seven Summits dream. By 1985, he had already reached the summits of Aconcagua, McKinley and Kosciuszko. Mike Dunn of Carson City, Nevada, also had an interesting record. He was the first to jump from an airplane and land via parachute on the North Pole! J. Stephen Fosset of Chicago, had also been a member of Morrow's previous expedition to Antarctica. Fosset additionally swam across the English Channel (a feat that greatly impressed Bill) and would later become the first man to fly solo around the world in a balloon.

In 1985, the most difficult aspect of a mountaineering expedition in Antarctica was not the climbing itself, but rather simple logistics. Transporting tons of men and supplies to the most remote region of the world is always difficult, but when compounded by the extreme cold temperatures of Antarctica, specialized equipment is needed. After careful research, Morrow had selected a Canadian DeHaviland Standard Twin Otter 300 aircraft to fly from South America to the Ellsworth Mountains. Morrow then hired Giles Kershaw, an English pilot who had logged more air miles in the Polar Regions than any other pilot. Dick Mason of Anchorage, Alaska, was hired on as co-pilot and engineer.

From his expedition a year earlier, Morrow had established contacts within the Chilean military establishment. Through a retired air force officer, General Don Javier Lopetegui, arrangements were made for refueling operations and even aerial supply drops over the base camp on Vinson Massif. In the unfortunate event of an accident, Lopetegui had assured Morrow that he would mount a rescue effort.

As an attempt on Vinson is one of the most expensive mountaineering ventures to undertake, Morrow showed his appreciation for Lopetegui's assistance by allowing a Chilean climber to join the expedition. Alejo J. Contreras, a metal worker from Santiago, would act as Expedition Liaison Officer. A well-known member of the Chilean Alpine Rescue Corps, Contreras had made numerous ascents in the Andes and was a well-respected member of the South American mountaineering community. He and Bill shared stories of their individual adventures on Cerro Aconcagua. Bill was amazed to discover that Contreras had made an ascent of the *White Sentinel* on skis nearly to Guanaco Ridge and from there, proceeded to the summit on foot.

Bill appreciated the skills and experience of pilots Kershaw and Mason. These men had flown the Twin Otter plane from Canada to Southern Chili in only four days! Once in Santiago, ski wheels were affixed to the aircraft, cutting her speed from 150mph down to 135. The pilots attempted to counter balance the lack of speed with increased fuel capacity. They managed to store a 250-gallon tank of fuel in the passenger compartment, thereby increasing their total fuel capacity to 813 gallons. Consuming ninety gallons of fuel an hour the Otter could remain aloft for nine straight hours. June would recall that after Kershaw had flown the team to Antarctica, he returned to South America and met her on the airport tarmac. Kershaw popped out of his aircraft wearing a white, straw Panama hat complete with a long red feather! He walked right up to her and pulled a letter from out of his left breast pocket.

"I have a letter here from Bill," he said as he handed the paper over to her, "I kept it close to my heart to keep it warm!" June laughed and was glad Bill was associated with such people. Kershaw reminded June of Errol Flynn, the movie star from the golden era of motion pictures.

Kershaw, having received favorable weather reports to the west of Vinson Massif, banked the plane over the Ellsworth Mountains. Should the team encounter foul weather, they would land at Siple Base, a nearby United States weather station. Kershaw made the decision to proceed to Base Camp. This was a critical move as the team could be in serious trouble if adequate room for a landing could not be found. Fuel was running low and the mathematics were not in their favor. Within minutes of making the decision however, cloud cover ahead parted and revealed Antarctica's highest mountain.

Vinson Massif stands at 16,023 feet in the Sentinel Range near Antarctica's Ronne Ice Shelf. Located on the 80th Parallel, the atmospheric pressure on her slopes is relatively thinner than that of peaks closer to the Equator. Climbers are therefore exposed to conditions more equivalent to mountains that exceed 18,000 feet. The average daily temperature in the region hovers at -20 degrees Fahrenheit. Perhaps the most inherent danger from climbing the mountain is its extreme remoteness. Only 750 miles from the South Pole, a broken leg while climbing here could mean a painful and lengthy evacuation. While not a technically challenging mountain, Vinson Massif is without a doubt, one of the coldest environments for mountaineering in the world.

Steve Bell, who completed the Seven Summits in May of 1997, described the region encompassing Vinson Massif:

> "In Antarctica, mountain ranges rise from seas of polar ice and the environment, devoid of all flora and fauna, is perhaps the most unforgiving in the world...Vinson is best attempted during the summer months of November, December and January, when there is 24-hour daylight. Unlike the climate of many of the world's great mountains, the Sentinel Range tends to be influenced by a stable air mass producing very good weather and mild, low temperatures. However, in practice life is never quite that simple. Atmospheric pressure at the Poles is lower that it is at other latitudes, resulting in air masses being sucked into these regions at high altitudes. As the air cools

over the South Pole it descends rapidly and rushes
outwards at high speed. Being caught in high winds
on the summit plateau of Vinson is probably the most
serious aspect of the climb. The interior of mainland
Antarctica can truly claim to be the last great expanse
of real wilderness. It is the world's highest, coldest,
and, perhaps surprisingly, driest continent, with
valleys that in all probability have not received any
precipitation for the last two million years."[7]

There are several benefits however, to making an attempt in
the Sentinel Range. Though ice screws are difficult to anchor, the
danger of rock fall is extremely minimal. One of the most treasured
benefits climbers depart the mountain with is memory of the splendid view. From east to west, ice fields stretch to the horizon.

Though climbers had barely heard of the Sentinel Range prior
to 1935, they became inspired by the efforts of Lincoln Ellsworth.
During that year, Ellsworth made a transcontinental flight over
Antarctica and brought back a host of photographic documentation
that intrigued western mountaineers. Members of the International
Geophysical Year exploratory expedition of 1957-58 instantly realized that the range held the highest mountains on the southernmost
continent. A whole series of unexplored peaks were just waiting to be
explored. It took nearly a decade of political negotiations before a
team of hand picked mountaineers was given the opportunity to
make an attempt in the range.

The first ascent of Vinson Massif occurred on December 17,
1966. The 1966-67 American Antarctic Mountaineering Expedition
was the first party to arrive on the continent with the sole purpose
of mountaineering exploration. They used a ski-equipped US Navy
Hercules, which landed the team on the Nimitz Glacier, a full eighteen miles away from Vinson's summit. Barry Corbet, John Evans, Bill
Long, and Pete Schoening of K2 fame were in the party that made
the first ascent. Later that same month, other members of the expedition made two subsequent ascents. When this highly experienced
team of climbers departed Antarctica after over a month's work, they
had made first ascents of six mountains; four of which were the
highest in the range.

No climber would set foot on the great peak for thirteen years. In 1979, members of an American team who were engaged in survey work accomplished the fourth ascent. The fifth and six ascents occurred in 1983, during the much-publicized Seven Summits expeditions undertaken by Dick Bass and Frank Wells. In 1983 and 1984 came Morrow's initial attempts. In 1985, the region was still rarely visited and nearly every peak in view held virgin terrain.

·— ≖◆≖ —·

Kershaw landed the Twin Otter aircraft at the base of Vinson near the 8,000-foot level. Skies were clearing, no wind could be detected and the temperature was below 0-degrees. Kershaw and Mason soon organized teams to dig several five-foot holes in the snow. Deadman anchors were used in these pits to anchor the aircraft. Kershaw then contacted the Chilean Air Force at Punta Arenas and verified that air drops of supplies and fuel would be occurring on schedule.

While Kershaw was working with the Chileans, the remainder of the expedition began to construct the first camp. Three North Star tents were quickly erected and Bill reached for his snow saw. Snow blocks had to be cut and fitted to make a five-foot wall surrounding each tent. An area of ice and snow was set aside for drinking water while another section, downhill, was designated as a latrine. Working in subzero temperatures was nothing new to Bill but he was concerned nevertheless about his old frostbite injury incurred on K2 a quarter century earlier. He made a mental note to keep an eye on his feet.

On the first full day of the expedition, Bill shouldered a 60-pound pack and made his way toward the base of Mount Shinn, a 14,954-foot peak sharing a snow saddle with Vinson. He was warm enough while working but would grow cold if he stood still for too long. A man of endless curiosity, he would continually check his thermometer and record the coldest temperatures during the day. He would note, for example, that on November 12, the ambient temperature dipped to -21 degrees Fahrenheit. Bill grew cold only during breaks or when his course caused the sun to drop below a ridge.

Hackett enjoyed the simple objective of the day, the establishment of a base camp 1,200 feet higher up the valley. The team found the route difficult to traverse. Freezing winds from the night before had caused sastrugi conditions. A hard outer shell would be broken through when a climber stepped forward. He would then sink up to his calves or deeper in soft snow underneath. After a considerable amount of work, Bill and others arrived at the proposed site for base camp. They cached their heavy loads and made the return journey to the Twin Otter.

Bill awoke on the morning of the thirteenth to the sound of aircraft overhead. It reminded him of his days on McKinley four decades earlier. A C-130 came into view at 6:00AM while six hundred feet above the ice field; air crewmen pitched five loads of cargo out the side door. Parachutes brought them safely to the glacier. Two passes later, a total of twenty pallets had been dropped. Upon closer examination, Bill noticed it was 1,980 gallons of fuel for their return journey. He did some quick math and discovered that at $40.40 per gallon, the expedition had just incurred a cost of $80,000. After taking stock of all provisions, Kershaw and Mason departed with the Twin Otter, bound for Punta Arenas. There, they would work with a team of Korean climbers and eventually return to evacuate Morrow's team.

The following morning, Morrow pushed the team to establish Camp II higher up the mountain. "We labored to the top of a col 1,300 feet above base camp," Bill would recall. "Laboring through a foot of loose snow atop sastrugi and ice. A fixed rope, set with ice pitons up the last 800 feet, allowed us to jumar upward, easing some of the pain of our heavy loads. We cached our material at the intended site of Camp II, then descended."[8], Bill was disgusted with the ice conditions but seemed pleased to be climbing on his seventh continent. Over a foot of loose snow was piled on top of a thick layer of ice. Perfect avalanche conditions.

On November 15, Camp I was occupied at the 10,300-foot level. Two North Star tents were erected, protected from the high winds by walls of snow-blocked ice. A field of large crevasses was conveniently located near camp, a potential haven from encroaching storms should the need arise. "The katabatic winds," Bill would note, "a rush of cold air from aloft, are common to this area. They can reach velocities of 200 miles per hour or more, and climbers carefully guard against being caught in their destructive force."[9] Bill was amazed that Caffrey, Dr. Mitchell, Williams, Fosset and Dunn had all brought their skis with them! It reminded him of Joe Leuthold and

Hjalmar Hvam back on Mount Hood during the 1930's. Bill had always enjoyed climbing and skiing but rarely mixed the two.

Up at 2:00 the following morning, November 16, Bill consumed some food and several cups of hot tea. Weather reports from officials at the South Pole's Scott-Amundsen Station seemed favorable. In an effort to cross-reference their data, Morrow insisted that they check with authorities at Siple Base. "Our radio," Bill remarked, "placed out in the open, raised no reply from our call sign, *Flamingo Mobila.*"[10] Finally, after several attempts, Siple Base confirmed that clear skies could be expected for the remainder of the night and well into the morning.

Within the hour, Bill was carrying a load up a 45-degree pitch towards Camp II. The morning was clear but quite cold. Only a light breeze was present but Bill welcomed it as it evaporated the sweat from his brow. He found himself roped to Mike Dunn while Caffrey and Alejo shadowed them. Carefully weaving through the icefall, these four climbers ascended 1,800 feet within a mile and-a-half and reached the summit of the Shinn-Vinson Saddle--the link between both peaks. Skis were employed early on during the climb and this helped with the speed of the ascent. It was hoped that the col could be reached before a significant amount of sunshine warmed the slopes and loosened the snow.

Upon reaching the safety of the col, they immediately began construction of snow walls to protect not only the loads they brought with them, but also the provisions they had cached there several days earlier. Once they felt the supplies were safe from inclement weather, they turned and made a hasty retreat to Camp I.

November 17 was a day expedition members dreaded but one Bill would look back on with fond memories. Few of the team members received any sleep the previous evening. Antarctica's fierce winds had risen and a sudden storm had descended on Camp I. High winds from the Shinn-Vinson Saddle removed snow from the slopes and deposited it in the icefall and throughout Camp I below. Bill himself had been kept up most of the night by the winds and the familiar sound of tent fabric flapping. The entire expedition was stuck in camp for the day and even went to bed for the night at 3:00pm! What was a single day lost to Bill Hackett? After his 1960 K2 Expedition, Bill would never feel uncomfortable in a tent again. After so many terrible weeks on the *Savage Mountain*, Antarctica seemed tame. But then there was the heels and toes of his feet. They had started to show the first signs of 'frost-nip' and Bill monitored them carefully (and privately) to ensure they would not become a liability.

On Monday, the day after the storm, Bill awoke and knew he had troubles. While cooking breakfast he took stock of his physical condition. His feet were not giving him as much trouble but his neck surprisingly ached. This pain became so serious that Bill felt compelled to bring the matter to Morrow's attention. "I was not feeling my best," Bill would later write, "My neck had plagued me during the entire trip into this frigid clime. I discussed my problem with the others, and they all urged me to continue, readily offering to share the weight of expedition equipment. They assured me that all I would need to carry would be my personal gear."[11] It was clear that Morrow and other members of the expedition wanted to see one of the pioneers of the Seven Summits dream obtain his sixth trophy. After considering the matter over breakfast, Bill decided to continue with the ascent and see if the higher altitudes would affect him further.

Hackett and Steve Fosset roped up together and began the ascent ahead of the others. Together, they broke trail and placed bamboo markers along their way. The footsteps they had created the day earlier were now obliterated due to high winds. It was during this ascent that Bill would make, "the most agonizing decision of my entire mountaineering career."

Bill explains:

"Even with my reduced load, the shoulder and neck pain soon crowded my tolerance level. A decision was imperative! I could continue forward with only the bare ability to get myself to the next camp, with little or nothing left to contribute to the survival of the party in this most inhospitable environment. If conditions should become more severe, I could become a serious detriment to the party. Camp II was at 12,000 feet; we were still 5,000 feet short of the summit. My slowness on the wind-swept ridges of exposed rock and ice near the summit could cause our party to bivouac. I would risk exposing myself and the other members of the party to serious hazard."[12]

Bill additionally felt a great deal of pain in his ankle. Years after the venture, he would confide to a friend, "Our feet were always in contact with the snow, and even with the best of boots, I began to feel the cold take its toll." It is interesting to note that what Bill considered 'the best of boots' was in reality, his old white felt Army boots (Bunny Boots) that he had first used on McKinley with Fred Beckey in 1954, over thirty years earlier! Bill had at least taken the time to have them re-soled but it is surprising to learn that he did not take advantage of the significant improvements made in footwear over the subsequent decades. He did, however, invest in a new pair of crampons that would see additional use on a memorable last ascent in the Cascades.[13]

On a wind swept snow slope near the Shinn-Vinson Saddle, Bill Hackett made the decision to retreat. In some regards, this decision was harder for him than the one he made on K2 years earlier. In the Karakoram, the monsoon had clearly arrived and Bill knew to continue would have meant suicide. Thoughts of retreating seem to come easier when faced with insurmountable obstacles. On Vinson Massif however, Bill *might* have been able to reach the summit given time and fair weather. He knew this but did not want to cause any problems to the team as a whole. Morrow, Caffrey and Alejo approached him from below. Morrow understood Bill's reasoning and took his place on the line. Bill turned and then headed back to Camp I alone with his thoughts.

When Bill arrived back in Camp I, he discovered that Dunn and Mitchell were ready to depart for Camp II. They exchanged pleasantries and went their separate ways, Dunn and Mitchell towards Camp II; Hackett and Rich Mason down to the landing camp. The journey between camps was uneventful and Bill took the time to reflect over his mountaineering career: McKinley, Aconcagua, Kilimanjaro, Logan and a host of other fascinating ascents. Even with a half a century of making alpine history under his belt, he still chose to re-evaluate his failures rather than revel in his success. Here, descending the lower slopes of Vinson Massif, thousands of miles from the comfort of his home, Bill felt the bitter taste of defeat once again. Even he would later acknowledge that he had made the right decision. "I did not emerge unscathed," he would write, "for a couple of my toes turned dark. Fortunately it was only the loss of the toe-nails which sloughed off later." He was also to learn that he had torn the rotator cuff in his left shoulder while trying to tighten his pack straps!

When Bill and Rich Mason reached the safety of the landing base camp, members of a Korean climbing team were already there to greet them. Giles Kershaw had flown them in from Punta Arenas a few days earlier. There were other climbers, journalists and even a cameraman in camp but the Koreans indicated those individuals were asleep in nearby tents. The Koreans invited Hackett and Mason in for some tea and a modest meal. Over dinner, the Koreans informed them they had carried loads up the mountain the day earlier and had successfully established their own Camp I. Bill was able to provide his new friends with detailed information concerning the route to Camp II and what to expect on the Shinn-Vinson Saddle. Bill would later state that he enjoyed the evening's conversation, shared over cups of hot noodles and tomato soup. Everyone exchanged climbing stories. Though the Koreans were fascinated by Bill's five pioneering expeditions to McKinley, Bill was just as impressed with their adventures in the Japanese Alps and other Asian mountaineering chains. It was a pleasant way to end a day that had weighed heavily on Bill's mind.

On the following morning, Tuesday, November 19, 1985, Morrow, Kershaw, Williams, Dr. Mitchell, Caffrey, Dunn, Fosset and Contreras succeeded in reaching the summit of Vinson Massif. Morrow temporarily placed a pink lawn flamingo on the summit for some novelty photographs. After many attempts, he had at last achieved one of the most difficult continental peaks. "Vinson was not so much a mountaineering success," Morrow would state, "As it was a *logistical* triumph."[14]

On the morning of November 22, three days after Morrow and his team had reached the summit, Bill was anxious to climb again. His feet seemed to be doing better, the pain in his left heel had vanished, and his spirits in general ran higher. He departed Camp I and hiked alone towards base camp.

Bill would write:

"After about 2.5 miles I left the trail near the 10,000 foot level, breaking snow towards an unnamed peak, ca 10,000+ feet, which I called Pyramid Peak, because of its configuration. It steepened, and I climbed without crampons, encountering sporting stretches of solid sedimentary rock, as well as light snow atop an icy base. Reaching the summit at 2:30pm, I found a small cairn marked with a bamboo pole. A note in a plastic bag indicated that an American party had made the first ascent in 1968 and that the Bass-Wells Seven Summit Expedition had been there in 1983."[15]

Bill ripped off a scratch piece of paper from a notebook and scribbled some general information on the page. He indicated that he had made this particular ascent as a representative of the American Alpine Club. After collecting his obligatory rock samples, he turned and descended back to base camp.

⸻

Shortly after his return to Oregon from Antarctica, Bill felt some pains in his chest that he at first, refused to address. Despite June's continual pleading to seek medical aid, Bill worked from home until he could no longer take the pain. He finally relented and agreed to be taken to St. Vincent's Hospital in Beaverton. It would take three cardiac specialists to convince him that he urgently needed quadruple bi-pass surgery. It became readily apparent why he had trouble climbing on Vinson Massif! If this wasn't enough, Bill did his best to get a new heart. "I don't want a patch job," he would say, "Let's just put a new one in." Again, it would take several physicians to convince him to go under the knife and get his 'patch-job.' Dr. Starr's world-famous cardiac team at St. Vincent's performed the honors on Valentine's Day, 1986. Bill recuperated nicely, but needed to undergo two carotid artery surgeries seven years later! It seemed as if the old bear was invincible.[16]

Giles Kershaw was not so lucky. Bill and June were saddened to learn a few years later that he had died in Antarctica. Apparently

some friends of his were going to make a film and they wanted
Kershaw to fly a gyro-copter while they shot some footage. Before the
cameras were turned on Kershaw wanted some time to experiment
with the aircraft. He was used to flying fixed-wing airplanes and was
naturally curious about this small, frail looking contraption. During
an experimental flight the gyro-copter experienced mechanical difficulties and crashed on the ice near Jones Sound.[17]

Kershaw remains there still.

—◄═╋═►—

CHAPTER XVII

Autumn

"Bill thought he would live forever."[1]

—Allan Striker

In the summer of 1999, Bill Hackett would oftentimes relax on his back deck, soaking in the sun. June would be busy in her garden just below, and they would talk well into the evening over a variety of subjects. In the distance was Mount Hood, where Bill had made his first ascent sixty-six years earlier. He couldn't believe that so much time had passed and now, at the age of eighty-one, it was only natural for him to reflect back upon his life and remember his achievements and disappointments.

In some regards, Bill couldn't believe that he had survived for so long! He had had so many 'close calls' over the years that many who knew him well were certain he would have met his end in a tragic plane crash or climbing accident. In February of 1958, he was involved in a serious plane accident in Alaska. He was up in the region for an annual military exercise and during some free time he contacted his friend, Terris Moore. Bill wanted to know if he would be interested in flying a ski-equipped plane over the Cook Inlet in order to climb a mountain. Terris Moore, Bill Hackett, Ernie Baumann, Frank Palmer and Don Steffa flew in two different planes bound for Mount Spurr. Baumann, Palmer and Hackett boarded a single-engine, Super Cruiser 135. "We flew toward Mt. Spurr," Bill would write, "and about 10:00 elected to try a landing. The glacier surface was sastrugi, extremely hard and bumpy, so Ernie took the plane up and banked to the left, which put us downwind, and at the same time we caught a downdraft so when the tip of the left wing touched first, the plane was thrown over onto the right wing which caused the fuselage to jackknife. After some moments of orientation and the discovery that nobody was injured, we crawled out of the wreckage."[2]

Another time Bill was flying aboard a plane in Alaska when the pilot, Ken Curry, was a bit hung over after a night on the town. Curry knew Bill had his civilian pilot's license and as a result, he asked Bill to take the controls while he caught some sleep. Reluctantly, Bill manned the controls until the plane was nearing Anchorage. At that time he tried to rouse Curry but encountered some difficulty. "Hey!" Bill shouted, "I don't have enough experience to land something this big so I need you to pull it together!" Curry miraculously landed the plane but Bill would later say that the passengers, teachers heading to Anchorage, had endured the roughest landing they had ever experienced!

Bill could easily have died or been seriously injured on several occasions during his lengthy climbing career. He had taken a serious fall down the Mazamas Old Chute on the southern side of Mount Hood in the late 1930's. Glenn Gullickson had died in a nearly identical fall there only a few years earlier.[3] Bill was fortunate enough to have landed in soft snow and on a good angle. He came to rest near Crater Rock and after checking to ensure he hadn't broken anything, he climbed back up and reached the summit.

There were other incidents in the hills that started out with Bill in pain but would always bring a smile to his face when he recalled the stories years later. He fell asleep on the summit of Mount Hood one time and sunburned his eyelids so bad he was unable to see for a week! In April of 1938, he was making a ski ascent of the same mountain with Joe Leuthold and Jim Harlow. Bill had forgotten to bring his ice axe and, during the final stretch up the mountain's inner crater wall, he employed a ski pole instead. High winds had gouged away the snow, leaving long, sword-like spurs of ice known as *ice feathers*. Because some of them seemed strong, Bill trusted his weight to them. Naturally, one broke and he fell backwards, bouncing off the gully wall. He would later say he 'fell like a wounded bird.' When Bill finally came to rest in a snowdrift above the Devil's Kitchen, he had the wind knocked out of him as well as his resolve to finish the ascent. On another occasion, in August of 1941, he was over halfway up the Mazamas Old Chute on Mount Hood. A sizeable rock overhead came loose and would have beaned him in the head had he not seen it coming. At the last moment, he threw himself to one side to avoid a direct hit. The rock struck a glancing blow to his rear but he managed to maintain his balance. Bill would eat his meals off the fireplace mantelpiece for a week![4]

Bill would acknowledge that one of his closest calls ever occurred during his Army service in 1944. During an ascent of Mount Bartlett in Colorado, he was in a party that was climbing unroped, just shy of the summit when they ran into some windslab. Windslab forms on the lee side of a mountain and its as hard as rock, with a finely grained surface resembling vanilla sherbet. The whole thing often collapses when least expected, shattering into a multitude of large, sharp-edged chunks of ice. Bill was the last of the party to climb over this windslab and when he reached the top, he wanted to catch up to his teammates. The snow suddenly let loose with a 'crack' sounding like a deep, cannon shot. The slab had cracked and it was collapsing directly underneath him! In a matter of seconds, several actions occurred simultaneously. The soldier who was closest to Bill ran back to the clearly evident crack in the ice and extended his ski pole out towards him. Bill, desperately trying to keep his balance, teetered on a large slab of ice, then ran up the side of it and leaped towards safety. Bill grabbed the extended ski pole and landed on the other side of the crack. He was then able to see the wall of ice falling 3,000 feet down the face of the mountain![5]

⊷ ⊷ ✠ ⊷ ⊷

Bill believed the climbers of today didn't appreciate the pioneering efforts *his* generation provided. He also couldn't understand why today's climbers merely made repeat ascents rather than strike out for new terrain. No clearer example could be had than the

changes seen on McKinley's West Buttress since 1951. As a member
of the party who made the first ascent, Bill naturally took pride in the
achievement but in the decades that followed, the route would
become the most popular path to the summit while Bill felt other
routes were more rewarding. Karstens Ridge, for instance, was a more
beautiful and interesting ascent, and the Northwest Buttress was certainly more challenging. By the late 1990's Bill could clearly see that
by far, today's climbers were flying out of Talkeetna, landing on the
Kahiltna Glacier and, weather permitting, completing their ascent and
returning inside of three weeks. It wasn't that Bill was adverse to
advances in transportation or gear; he just missed seeing that pioneering *spirit* in most of the climbers he encountered in his later years.
He would rather see a climber attempt virgin routes or at the very
least, make repeat ascents of routes that had a historical significance.

Though Bill marveled at the advances in climbing supplies
and equipment, he nevertheless used the same gear he had packed on
his back for half a century. He was a man who carefully monitored
his food intake at higher altitudes and was astonished when he read
how many calories and nutrients were packed into small bars of food.
Gone were the days when Bill consumed great quantities of liver
before a serious ascent, as he believed the practice would assist in his
acclimatization. He recalled the massive packs he had carried in the
past, jam-packed with food! These advances, Bill knew, would mean
fewer carries between camps or longer periods of time the team could
spend on a mountain. Bill recalled meeting a climber in Alaska during the 1950's who was packing a cast-iron skillet to the higher
camps! Today, a climber could carry titanium pots that fit snugly, one
inside the other, and weigh next to nothing. Better headlamps,
warmer bags, stronger tents, and advanced fabrics were always interesting topics for Bill, but he would naturally need to compare them
to the equipment he employed in the past.

Bill also wondered, on occasion, how the mountaineering
community might remember him. Most people who were familiar
with the name of Hackett associated it with early ascents of
McKinley. Few knew he had led an expedition to K2 and fewer still
knew he was one of the first climbers in history to avidly pursue the
dream of the Seven Summits. He never lost a man on an expedition,
never passed up an opportunity to make mountaineering history, and

climbed beside some of the most talented climbers of his generation: Jules Eichorn, Brad Washburn, Bob Craig, Fred Beckey and Achille Compagnoni to name a few. But would the climbing community remember a man like Bill? On November 4, 1989, he received his answer--a tribute that was dear to his heart. Bill was made an Honorary Member of the Mazamas. This honor had been bestowed on only twenty-nine people during the clubs ninety-five year exis-tence, and Bill felt privileged to be associated with the likes of John Muir, Teddy Roosevelt, and Lewis A. McArthur.[6]

As he had never completed his goal of the Seven Summits, Bill wondered if anyone would remember, or even care about his early attempts. Steve Bell paid tribute to Hackett's continental vision and achievements in his *Seven Summits: The Quest to Reach the Highest Point on Every Continent* (2000). He would note, "The concept of the Seven Summits has evolved with the improvement in accessibility and knowledge. This evolution has been steered by the activities of a handful of ambitious climbers, who together can claim to be the architects of the Seven Summits challenge...In September 1956 William D. Hackett, a soldier from Oregon, USA, reached the top of Mont Blanc to become probably the first person to reach the top of five continents. This of course assumes that Mont Blanc, the highest mountain in Western Europe, is the overall European summit. For most people, the now accepted European summit of Elbrus was out of reach behind the Iron Curtain of the Soviet Union, together with the rest of the Caucasus Mountains, until the mid 1980s. Bill Hackett's other summits were McKinley (1947), Aconcagua (1949), Kilimanjaro (1950), and Kosciuszko (1956). There is no doubt that Hackett did have aspirations to complete the rest."[7] There have probably been scores of climbers over the previous two centuries who have inde-pendently come up with the idea to ascend the highest peak on each continent, but Bill was one of the first to have the means, motive and opportunity to make the attempt. Pat Morrow thought of the idea in 1982, Dick Bass in 1981, and Frank Wells back in 1954.[8] We have Bill's diary entries, and more importantly, his letter to Hal Burton of New York which show he had undertaken his pursuit as early as 1949. Bill felt fortunate to have entertained Dick Bass in his home and to have climbed with Pat Morrow in Antarctica. He was grateful to have lived long enough to see the Seven Summits dream come to fruition.

Bill always believed that one should stay as active as possible for as long as possible. This wasn't mere philosophy for him but a way of life. When he found that he could no longer handle the rigors of mountaineering, he turned his attention to athletic endeavors that he had always placed on the 'back burner'; adventures he wanted to undertake if climbing was no longer feasible. He had always wanted to make a parachute jump but was denied permission by the Army because of his official duties. Apparently, Bill was too *valuable*. So, in 1987, at the age of sixty-nine, he made his one and only jump and said he 'better do it before his bones got too brittle.' After six hours of instruction at a small airfield near Aloha, Oregon, he jumped. He used one of the new design chutes and landed feet first, dead center on target. June would joke that when Bill made the leap she took out a bottle of champagne, a bible and a band-aid, not sure which one she would need. They drank the champagne.

Bill had a very keen interest in the US Space Program and in the early 1980's; he signed up for the first commercial space shot, slated for October 12, 1992. Bill hoped it would take place as scheduled as it would fall on his seventy-fourth birthday! Always the historian, Bill recognized the date as the 500th anniversary of Columbus discovering America. In November of 1988, he attended the Adult Program at the US Space Academy in Huntsville, Alabama. Bill passed physical and psychological tests, spent time in flight simulators and attended lectures covering a wide variety of topics on space exploration. When the space shuttle Challenger was lost, the program was put on indefinite hold. When his deposit of $5,000 was returned, Bill said it was the saddest check he ever received.

During the summer of 1985, Bill decided to make another ascent of Mount Hood but this time he wanted to take June in order to show her the alpine environment that he had devoted his life to exploring. This trip would mark his eighty-eighth and final ascent of the peak, where his extensive career began in 1933. He hadn't climbed the peak in twenty years, but June naturally felt safe in the hands of a man with Bill's resume.[9] June wanted to learn more about Bill and see if she could discover part of the reason why he loved the mountains so much. They drove to Timberline Lodge and carefully made the long pilgrimage up the traditional South Side Route. They took a break for a meal on the Hogsback and Bill was able to direct

June to several points of interest. He showed her where he had fallen down the chute, he motioned towards the volcanic fumarole where Victor von Norman had met his end in 1934, and he described what it was like to climb the nearby pinnacles and features; Crater Rock, Illumination Rock and the inner crater wall itself. When they reached the summit, Bill saw that the snow pack had receded enough to reveal the remnants of Elijah Coalman's US Forest Service cabin that had stood on the summit from 1917 to 1942. Nearby was the summit register and Bill and June proudly signed their names. For both participants, the trip would be one of their lasting memories. Only with the passing of time would Bill come to realize that the ascent would mark his last adventure on Mount Hood. For June, the view from the summit was worth all the hard work to get there. She also received a better understanding of her new beau and why the mountains were so essential to his life. When they finally reached their car in the parking lot, Bill turned to her and said with clear pride and affection, "You're a tough little shit, I better take good care of you."

Bill even found time to fly to both geographical poles of the Earth. His time in Antarctica had wet his appetite for further polar adventures. As a result, Bill signed on with fourteen others to make a journey to the North Pole in 1987. They piled into two DeHaviland Twin Otter airplanes and made a series of flights that took them closer and closer to the pole. One of Bill's companions on this journey was Captain James Lovell, US Navy (Retired), who had flown missions during both the Gemini and Apollo programs. Though he had countless military and civilian flights to his credit, most people remember Lovell from the miraculous journey of Apollo 13 in 1970. Though there were no serious physical requirements made of the passengers, Bill was pleased to be assaulted by a multitude of sensations: sights, sounds, and smells. New experiences, for Bill, were the key to staying young. He would write:

> "Our proposed round trip to the pole and back to Eureka entailed 1,250 miles. Since the Twin Otter's range was about 900 miles, a refueling stop was required at Lake Hazen, another 280 miles to the northeast at 82 degrees North latitude. A Bradley Air Service Douglas DC-3 had previously flown into Lake

Hazen and unloaded approximately 30-55-gallon barrels of aviation fuel for us. We landed on the frozen surface of the lake and taxied over to the fuel cache, where pumping the gasoline from the drums took 63 minutes. Many remained in the plane, but I got out for some photography to encounter the most severe weather of the entire trip. While walking, I saw tracks of the Arctic hare. I thought this remarkable, since the temperature was -40 degrees Fahrenheit and a fierce wind pummeled us from the west, an astonishingly uncomfortable demonstration of the wind chill factor."[10]

On April 13, 1987, Bill stood at the North Pole with Jim Lovell. Bill would later remark that the experience was one of the most significant moments of his life, the 'fulfillment of a lifelong dream.'[11]

Bill also raised the *Stars & Stripes* at the South Pole on January 21, 1988.[12] Six years later, in 1993, he was able to travel through the Northwest Passage. This adventure took place while he stayed aboard the *Kapitan Khebnikov*, a Russian icebreaker based out of Provideniya in eastern Siberia.[13] Bill and June traveled through Africa, Europe, South America and Asia. They explored Mount McKinley's Kahiltna Glacier and always talked of further adventures. Bill was living his credo that one should stay as active as possible, mentally as well as physically.

On August 18, 1992, Bill dispatched a letter to the Colorado Mountain Club, indicating that he was about to embark on another adventure. "Since I've climbed about forty of your state's Fourteen Thousanders during the years 1943 thru 1954," he would state, "I've decided that I should climb the remaining ones before old age really sets in in earnest!"[14] Bill had made several of these ascents with 10th Mountain reconnaissance troops during the war. Other companions during that time period were Bob Anderson, Coleman Leuthy, Smoke Blanchard and his wife, Naydene. He had soloed twenty-two of the forty peaks and was accompanied by a handful of climbers while climbing the others.[15] Bill hoped to complete the remaining peaks to add another record to his list of historic achievements. His initial interests were those peaks to be found in the Sawatch and San Juan Ranges.

Bill got ahold of his old friend, Allan Striker, in Colorado and asked if he might be interested in such a venture. In 1979, Striker had bought an outdoor equipment manufacturing company that Bill had already worked with after his Army service. During the years that followed, Allan and Bill became close personal friends but had never climbed together. Striker had climbed around the world and was young enough to provide Bill the physical and mental support he would need during the proposed adventure. Bill sent Allan a letter outlining a sample schedule and the sheer volume of peaks Bill was hoping to climb immediately took Allan aback. From Bill's itinerary, he wanted to climb sixteen peaks, all over 14,000 feet high, in the space of twelve days![16]

When Bill and June arrived in Denver, they stayed with Bill's son, Pete, and his wife, Dorothy. A meeting was arranged with Allan Striker but when Bill was engaged in conversation in another room, June and Pete took Allan aside. They quietly informed Allan that Bill had a quadruple bi-pass in the late 1980's and could he, Allan, please monitor Bill's condition during the course of the trip. Allan readily agreed and the pair was soon heading into the hills.[17]

The journey began on September 18, with an attempt on Missouri Mountain in the Sawatch Range. Both Bill and Allan were impressed with the Aspen trees. Their leaves were falling and Allan likened them to 'walking on a golden carpet.' It had rained all morning and when the pair of climbers came upon a swollen river they hunted about for an adequate location to cross. Bill made the determination that he had found the spot but within a few minutes he had accidentally 'taken the swim' and was soaked to the bone! They would lose an hour while trying to dry out Bill's clothing. Allan noticed that Bill was wearing cotton pants and offered a pair of wool pants he had in his pack. Bill declined, stating he had climbed in cotton for years. The last few thousand feet of the route were comprised of extensive talus slopes. These large fields of loose rock are murder on the ankles and they caused Bill to slacken his pace considerably. "My pins are gone!" Bill would say, in reference to his shaking legs. Eventually, Bill could go no further and was forced to turn around a mere 500 feet from the summit.[18]

On the 19th, Bill and Allan made an attempt on Huron Peak within the same mountain range. They initially lost the trail but spied a pack trail farther downhill. They made their way to this land-mark and met some hunters who directed them towards the correct path. This detour meant Bill and Allan made a triangle towards their destination instead of a straight line. Again, Bill was faced with another extensive talus field that stretched clear to the summit. The weather turned foul and snow was soon falling. Roughly 200 to 300 feet from the summit, Bill paused and came to the realization that he had just enough reserve energy to make the descent. He advised Allan that he would need to turn back and Allan took up a position direct-ly in front of Bill, in the event that he should fall. The descent was tricky since the rocks were wet and quite slippery. "Bill stumbled and would fall on occasion," Allan recalled, "He fell a number of times, once very badly. He had his old K2 ice ax slung on the back of his rucksack and it was fortunate that he did so. When he fell the ax kind of wedged between some rocks and prevented him from striking his head." It would take Allan a few moments to get Bill back on his feet. What would normally take a climber fifteen minutes to descend, now took Bill a considerably longer time.[19]

On September 21, Bill and Allan were refreshed from a day of rest and ready to tackle two peaks in the San Juan Range: Red Cloud, at 14,034 feet, via the Northeast Ridge and Sunshine Peak, at 14,001 feet via the North Ridge. Located in the southwest corner of Colorado, the peaks were situated along the most westerly advance of the Continental Divide. Red Cloud got its name from the rouge color of many of its rocks, a rhyolite seen for many miles. Sunshine Peak, situated directly next to Red Cloud, is usually reached by hiking two miles south from the latter's summit.[20]

Bill and Allan departed the trailhead at 5:00am and reached the summit of Red Cloud just over seven hours later. After stopping for some photographs and conversation, the pair descended onto the saddle that led to Sunshine Peak. Bill fatigued quickly but *thought* he was moving along at an adequate pace. It was only after Allan showed him their progress on a topographic map that Bill began to realize just how slow he was moving. Once on the summit of Sunshine Peak, Bill looked around and enjoyed the view, unaware that it would be his last summit in a lengthy career.

Allan Striker would be Bill's last climbing partner and he recalled his adventures with Bill with mixed emotions. On the one hand he felt privileged to be hiking beside a man that had made so much history on McKinley and K2. On the other hand, Allan couldn't ignore the fact that he was standing beside a man who clearly believed his heart and physique were those of a man forty years younger! "Bill thought he would live forever," Striker recalls, "He could be so excited and full of fire but his mind was too active for his body. In his head Bill was still in his prime and refused to believe that his body couldn't keep up. He was having great difficulty coming to the realization that he was mortal after all. He was truly a world-class mountaineer but he was living in the past. No one was harder on himself than Bill Hackett." Allan thought his journey with Bill was a 'marvelous experience' and was quite meaningful to him personally.[21]

On the afternoon of Thursday, August 5, 1999, June was out in her garden while Bill was at his desk working on invitations for their upcoming New Years Eve celebration for the year 2000. When June came inside to take a break, Bill approached her and asked her if he looked any different. She said he looked a bit pale and inquired if anything was the matter. He said that his heart was acting funny but that he thought he would be okay if he just rested a while. Within a few minutes he stated that he did not feel any improvement but refused to let June call 911 to receive medical attention. June had to privately telephone a nurse and when June described her husband's symptoms, the nurse demanded that Bill be handed the telephone receiver. It would take a few minutes of dialogue but the nurse was able to convince Bill to allow June to contact emergency services. During the ten minutes it would take the ambulance to locate the Hackett residence amongst the sprawling West Hills of Portland, Bill went back downstairs to his office. Concerned, June followed him shortly afterwards to discover him still revising the text of the invitations.

"The ambulance is going to be here any minute." June pleaded, "We need to go upstairs!" But Bill simply had to finish what he started. He typed a few more lines, pulled the sheet from the typewriter and then continued to print the heading. As he placed the dot on an exclamation point he said, "Okay, I'm ready." The ambulance was pulling up to the house at the same time. The paramedics checked Bill's pulse and were not pleased with their findings. They stated that he needed to go to the hospital for evaluation and asked whether they should bring in a stretcher.

"Hell no!" came Bill's response. When asked if a wheelchair wouldn't be better, he responded in kind. "Hell no, I'm going to walk out of my own home!"

He was transported to St. Vincent's Hospital, the same facility where he had his quadruple bi-pass surgery thirteen years earlier. Dr. Starr's team, the same medical personnel who had worked on Bill years earlier, were called to take another look at the elderly mountaineer. What they found was discomforting. Bill had so much scar tissue due to his previous operations that he would need to undergo an additional quadruple bi-pass surgery to clear things up.

Preparations needed to be taken before Bill could enter surgery. That weekend, he remained at St. Vincent's while his doctors started him on blood thinners and other necessary drugs. June learned that her husband was scheduled to undergo his operation on Monday morning. She arrived early enough in order to ensure that she would be able to spend more time with Bill before the procedures would begin. Bill wouldn't allow June to contact his children or any of his friends. He didn't want anyone to be concerned about him and he didn't want to be the center of any 'fuss' or unnecessary attention.

Bill got along great with the doctor who would be his anesthesiologist. He was also a climber and the two shared stories of familiar peaks and cold nights out under the stars. Bill was interested in the fact that the doctor had just returned from climbing in Patagonia, a region he had never visited.

When it came time for surgery on Monday, August 9, 1999, June was at Bill's side. She leaned over, kissed him on the cheek and said, "Goodbye, I'll see you later." While Bill was being wheeled away on the gurney, he turned his head slightly.

"Not goodbye," Bill responded, *"Au'Revoir"*.

Bill Hackett passed away that afternoon due to heart complications. He would be missed by those who climbed with him... and those who wished they had.

⚹

Their spirits linger
In the campfire smoke,
Near the weathered tent,
On the heather slope,
By the waterfall.

We feel their presence
In the fog-bound trees,
On the mountain path,
In the morning breeze,
In the soft nightfall.

They have gone away.
Through eternity,
For these absent friends
Let the mountains be
Their memorial.[22]

—Vera Dafoe
Mazamas Historian

GLOSSARY

ACCLIMATIZE: The act of gradually becoming accustomed to higher altitudes.

AID CLIMBING: A climbing technique which employs the use of chocks, bolts, pitons or other such hardware for the support of a climber's weight.

AIGUILLE: A needle-shaped rock mass.

ALPINE STYLE: A quick, lightweight method of ascending larger mountains. A climber carry's all of his/her equipment with them rather than establish stocked camps. Though this may make for a faster ascent it also increases the danger.

ANCHOR: A point to which ropes or belays can be secured by pitons, cams, ice screws or some other form of protection.

ANORAK: A pullover jacket without a front zipper.

BALACLAVA: A wool, polyester or fleece cap that covers the neck and head, leaving the face exposed.

BELAY: A technique used by climbers to safeguard one another while ascending. The belayer, anchored by pitons, snow pickets, rock horns or other natural formations, pays out the climbing rope for his/her partner. The belayer holds fast to the rope in the event his partner slips.

BERGSCHRUND: An expansive, deep crevasse at the head of a glacier. The upper lip of the bergschrund is normally higher than the lower lip.

BIVOUAC: An overnight, hastily erected emergency shelter.

BIVOUAC (BIVY) SACK: A nylon sack climbers can use to protect themselves from the elements. Normally used for emergency purposes.

BOULDERING: Climbing or scrambling on sizeable rocks and boulders that are close to the ground.

BUTTRESS: A steep mountain mass or wall jutting out from the mountain proper.

CACHE: A temporary storage place for food, equipment or other provisions.

CAIRN: A stack or pile of rocks constructed to mark a trail. Often used to prove a first ascent before the use of photography or in the absence of written documentation.

CARABINER: A metal or aluminum snap-link used to connect ropes, slings or anchors to one another.

CEREBRAL EDEMA: An altitude-induced illness marked by an accumulation of fluids in the brain. Fatal if a climber is not immediately evacuated to lower elevations.

CHIMNEY: Any crack in rock or ice that is large enough for someone to climb inside and continue climbing.

CHOCKSTONE: Rocks that are firmly lodged in cracks. Chockstones vary in size.

CIRQUE: A valley or amphitheater at the head of a valley, normally with steep walls.

COL: A saddle between two mountain peaks, a mountain pass.

CORNICE: Overhanging snow and ice on the leeward side of a ridge. Formed by strong winds. They may buckle under the weight of a climber standing or crossing over them.

COULOIR: A steep rock or ice gully.

CRAMPONS: Steel or aluminum spikes attached to the bottom of climbing boots to prevent sliding on ice.

CREVASSE: A fracture in a glacier's surface, caused by the movement of the ice over uneven bedrock. A hidden crevasse is one that is covered by a thin layer of ice and snow.

CRUX: Considered the most difficult section of a pitch or route.

DIHEDRAL: Inside corners where two walls of rock or ice meet. Stemming techniques are normally used to ascend up dihedrals.

FIXED ROPE: Rope that has been anchored to a snow slope or rock face that enables climbers to ferry gear up the mountain. Use of fixed ropes additionally helps a team descend a mountain quickly in the event of an emergency (storm, injured party member, etc).

FREE CLIMBING: A climbing style that places strict emphasis on the use of natural hand and footholds. Climbing hardware is used only for the possibility of a fall, not to support the climber or assist in the climber's progress.

FRONT POINTS: Two points on crampons that face forward. They enable a climber to ascend steep walls of ice.

GAITERS: Nylon, polyester or similar fabric wrapped around the lower ankles to keep rock and other debris from entering a climber's boots.

GLACIER: A river of ice flowing slowly down a mountainside.

GLISSADE: One of the fastest and easiest methods of descending dependable snow. There is the standing, sitting or crouching method of glissading, each enabling a climber to slide down the mountain. The ice axe is used as a breaking device.

HEADWALL: A prominent rock face on a mountain.

HYPOTHERMIA: A medical condition where a climbers body core temperature drops below normal. Hypothermia is caused by exposure to extreme cold temperatures.

ICE AX: A climber's tool used for cutting steps. It has a sharp pick and broad adze that can be used for digging or chopping. Additionally used to self-arrest, or slow a climber's speed during an uncontrolled slide.

LEAD CLIMBER: The climber who first ascends, placing rock or ice protection along the way for those who follow.

LIEBACK: A technique using counterforce to enable a climber to move up rock. Using the feet and hands, the climber pushes and pulls in opposing directions to keep a climber in position. Very taxing on the limbs!

MORAINE: A ridge or mass of boulders and sand deposited on the sides of a glacier.

NIEVE PENITENTES: Pillars of ice produced when atmospheric conditions and radiation are conducive to sun cup production. Most prevalent in the high Andes or Himalaya.

PARKA: A fur jacket with full frontal zipper and hood.

PINNACLE: A tower of rock. See Spire.

PITCH: A measurement of vertical distance, normally one rope length.

PITON: A metal blade or spike forcefully driven into cracks in the rock. A ring at the back end allows a carabineer and rope to be attached for a climber's protection.

PROBING: Checking a suspected snowfield for crevasses by use of an ice ax shaft.

RAPPEL: A method of descending steep terrain with the use of ropes. During Hackett's early years of climbing in the Cascades, he rappelled by passing his rope under one of his legs, across his body, and then over the opposite shoulder. By the time he entered the service, he had become proficient in the use of mechanical devices for rappelling.

RIB: A steep ridge leading to the mountain's summit.

RIME ICE: A type of ice that lacks crystalline pattern and may form large feathery flakes.

RUNNERS: Loops of cord or rope that are used for safety anchors or for assisting in rappels. Hackett continually referred to his runners as 'slings.'

SASTRUGI: Surface snow that has been compacted and scoured by high winds into irregular ripples.

SCHIST: Rock that has several layers of different minerals. Very brittle and can split into thin plates.

SCREE: Small stones or rock debris normally resting in a gully.

SELF-ARREST: A method of slowing or stopping a climber from falling on steep snow. A climber digs into the passing snow with his ice axe, which may act as a breaking device.

SERAC: A tower or wall of ice that has broken away from a glacier that will eventually topple due to gravity.

SLING: A nylon loop that a climber can stand in while ascending. Also used for belay and anchor points.

SOLO: The art of climbing alone. Generally frowned upon for generations of climbers, solo mountaineering has slowly gained acceptance in the mountaineering community. Most solo ascents are proven through photographic documentation.

SPINDRIFT: Powder snow that is blown by the wind.

SPIRE: A column of rock, tapering to its summit.

STEMMING: A technique that uses counterforce to support a climber between two points on rock or ice. Enables a climber to ascend steep rock when no holds appear evident.

TRAVERSE: The act of crossing a slope. Also used to define the complete crossing of a mountain, up one side and down the other.

VERGLAS: A clear layer of thin ice, formed when water freezes on rock.

WAND: A bamboo staff, normally four feet in length, used by climbers to mark their trail.

WIND SLAB: A snow layer that, after metamorphic hardening, is easily fractured when a climber passes over. If cold enough, a climber can gain a tremendous amount of ground on such terrain, but if conditions are poor, wind slab can fracture into slab avalanches that are particularly hazardous.

APPENDIX

END NOTES

CMC=Colorado Mountain Club.
MCJ=Mazama Club Journals (Portland).
OC=Oral Communication. Unrecorded conversation. Author's Collection.
RS=Recorded Statement. Author's Collection.
TAJ=The Alpine Journal (London).
TCC=The Conrad Collection. Author's Collection.
TMN=The Mountaineers Journals (Seattle).
WC=Written Communication. Letter or other such documentation.
WDHD=William D. Hackett Diaries (1939-1965).
WDHP=William D. Hackett Papers (1918-1999).

Chapter I "The Apprentice"
1.) Hackett, William D. & Grauer, Jack, *Hackett's Odyssey*, unpublished manuscript, circa 1992. WDHP.
2.) Hackett, June, OC, 09-17-2001. TCC.
3.) Scott, John D., *We Climb High: A Chronology of the Mazamas (1894-1964)*. Mazamas Special Edition, 1969.
4.) Hackett, William D., *Mountaineering Record of Major William D. Hackett, USA (ret.)*. WDHP.
5.) Hackett, William D. & Grauer, Jack, *Hackett's Odyssey*, unpublished manuscript, circa 1992, as are any additional quotes in this chapter. WDHP.
6.) Kester, Randall, RS III, *The Wy'East Climbers*, 10-01-1999, TCC. Lewis, Hank, RS VI and VII, *The Wy'East Climbers*, 09-17-1999, TCC. Norene, Lu, RS II, *The Wy'East Climbers*, 09-21-1999, TCC.
7.) Lewis, Hank, OC, 08-29-1999. TCC. Carter, John, OC, 12-03-2001. TCC.
8.) Lewis, Hank, RS V, *Mount Hood Ski Patrol*, 09-17-1999, and RS II, *Mount Hood Personalities*, 09-23-1998, TCC. Kester, Randall, RS II, Mount Hood (1935-1955), 08-06-1999, TCC.
9.) Kester, Randall, RS IV, *Mount Hood Ski Patrol (1944-1955)*, 10-06-1999, TCC.
10.) Lockerby, Robert, OC, 11-27-2001. TCC. Scott, John D., *We Climb High: A Chronology of the Mazamas (1894-1964)*. Mazamas Special Edition, 1969.
11.) Blanchard, Smoke, *Memories of a Mountain Rambler*, Sierra Club Books, San Francisco, 1985.
12.) Loveland, Charles, OC, 08-02-1998. TCC.
13.) Hackett, June, OC, 10-05-1999. TCC.
14.) Carter, John, OC, 12-03-2001. TCC.
15.) Carter, John, OC, 12-03-2001. TCC.
16.) Hackett, June, OC, 09-27-2001. TCC.
17.) Loveland, Charles, RS III, *Mount Hood*, 03-27-1998. TCC.
18.) Hackett, June, OC, 09-27-2001. TCC.

Chapter II "The Road to Italy"
1.) Earle, Captain George F., *History of the 87th Mountain Infantry, Italy, 1945*, privately published, 1945.
2.) Carter, John, OC, 12-03-2001. TCC.
3.) WDHD, January 11, 1942.
4.) Carter, John, OC, 12-03-2001. TCC.
5.) Hackett, William D., *Mountaineering Record of William D. Hackett*, WDHP.
6.) McJury, Russ, OC, 02-06-2000. TCC.

7.) Powers, Dick, OC, 10-01-2001. TCC.
8.) Hackett, William D. & Grauer, Jack, *Hackett's Odyssey*, Unpublished Manuscript, circa, 1992. Hackett, William D., *Personal Army Record of Major William D. Hackett*, USA, (ret.), WDHP.
9.) WDHD, July 25, 1942.
10.) WDHD, August 1, 1942.
11.) Hackett, William D, *Mountaineering Record of Major William D. Hackett, USA (Ret.)*, WDHP.
12.) WDHD, December 29, 1942.
13.) Earle, Captain George F., *History of the 87th Mountain Infantry: Italy, 1945*, privately published, 1945.
14.) WDHD, April 11, 1944.
15.) WDHD, November 27, 1944.
16.) WDHD, January 3, 1945.
17.) WDHD, January 11, 1945.
18.) WDHD, January 4-13, 1945.
19.) Earle, Captain George F., *History of the 87th Mountain Infantry, Italy, 1945*, privately published, 1945.
20.) WDHD, January 13, 1945.
21.) *A Soldier's Guide to Naples*, US Army publication, 1944. WDHP.
22.) Powers, Dick, OC, 10-01-2001. TCC.
23.) WDHD, January 14-15, 1945.
24.) WDHD, January 19, 1945.
25.) Casewit, Curtis, *Mountain Troopers: The Story of the Tenth Mountain Division*, Thomas Y. Crowell Company, New York, 1972.
26.) Earle, Captain George F., *History of the 87th Mountain Infantry, Italy, 1945*, privately published, 1945.
27.) WDHD, February 12, 1945.
28.) WDHD, February 19, 1945.
29.) Putnam, William Lowell, *Green Cognac: The Education of a Mountain Fighter*, The American Alpine Club Press, New York, 1991.
30.) Burton, Hal, *The Ski Troops*, Simon and Schuster, New York, 1971.
31.) WDHD, February 26, 1945.
32.) Powers, Dick, R/S. I, 10-01-2000. TCC.
33.) Casewit, Curtis, *Mountain Troopers: The Story of the Tenth Mountain Division*, Thomas Y. Crowell Company, New York, 1972.

Chapter III "Brothers in Arm"

1.) Hackett, William D, & Grauer, Jack, *Hackett's Odyssey*, Unpublished Manuscript, Circa, 1992.
2.) Earle, Captain George F., *History of the 87th Mountain Infantry, Italy, 1945*, privately published, 1945.
3.) Earle, Captain George F., *History of the 87th Mountain Infantry, Italy, 1945*, privately published, 1945.
4.) WDHD, April 3, 1945.
5.) Earle, Captain George F., *History of the 87th Mountain Infantry, Italy, 1945*, privately published, 1945.
6.) Hackett, William D, & Grauer, Jack, *Hackett's Odyssey*, Unpublished Manuscript, Circa 1992.
7.) Hackett, William D, & Grauer, Jack, *Hackett's Odyssey*, Unpublished Manuscript, Circa 1992.
8.) WDHD, April 19, 1945.
9.) Earle, Captain George F., *History of the 87th Mountain Infantry, Italy, 1945*, privately published, 1945.
10.) Earle, Captain George F., *History of the 87th Mountain Infantry, Italy, 1945*, privately published, 1945.
11.) Earle, Captain George F., *History of the 87th Mountain Infantry, Italy, 1945*, privately published, 1945. Italics are the author's.
12.) General Order Number 85, *Award of Silver Star*, 22 May 1945, APO 345, US Army, by command of Major General Hays, WDHP.
13.) WDHD, April 20, 1945.
14.) Hackett, William D, & Grauer, Jack, *Hackett's Odyssey*, Unpublished Manuscript, Circa, 1992, WDHP.

15.) WDHD, April 21, 1945.

16.) WDHD, April 22, 1945.

17.) Hackett, William D, & Grauer, Jack, *Hackett's Odyssey*, Unpublished Manuscript, Circa, 1992, WDHP. WDHD, April 23, 1945.

18.) WDHD, April 27, 1945.

19.) Dusenbery, Harris, The North Apennines and Beyond with the 10th Mountain Division, Binford & Mort, Portland, 1998.

20.) WDHD, April 29, 1945.

21.) WDHD, May 2-7, 1945.

22.) Hackett, William D, & Grauer, Jack, *Hackett's Odyssey*, Unpublished Manuscript, Circa, 1992, WDHP.

23.) Lewis, Hank, R/S IX, *The 10th Mountain Division*, 09-29-1999. TCC.

24.) Powers, Dick, Written Statement, *The First Ascent*, circa, 2000.

25.) Powers, Dick, R/S I., *The 10th Mountain Division*, 10-01-2001. TCC.

Chapter IV "Operation White Tower"

1.) Washburn, Dr. Bradford, *Over the Roof of Our Continent*, The National Geographic Magazine, LXXIV, July 1938.

2.) WDHD, May 8, 1946.

3.) WDHD, May 11, 1946.

4.) WDHD, May 13, 1946.

5.) Hackett, William D. & Grauer, Jack, *Hackett's Odyssey*, Unpublished Manuscript, Circa, 1992.

6.) WDHD, May 15, 1946.

7.) WDHD, May 18, 1946.

8.) WDHD, May 19, 1946.

9.) Hackett, William D, & Grauer, Jack, *Hackett's Odyssey*, Unpublished Manuscript, circa, 1992.

10.) Hackett, William D, & Grauer, Jack, *Hackett's Odyssey*, Unpublished Manuscript, circa, 1992.

11.) Washburn, Bradford, OC, 12-12-2001. TCC.

12.) NKA, *Bill Hackett to Climb Mt. McKinley*, MCJ, Vol. XXIX, No. 4, 1947.

13.) Washburn, Dr. Bradford and David Roberts, *Mount McKinley: The Conquest of Denali*, Abradale Press, New York, 1991.

14.) Stuck, Hudson, *The Ascent of Denali*, Charles Scribner's Sons, New York, 1914. Pearson, Grant H., *My Life of High Adventure*, 1962. Washburn, Dr. Bradford, Note to the Editor, Appalachia, XXIV, Boston, June 1943.

15.) NKA, *Bill Hackett to Climb Mt. McKinley*, MCJ, Vol. XXIX, No. 4, 1947.

16.) Hackett, William D, *Mt. McKinley; 1947 Climbs of North and South Peaks*, MCJ, Vol. XXIX, No. 13, 1947.

17.) Washburn, Dr. Bradford, *Operation White Tower*, TAAJ, VII, New York, 1948. Craig, Robert, *Operation White Tower*, TMN, Volume XXXIX, No. 13, 1947.

18.) Pearson, Grant H., *My Life of High Adventure*, 1962.

19.) WDHD, March 28, 1947.

20.) WDHD, March 31, 1947.

21.) WDHD, April 6, 1947.

22.) Craig, Robert, *Operation White Tower*, TMN, Volume XXXIX, No. 13, 1947.

23.) WDHD, April 9, 1947.

24.) WDHD, April 12, 1947.

25.) WDHD, April 12, 1947.

26.) WDHD, April 18, 1949.

27.) Craig, Robert, *Operation White Tower*, TMN, Volume XXXIX, No. 13, 1947.

28.) Bob Craig placed the date that Camp II was established as 21 April, a full eight days earlier than Hackett's recollection.

29.) Stuck, Hudson, *The Ascent of Denali*, Charles Scribner's Sons, New York, 1914.

30.) Hackett, William D., *Mt. McKinley; 1947 Climbs of North and South Peaks*, MCJ, Vol. XXIX, No. 13, 1947.

31.) WDHD, May 12, 1947.

32.) Hackett, William D., *Mt. McKinley; 1947 Climbs of North and South Peaks*, MCJ, Vol. XXIX, No. 13, 1947.

33.) WDHD, May 26, 1947.

34.) NKA, *Bill Hackett Scales Mt. McKinley*, MCJ, Vol. XXIX, No. 7, 1947.

35.) Browne, Belmore, *The Conquest of Mt. McKinley,* Putnam's, New York, 1913.
36.) NKA, *Bill Hackett Scales Mt. McKinley*, Vol. XXIX, No. 7, 1947.
37.) WDHD, June 18, 1947.

Chapter V "The White Sentinel"

1.) Hackett, William D., *I Can't Stop Climbing*, Undated letter to Hal Burton of New York, circa, 1949. WDHP.
2.) *Resumen de Ascensiones, Revista Andina,* No. 50, Santiago, Chile, 1946. Translated by Maria Gamon. WDHP.
3.) WDHD, February 13, 1949.
4.) *Expedition Chileno-Argentina Llega a la cima norte del Monte Aconcagua*: Humberto Escobar de Chile y Miguel Caffaro de Argentina se dieron un abrazo simbolico en la cumbre del coloso. Es la 26.a expedition que llega a esa cumbre, *Revista Andina,* No. 56, Santiago, Chile, 1947. Gonzalez, *Ascension al Aconcagua, La Montana,* No. 190, Mexico, 1948. Translated by Maria Gamon. WDHP.
5.) NKA, *Dr. Gussfeldt in South America, TAJ,* Vol. XI, London, 1884.
6.) Fitzgerald, *The Highest Andes: A Record of the First Ascent of Aconcagua and Tupungato in Argentina, and the Exploration of the Surrounding Valleys,* Charles Scribner's Sons, New York, 1899. *The Ascent of Aconcagua, TAJ,* Vol. XVIII, London, 1897. *Aconcagua, TAJ,* Vol.. 37, London, 1925.
7.) WDHD, February 7, 1949.
8.) Hackett, June, OC, 03-01-2000 TCC.
9.) NKA, *For First Time a North American, Hackett, Reaches Highest Peak on Continent: Mottet Makes Ascent for Second Time,* Los Andes newspaper, Mendoza, February 23, 1949.
10.) WDHD, February 14, 1949.
11.) Hackett, June, OC, 03-01-2000 TCC. WDHD, February 15, 1949.
12.) Hackett, William D, *Aconcagua Expedition Equipment List,* MCJ, 1949.
13.) Conway, Sir Martin, *Aconcagua and Tierra del Fuego: A Book of Climbing, Travel and Exploration,* Cassell and Company, London, 1902.
14.) WDHD, February 16, 1949.
15.) Hackett, William D, *I Can't Stop Climbing*, Undated letter to Hal Burton of New York, circa, 1949. WDHP.
16.) WDHD, February 18, 1949.
17.) Hackett, William D, *First U.S. Ascent of Aconcagua,* MCJ, 1949. Hackett, William D, *I Can't Stop Climbing*, Undated letter to Hal Burton of New York, circa, 1949. WDHP.
18.) WDHD, February 19, 1949.
19.) Hackett, June, OC, 03-01-2000 TCC.
20.) Hackett, William D, *I Can't Stop Climbing*, Undated letter to Hal Burton of New York, circa, 1949.WDHP.
21.) Hackett, William D., *I Can't Stop Climbing*, Undated letter to Hal Burton of New York, circa, 1949. WDHP. NKA, *Aconcagua, AAJ,* Vol. VII, No. 3, 1949.
22.) Hackett, June, OC, 03-01-2000. TCC.
23.) NKA, *Hackett Made It,* MCJ, Vol. XXXI, No. 3, 1949.
24.) WDHD, February 19, 1949.
25.) Hackett, June, OC, 03-01-2000. TCC.
26.) WDHD, February 26, 1949.
27.) WDHD, March 2, 1949.
28.) Perón's Address, 1949. WDHP.

Chapter VI "The Dark Continent"

1.) Hackett, June, OC, 01-18-2000. TCC..
2.) WDHD, January 24, 1950.
3.) Hackett, June, OC, 01-18-2000. TCC.
4.) Hackett, June, OC, 01-18-2000. TCC.
5.) WDHD, February 7, 1950.
6.) WDHD, February 7, 1950.
7.) Now named *Mandara* and still in use to this day. The Kibo Hut also remains but Peter's Hut is unfortunately gone. In its place is a sprawling collection of shacks that can house over fifty people. Griffin, *Kilimanjaro-33 Years On,* Die Joernaal van die Bergklub van Suid-Afrka, Cape Town, 1994.

8.) Hackett, June, OC, 01-18-2000. TCC.
9.) *Mountain Exploration in Africa*, TAJ, Vol. VI, London, 1874.
10.) It was a variation of Meyer's route that Hackett would use in 1950. Lange and Weigele pioneered the present-day Marangu Route in July of 1909. Meyer, *Across East African Glaciers*, George Philip & Son, Liverpool, 1891. *Ascent of Kilimanjaro* (report of the First Ascent), TAJ, Vol. XIII, London, 1887.
11.) WDHD, February 8, 1950.
12.) Hackett, June, OC, 01-18-2000. TCC.
13.) Loveland, Dr. Charles, OC, 09-12-1997. TCC.
14.) WDHD, February 9, 1950.
15.) Hackett, June, OC, 01-18-2000. TCC.
16.) WDHD, February 10, 1950.
17.) Hackett, June, OC, 01-18-2000. TCC.
18.) Hackett, William D. & Grauer, Jack, *Hackett's Odyssey*, unpublished manuscript, circa 1992. WDHP.
19.) WDHD, February 10, 1950.
20.) Hackett, June, OC, 01-18-2000. TCC.
21.) *Kilimanjaro and Kenya*, AAJ, Vol. VII, New York, 1950.
22.) Mackinder, John, *The Ascent of Mount Kenya*, TAJ, Vol. XX, 1900.
23.) K.M. Barbour's "Editor's Introduction" to *The First Ascent of Mount Kenya* by H.J. Mackinder, Ohio University Press, Athens, 1991.
24.) WDHD, February 14, 1950, Hackett, William D. & Grauer, Jack, *Hackett's Odyssey*, unpublished manuscript, circa 1992. Most of the information we have on Hackett's ascent of Mount Kenya comes from Grauer's unpublished manuscript. Bill recorded events in his diary but never wrote at great length of the venture.
25.) WDHD, February 16, 1950.
26.) WDHD, February 17, 1950. Additionally includes details concerning their descent.

Chapter VII "The West Buttress"

1.) Washburn, Bradford, *Mount McKinley Conquered by New Route*, The National Geographic Magazine, Vol. CIV., No. 2, Washington, 1953.
2.) Washburn, Bradford, *Mount McKinley from the North and West*, AAJ, Vol. VI, 1947.
3.) This work was carried on in collaboration with the United States Coast and Geodetic Survey.
4.) Washburn, Bradford, *Mount McKinley Conquered by New Route*, The National Geographic Magazine, Vol. CIV., No. 2, Washington, 1953.
5.) Alaskan politicians and government officials were well aware of his mapping flights, photographic expertise, and more recently, his first ascents of Mount Deception and Silverthrone. Washburn, Bradford, *Mount McKinley: The West Buttress, 1951*, AAJ, Vol. VIII, No. 2, 1952.
6.) Captain Hackett would later officially report to the US Army that, "Without Dr. Moore, the degree of success and accomplishment of the expedition would have been virtually impossible to achieve." Report on *1951 Mount McKinley Expedition*, WDHP.
7.) Washburn, Bradford, *Mount McKinley Conquered by New Route*, The National Geographic Magazine, Vol. CIV., No. 2, Washington, 1953.
8.) Washburn, Bradford, *Mount McKinley Conquered by New Route*, The National Geographic Magazine, Vol. CIV., No. 2, Washington, 1953.
9.) Washburn, Bradford, *Mount McKinley Conquered by New Route*, The National Geographic Magazine, Vol. CIV., No. 2, Washington, 1953.
10.) More, Jerry, *To The Top of McKinley*, Trail and Timberline, CMC, No. 397, 1952. Washburn, Bradford, *Mount McKinley: The West Buttress, 1951*, AAJ, Volume VIII. No. 2., 1952.
11.) Washburn's *A Brief History of the West Buttress Route's Origins & Photographs*, found in Coombs', *Denali's West Buttress; A Climber's Guide to Mount McKinley's Classic Route*, The Mountaineers, Seattle, 1991.
12.) More, Jerry, *To The Top of McKinley*, Trail and Timberline, CMC, No. 397, 1952. Washburn, Bradford, *Mount McKinley: The West Buttress, 1951*, AAJ, Volume VIII. No. 2., 1952.
13.) Hackett, William D, *Description of Camps*, Report on *1951 Mount McKinley Expedition*, sponsored by the Boston Museum of Science, University of Denver and the University of Alaska, Fort Richardson Headquarters, Alaska, October 31, 1951.
14.) Washburn, Bradford, *Mount McKinley Conquered by New Route*, The National Geographic Magazine, Vol. CIV., No. 2, Washington, 1953.

15.) WDHD, June 22, 1951.
16.) Washburn, Bradford, *Mount McKinley Conquered by New Route*, The National Geographic Magazine, Vol. CIV., No. 2, Washington, 1953.
17.) WDHD, June 23, 1951.
18.) WDHD, June 23, 1951.
19.) WDHD, June 24, 1951.
20.) Washburn, Bradford, *Mount McKinley Conquered by New Route*, The National Geographic Magazine, Vol. CIV., No. 2, Washington, 1953.
21.) WDHD, July 5, 1951.
22.) Washburn, Bradford, *Mount McKinley: The West Buttress, 1951*, AAJ, Vol. VIII, No. 2, 1952.
23.) Washburn, Bradford, *Mount McKinley Conquered by New Route*, The National Geographic Magazine, Vol. CIV., No. 2, Washington, 1953.
24.) WDHD, July 6, 1951.
25.) More, Jerry, *To The Top of McKinley*, Trail and Timberline, CMC, No. 397, 1952.
26.) WDHD, July 7, 1951.
27.) Washburn, Bradford, *Mount McKinley: The West Buttress, 1951*, AAJ, Vol. VIII, No. 2, 1952.
28.) WDHD, July 8-10, 1951.
29.) WDHD, July 10, 1951.
30.) Washburn, Bradford, *Mount McKinley Conquered by New Route*, The National Geographic Magazine, Vol. CIV., No. 2, Washington, 1953.
31.) Washburn, Bradford, *Mount McKinley Conquered by New Route*, The National Geographic Magazine, Vol. CIV., No. 2, Washington, 1953.
32.) More, Jerry, *To The Top of McKinley*, Trail and Timberline, CMC, No. 397, 1952.
33.) Washburn, Bradford, *Mount McKinley: The West Buttress, 1951*, AAJ, Vol. VIII, No. 2, 1952.

Chapter VIII "The Recalcitrant"

1.). Anderson, Robert L., *Mt. McKinley-An Adventure in Expeditionary Mountaineering*, MCJ, Vol. XXXIV, No. 13, 1952.
2.) Hackett even met with Cliff Cernick of the *Anchorage News* and provided him with details of the expedition for immediate release to the United Press. WDHD, June 15, 1952.
3.) Anderson, Robert, R/S II, *Mount McKinley* (1952) TCC.
4.) Even less than a week prior to departure, Hackett had still not settled on the principal players of his expedition. Hackett's diaries record that he had asked, at one time or another, Truman Billingsley, Dan Hartley, Andy Brockley and Chuck Hightower to join the team. All were unable to go but someone suggested Jerry Gholson. Bill felt Gholson's climbing resume wa 'insufficient' so he declined to approve him. In his stead, Bill went with Ernie Baumann, a climber recommended to Bill by Chuck Hightower. WDHD June 8-9, 1952. Material concerning Bob Anderson and the background on other party members comes from Anderson, Bob, OC, 12-27-2001. TCC.
5.) WDHD, June 7, 1952.
6.) Anderson, Robert L., *Mt. McKinley-An Adventure in Expeditionary Mountaineering*, MCJ, Vol. XXXIV, No. 13, 1952.
7.) Anderson, Robert L., *Mt. McKinley-An Adventure in Expeditionary Mountaineering*, MCJ, Vol. XXXIV, No. 13, 1952.
8.) Hulten, Eric, *Flora of Alaska and Neighboring Territories*, Stanford University Press, 1968.
9.) WDHD, June 22, 1952.
10.) Anderson, Robert L., *Mt. McKinley-An Adventure in Expeditionary Mountaineering*, MCJ, Vol. XXXIV, No. 13, 1952.
11.) WDHD, June 20, 1952.
12.) WDHD, June 26, 1952.
13.) WDHD, June 28, 1952.
14.) Anderson, Robert L., *Mt. McKinley-An Adventure in Expeditionary Mountaineering*, MCJ, Vol. XXXIV, No. 13, 1952.
15.) WDHD, June 29-30, 1952.
16.) Anderson, Robert L., *Mt. McKinley-An Adventure in Expeditionary Mountaineering*, MCJ, Vol. XXXIV, No. 13, 1952.
17.) WDHD, July 3, 1952.
18.) Anderson, Robert L., *Mt. McKinley-An Adventure in Expeditionary Mountaineering*, MCJ, Vol. XXXIV, No. 13, 1952.

19.) WDHD, July 6-7, 1952.
20.) WDHD, July 8, 1952.
21.) WDHD, July 9, 1952.
22.) The authors had the privilege of meeting with Bob Anderson in his Milwaukie home during the research portion of this project. Anderson showed us the parka he wore during this stretch of the ascent and to the very summit. We were amazed that his parka was nearly paper-thin and should more appropriately be labeled as a *windbreaker*.
23.) Anderson, Robert L., *Mt. McKinley-An Adventure in Expeditionary Mountaineering*, MCJ, Vol. XXXIV, No. 13, 1952.
24.) WDHD, July 8, 1952.
25.) Anderson, Robert, R/S II, *Mount McKinley* (1952) TCC.

Chapter IX "The Northwest Buttress"

1.) WDHD, May 30, 1954.
2.) Wickersham, James, *Old Yukon-Tales, Trails and Trials*, Washington Law Book Company, Washington, 1938.
3.) McLean, Donald H.O., *McKinley, Northwest Buttress*, AAJ, Vol. IX, No. 2, 1955.
4.) Hackett, June, OC, 11-12-1999. TCC.
5.) This information comes from Beckey's *Mount McKinley: Icy Crown of North America* (1993). Beckey was able to read his companions diaries years later and discovered that Wilson thought Hackett might be a 'steadying influence' on him, stopping him from selecting more difficult rock pitches in favor of practical snow couloirs and standard ice climbing.
6.) WDHD, May 2, 1954.
7.) WDHD, May 3, 1954.
8.) Beckey, Fred, *Mt. Deborah and Mt. Hunter: First Ascents*. AAJ, Vol. IX, No. 2, 1955.
9.) Beckey, Fred, *Mount McKinley: Icy Crown of North America,* The Mountaineers, Seattle, 1993.
10.) McLean, Donald H.O., *McKinley, Northwest Buttress*, AAJ, Vol. IX, No. 2, 1955. All other quotes from McLean are from the same source.
11.) WDHD, May 6, 1954.
12.) Hackett, June, OC, 11-12-1999. TCC.
13.) WDHD, May 6, 1954.
14.) WDHD, May 7, 1954.
15.) Beckey, Fred, *Challenge of the North Cascades*, The Mountaineers, Seattle, 1969.
16.) Beckey, Fred, *Mount McKinley: Icy Crown of North America,* The Mountaineers, Seattle, 1993.
17.) WDHD, May 6, 1954, and Beckey, Fred, *Mount McKinley: Icy Crown of North America*, The Mountaineers, 1993.
18.) McLean, Donald H.O, *McKinley, Northwest Buttress*, AAJ, Vol. IX., No. 2, 1955.
19.) Both Beckey's book and McLean's article in the American Alpine Journal indicate that it was Beckey, Hackett and Meybohm who pioneered the route to the crest of Cook's Shoulder. Hackett's diary entry for May 9, 1954, however indicates he and Beckey made the path alone. An interesting oversight.
20.) McLean, Donald H.O, *McKinley, Northwest Buttress*, AAJ, Vol. IX. No. 2, 1955.
21.) Loveland, Charles, OC, 08-02-1998. TCC.
22.) WDHD, May 11, 1954.
23.) WDHD, May 13, 1954.
24.) McLean, Donald H.O, *McKinley, Northwest Buttress*, AAJ, Vol. IX. No. 2, 1955 and any further quotes from McLean in this chapter.
25.) Beckey, Fred, *Mount McKinley: Icy Crown of North America,* The Mountaineers, Seattle, 1993.
26.) WDHD, May 19, 1954.
27.) WDHD, May 20-21, 1954.
28.) WDHD, May 22, 1954. Beckey, Fred, *Mount McKinley: Icy Crown of North America,* The Mountaineers, Seattle, 1993.
29.) Beckey, Fred, *Mount McKinley: Icy Crown of North America*, The Mountaineers, 1993.
30.) WDHD, May 30, 1954.
31.) WDHD, May 31, 1954.
32.) WDHD, June 1, 1954.
33.) WDHD, June 1, 1954.
34.) WDHD, June 6, 1954.
35.) Beckey, Fred, *Mount McKinley: Icy Crown of North America*, The Mountaineers, 1993.

Chapter X "The Journeyman"

1.) Hackett, William D. & Grauer, Jack, *Hackett's Odyssey*, Unpublished Manuscript, Circa, 1992.
2.) WDHD, August 1-9, 1955.
3.) WDHD, August 22, 1955.
4.) WDHD, August 25, 1955.
5.) WDHD, August 27, 1955.
6.) Hackett, June, OC, 01-02-2002. TCC.
7.) Hackett, June, OC, 01-02-2002. TCC. WDHD, August 28, 1955.
8.) Hackett, William D., Letter to Miss Jean Chase, Assistant Secretary for The American Alpine Club, February 28, 1956. WDHP.
9.) WDHD, February 6, 1956.
10.) Hackett, William D. & Grauer, Jack, *Hackett's Odyssey*, Unpublished Manuscript, Circa, 1992.
11.) Hackett, William D. & Grauer, Jack, *Hackett's Odyssey*, Unpublished Manuscript, Circa, 1992.
12.) The author has additionally found this peak to be spelled, 'Kosciusko'.
13.) WDHD, January 11, 1956.
14.) Hackett, William D. & Grauer, Jack, *Hackett's Odyssey*, Unpublished Manuscript, Circa, 1992.
15.) Hackett, William D, Letter to Maurice Herzog dated August 31, 1956. WDHP.
16.) Herzog, Maurice, *Annapurna*, E.P Dutton, New York, 1953.
17.) Letter from Maurice Herzog to *Club Alpin Francais* (in French), dated September 12, 1956. WDHP.
18.) Letter from Jean Morin to William D. Hackett, dated September 17, 1956. WDHP.
19.) Whymper, Edward, *Chamonix and the Range of Mont Blanc*, John Murray, London, 1896.
20.) Hackett, William D., Letter to Maurice Herzog, dated November 21, 1956.
21.) WDHD, September 28, 1956.
22.) WDHD, September 29, 1956.
23.) WDHD, September 30, 1956.
24.) NKA, *Infantryman Plans Antarctic Hike*, Newspaper Clipping from the collection of Maj. William D. Hackett. WDHP.
25.) Letter from Alfred Four to William D. Hackett, dated November 24, 1956. WDHP.
26.) Hackett, William D, Letter to Maurice Herzog, dated November 21, 1956.WDHP.

Chapter XI "Veteran"

1.) Blanchard, Smoke, *Walking Up & Down in the World: Memories of a Mountain Rambler*, Sierra Club Books, San Francisco, 1985.
2.) WDHD, June 7, 1958.
3.) Ullman, James Ramsey, *Americans on Everest*, J.B. Lippincott Company, New York, 1964.
4.) Blanchard, Smoke, *Walking Up & Down in the World: Memories of a Mountain Rambler*, Sierra Club Books, San Francisco, 1985.
5.) Blanchard, Smoke, *Walking Up & Down in the World: Memories of a Mountain Rambler*, Sierra Club Books, San Francisco, 1985.
6.) Hackett, William, D, *Mount McKinley*, MCJ, Vol. XL, No. 13, 1958.
7.) WDHD, June 11, 1958.
8.) Blanchard, Smoke, *Walking Up & Down in the World: Memories of a Mountain Rambler*, Sierra Club Books, San Francisco, 1985.
9.) WDHD, June 11, 1958.
10.) WDHD, June 12, 1958.
11.) Hackett, William D, & Grauer, Jack, *Hackett's Odyssey*, Unpublished Manuscript, Circa, 1992.
12.) WDHD, June 14, 1958.
13.) WDHD, June 14, 1958.
14.) Hackett, William D, & Grauer, Jack, *Hackett's Odyssey*, Unpublished Manuscript, Circa, 1992.
15.) Hackett, William D, & Grauer, Jack, *Hackett's Odyssey*, Unpublished Manuscript, Circa, 1992.
16.) WDHD, June 18, 1958.
17.) WDHD, June 19, 1958.
18.) Blanchard, Smoke, *Walking Up & Down in the World: Memories of a Mountain Rambler*, Sierra Club Books, San Francisco, 1985.
19.) Hackett, William D, & Grauer, Jack, *Hackett's Odyssey*, Unpublished Manuscript, Circa, 1992.
20.) WDHD, June 20, 1958.
21.) Hackett, William D, & Grauer, Jack, *Hackett's Odyssey*, Unpublished Manuscript, Circa, 1992.
22.) WDHD, June 22, 1958.

23.) Hackett, William D, & Grauer, Jack, *Hackett's Odyssey*, Unpublished Manuscript, Circa, 1992.
24.) Blanchard, Smoke, *Walking Up & Down in the World: Memories of a Mountain Rambler*, Sierra Club Books, San Francisco, 1985.
25.) WDHD, July 1, 1958.
26.) Hackett, William, D, *Mount McKinley*, MCJ, Vol. XL, No. 13, 1958.
27.) Blanchard, Smoke, *Walking Up & Down in the World: Memories of a Mountain Rambler*, Sierra Club Books, San Francisco, 1985.

Chapter XII "The Logan Massif"

1.) Blanchard, Smoke, *Memories of a Mountain Rambler*, Sierra Club Books, San Francisco, 1985.
2.) Lambart, H.F, *The Conquest of Mount Logan*, The National Geographic Magazine, Vol. XLIX, No. 6, 1926.
3.) Hackett, June, OC, 10-03-2001. TCC.
4.) Staender, Vivian, *First Ascent of Monkey Face*, MCJ, Vol. XLII, No. 13, 1960.
5.) Bohn, Dave, *The High Yukon*, MCJ, Vol. XL, No. 14, 1959.
6.) Correspondence between William D. Hackett and William E. Blanchard, March 14, 1961. WDHP.
7.) Hackett, William D, *Mount Logan 1959*, unpublished article, circa, 1959.
8.) Bohn, Dave, *The High Yukon*, MCJ, Vol. XL, No. 14, 1959.
9.) Blanchard, Smoke, *Memories of a Mountain Rambler*, Sierra Club Books, San Francisco, 1985.
10.) WDHD, June 10, 1959.
11.) Hackett, June, OC, 11-13-2001. TCC. WDHD, June 11, 1959.
12.) WDHD, June 11, 1959.
13.) Hackett, William D. & Grauer, Jack, *Hackett's Odyssey*, unpublished manuscript, circa, 1992.
14.) WDHD, June 12, 1959.
15.) Hackett, William D, *Mount Logan 1959*, unpublished article, circa, 1959.
16.) Bohn, Dave, *The High Yukon*, MCJ, Vol. XL, No. 14, 1959.
17.) WDHD, June 13, 1959.
18.) Bohn, Dave, *The High Yukon*, MCJ, Vol. XL, No. 14, 1959.
19.) Bohn, Dave, *The High Yukon*, MCJ, Vol. XL, No. 14, 1959.
20.) WDHD, June 18, 1959.
21.) Bohn, Dave, OC, 10-31-2000. TCC.
22.) Bohn, Dave, OC, 10-31-2000. TCC.
23.) Hackett, William D, *Mount Logan 1959*, unpublished article, circa, 1959.
24.) On the debit side, Hackett had written in his diary on June 19 that, "This is the weakest party I have ever to see on a big mountain" and noted on June 20, that other members of the party were, "in stages of physical collapse." It could be argued that Hackett was performing as he had on Aconcagua in 1949, climbing so fast that he left everyone else in his wake. On the plus side however, Hackett's diary states that as soon as he saw that something was amiss below, he, "...rushed down the 500-600' to find that nothing was wrong except that our boys had gotten cold & wanted a refuge from the weather. I blew my stack." WDHD, June 20, 1959.
25.) WDHD, June 21, 1959.
26.) WDHD, June 22, 1959.
27.) Blanchard, Smoke, *Memories of a Mountain Rambler*, Sierra Club Books, San Francisco, 1985.
28.) Church, *Famed Climber Places Flag Atop Mt. Logan; Conquers Second Largest Peak in North America, The Pioneer*, Anchorage, July 17, 1959.
29.) Hackett, William, D, *American Mount Logan Expedition*, AAC, Vol. XII, No. 1. 1960. Lyhne, *Local Men Fail, but Friends Reach Summit, Advance-Star* (Second Section), Burlingame, California, July 19, 1959.
30.) Blanchard, Smoke, *Memories of a Mountain Rambler*, Sierra Club Books, San Francisco, 1985.

Chapter XIII "The Black Pyramid"

1.) WDHD, July 31, 1960.
2.) NKA, *2 Oregon Mountain Climbers Gird For Assault on 28,500 Foot Peak, The Oregonian*, May 13, 1960.
3.) Conway, William M, *Climbing in the Himalayas*, T. Fisher Unwin, London, 1894. Keay, John, *Explorers of the Western Himalayas (1820-1895)*, John Murray, London, 1996 Edition.
4.) Crowley, Aleister, *The Confessions of Aleister Crowley*, Penguin Books, London, 1969.
5.) De Filippi, F, *La spedizione nel Karakoram e nell' Himalaya Occidentale*, Bologna, 1911.

280 Climb to Glory

6.) Houston, Dr. Charles & Bates, Robert, *Five Miles High*, Dodd, Mead and Company, Inc., New York, 1939.
7.) Cranmer, Chappell, and Wiessner, Fritz H., *The Second American Expedition to K2*, AAJ, Vol. IV, No. 1., 1940.
8.) Houston, Dr. Charles and Bates, Robert, *K2; The Savage Mountain*, McGraw-Hill, London, 1954.
9.) WDHD, May 25-28, 1960.
10.) Bohn, Dave, *K2-Giant of the Karakoram*, AAJ, Vol. I., No.12, 1961.
11.) Hackett, William D, *Individual Clothing En route to Skardu and Return*, WDHP. Hackett, William D, *Crate List, 1960 American/German Karakoram Expedition to K2*, WDHP. Hackett, William D, *Food Procured from US Army, 1960, American/German Karakoram Expedition to K2*, WDHP. Hackett, William D, *Porter Load List, 1960 American/German Karakoram Expedition to K2*, WDHP.
12.) WDHD, June 14, 1960.
13.) WDHD, June 15, 1960.
14.) Bohn, Dave, *K2-Giant of the Karakoram*, AAJ, Vol. I., No.12, 1961.
15.) WDHD, June 16, 1960.
16.) Bohn, Dave, *K2-Giant of the Karakoram*, AAJ, Vol. I., No.12, 1961.
17.) WDHD, June 19, 1960.
18.) Bohn, Dave, *K2-Giant of the Karakoram*, AAJ, Vol. I., No.12, 1961.
19.) WDHD, June 19, 1960.
20.) WDHD, June 20, 1960.
21.) Bohn, Dave, *K2-Giant of the Karakoram*, AAJ, Vol. I., No.12, 1961.
22.) WDHD, June 20, 1960.
23.) WDHD, June 22, 1960.
24.) WDHD, June 24, 1960.
25.) WDHD, June 29, 1960.
26.) WDHD, June 28, 1960.
27.) WDHD, June 30, 1960.
28.) WDHD, July 2, 1960.
29.) WDHD, July 3, 2001.
30.) Bohn, Dave, *K2-Giant of the Karakoram*, AAJ, Vol. I., No.12, 1961.
31.) WDHD, July 4, 1960.
32.) WDHD, July 10, 1960.
33.) WDHD, July 11, 1960.
34.) Bohn, Dave, *K2-Giant of the Karakoram*, AAJ, Vol. I., No.12, 1961.
35.) WDHD, July 23, 1960.
36.) WDHD, July 30, 1960.
37.) WDHD, July 31, 1960.
38.) Bohn, Dave, OC, 10-31-2000. TCC.
39.) WDHD, July 31, 1960.

Chapter XIV "New Year's Eve"
1.) WDHD, December 31, 1961.
2.) WDHD, September 7, 1960.
3.) WDHD, September 29-30, 1960.
4.) WDHD, September 9, 1960.
5.) WDHD, October 10, 1960.
6.) WDHD, October 16, 1960.
7.) WDHD, December 13, 1960.
8.) Ullman, James Ramsey, *Americans on Everest*, J.B. Lippincott Company, New York, 1964.
9.) WDHD, October 16, 1960.
10.) WDHD, November 5, 1960.
11.) WDHD, November 10, 1960.
12.) WDHD, October 12, 1961.
13.) WDHD, December 31, 1961.

Chapter XV "Eye of the Hurricane"

1.) Rebuffat, Gaston, *Men and the Matterhorn*, Nicholas Vane Publishers, London, 1967.
2.) WDHD, October 22, 1960, November 6, 1960, July 22-23, 1961.
3.) Desio, Ardito, *Ascent of K2*, Elek Books, London, 1955.
4.) WDHD, September 2, 1961.
5.) Rebuffat, Gaston, *Men and the Matterhorn*, Nicholas Vane Publishers, London, 1967.
6.) Whymper, Edward, *Scrambles Amongst the Alps in the Years 1860-69*, John Murray, London, 1900 Edition.
7.) Whymper, Edward, *Scrambles Amongst the Alps in the Years 1860-69*, John Murray, London, 1900 Edition.
8.) WDHD, September 2, 1961.
9.) WDHD, September 3, 1961.
10.) Whymper, Edward, *Scrambles Amongst the Alps in the Years 1860-69*, John Murray, London, 1900 Edition.
11.) Carter, John, OC, 12-03-2001. TCC.
12.) WDHD, September 22, 1943.
13.) WDHD, September 22-October 5, 1943.
14.) WDHD, November 23, 1944.
15.) WDHD, August 20, 1962.
16.) WDHD, November 28, 1962.

Chapter XVI "Vinson Massif"

1.) Hackett, William D, *Canadian-American Antarctic Expedition*, MCJ, Vol. LXVIII, No. 13, 1986.
2.) Morrow, Pat, OC, 01-05-2002. TCC.
3.) Morrow, Pat, OC, 01-04-2002. TCC.
4.) Hackett, June, OC, 01-04-2002. TCC.
5.) Hackett had designs on an attempt on Vinson Massif as early as 1957. He announced his intentions to *Stars & Stripes* and other publications. His diaries note the idea yet fails to indicate why he abandoned the attempt.
6.) Hackett, William D, *Canadian-American Antarctic Expedition*, MCJ, Vol. LXVIII, No. 13, 1986.
7.) Bell, Steve, *Seven Summits: The Quest to Reach the Highest Point on Every Continent*, Little, Brown and Company, New York, 2000.
8.) Hackett, William D, & Grauer, Jack, Hackett's Odyssey, *Unpublished Manuscript*, Circa, 1992.
9.) Hackett, William D, & Grauer, Jack, Hackett's Odyssey, *Unpublished Manuscript*, Circa, 1992.
10.) Hackett, William D, & Grauer, Jack, Hackett's Odyssey, *Unpublished Manuscript*, Circa, 1992.
11.) Hackett, William D, & Grauer, Jack, *Hackett's Odyssey*, Unpublished Manuscript, Circa, 1992.
12.) Hackett, William D, *Canadian-American Antarctic Expedition*, MCJ, Vol. LXVIII, No. 13, 1986.
13.) Hackett, June, OC, 04-23-2000. TCC.
14.) Morrow, Pat, OC, 01-05-2002. TCC.
15.) Hackett, William D, & Grauer, Jack, *Hackett's Odyssey*, Unpublished Manuscript, Circa, 1992.
16.) Hackett, June, OC, 01-04-2002. TCC.
17.) Morrow, Pat, OC, 01-04-2002. TCC.

Chapter XVII "Autumn"

1.) Striker, Allan, OC, 01-14-2002, TCC. Anderson, Robert, R/S II, *Mount McKinley* (1952) TCC. Carter, John, OC, 12-03-2001. TCC
2.) Hackett, William D, Letter to Dr. Rodman Wilson, August 5, 1998. WDHP.
3.) NKA, Portland Youth Killed on Hood; Glen Gullickson Falls 800 Feet in "Chute." The Oregonian, July 6,1932.
4.) WDHD, August 17, 1941.
5.) WDHD, January 12, 1944.
6.) NKA, Honorary Membership for Distinguished Achievement: William D. Hackett, MCJ, Vol. LXXI, No. 13, 1989.
7.) Bell, Steve, Seven Summits: The Quest to Reach the Highest Point on Every Continent, Little, Brown & Company, New York, 2000.

8.)   Ridgeway, Bass, Wells, *Seven Summits*, Warner Books, New York, 1986.
9.)   WDHD, March 13-14, 1965.
10.) Hackett, William D & Grauer, Jack, *Hackett's Odyssey*, Unpublished Manuscript, Circa, 1992.
11.) Hackett, William D & Grauer, Jack, *Hackett's Odyssey*, Unpublished Manuscript, Circa, 1992.
12.) *Banquet to hear 2-Pole Traveler*, MCJ, Vol. 70, No. 10, 1988.
13.) WDHD, July 19-August 5, 1993.
14.) Hackett, William D, Letter to the Colorado Mountain Club, August 18, 1992. WDHP.
15.) Hackett, William D, Colorado Rocky Mountains Fourteen Thousanders, WDHP.
16.) Hackett, William D, Letter to Allan Striker, August 30, 1992. WDHP.
17.) Striker, Allan, OC, 01-14-2002. TCC.
18.) Striker, Allan, OC, 01-14-2002. TCC.
19.) Striker, Allan, OC, 01-14-2002. TCC.
20.) Ormes, Robert M., and the Colorado Mountain Club, *Guide to the Colorado Mountains* (9th Edition), Colorado Mountain Club, 1992.
21.) Striker, Allan, OC, 01-14-2002. TCC.
22.) Dafoe, Vera, *Gone Away* (Poem), MCJ, Vol. LXXI, No. 13, 1989.

MOUNTAINEERING RECORD OF
MAJOR WILLIAM D. HACKETT, USA (RET.)

Compiled by William D. Hackett with Additions and Route Notes by Ric Conrad

The William D. Hackett Papers (WDHP0001).

MOUNTAIN	ELEVATION	DATE	ROUTE
Mt. Hood	11,239'	23 JUL 1933	South Side/Mazamas Old Chute
Mt. Hood	11,239'	26 MAY 1935	South Side/Mazamas Old Chute
Mt. Shasta	14,162'	31 MAY 1935	Horse Camp Route
Middle Sister	10,047'	05 JUL 1935	Hayden Glacier/Northwest Ridge
North Sister	10,085'	06 JUL 1935	South Ridge
Middle Sister	10,047'	06 JUL 1935	North Ridge
Mt. Hood	11,239'	25 AUG 1935	South Side/Mazamas Old Chute
Mt. Washington	7,794'	01 SEP 1935	North ArLte
Three Fingered Jack	7,841'	02 SEP 1935	Southwest ArLte
Mt. Hood	11,239'	14 JUN 1936	South Side/Mazamas Old Chute
Mt. Hood (First Ascent)	11,239'	28 JUN 1936	Eliot Glacier Cirque Wall
Mt. Hood	11,239'	05 JUL 1936	South Side/Mazamas Old Chute
Mount St. Helens (First Ascent)	9,677'	12 JUL 1936	Forsyth Glacier Cirque
Mt. Hood	11,239'	19 JUL 1936	Wy'East Route (Steel Cliff)
Mt. Jefferson	10,497'	26 JUL 1936	East Face
Mt. Adams	12,276'	02 AUG 1936	Ridge of Wonders
Mt. Hood (Solo)	11,239'	09 AUG 1936	South Side (Inner Crater Wall)
Mt. Hood	11,239'	16 AUG 1936	Steel Cliff (Modified Wy'East)
Mt. Hood	11,239'	23 AUG 1936	South Side/Mazamas Old Chute
Mt. Hood	11,239'	30 AUG 1936	South Side/Mazamas Old Chute
Mt. Washington	7,794'	06 SEP 1936	North ArLte
Three Fingered Jack	7,841'	07 SEP 1936	Southwest ArLte
Mt. Hood	11,239'	20 SEP 1936	South Side/Mazamas Old Chute
North Sister	10,085'	11 OCT 1936	South Ridge
Mt. Hood	11,239'	08 NOV 1936	South Side/Mazamas Old Chute
Mt. Hood	11,239'	02 MAY 1937	South Side/Mazamas Old Chute
Mt. Hood	11,239'	16 MAY 1937	South Side/Mazamas Old Chute
Mount St. Helens	9,677'	31 MAY 1937	Lizard Ridge
Mt. Hood	11,239'	06 JUN 1937	South Side/Mazamas Old Chute
Mt. Hood	11,239'	13 JUN 1937	South Side/Mazamas Old Chute
Mt. Hood	11,239'	04 JUL 1937	South Side/Mazamas Old Chute
Mt. Hood	11,239'	05 JUL 1937	South Side/Mazamas Old Chute
Mt. Hood (Solo Traverse)	11,239'	11 JUL 1937	Cooper Spur/Descent of Old Chute
Illumination Rock (Mt. Hood)	9,500'	18 JUL 1937	East Ridge
Mt. Hood	11,239'	25 JUL 1937	South Side/Mazamas Old Chute
Mt. Jefferson	10,497'	08 AUG 1937	Jefferson Park Glacier Cirque
Mt. Hood	11,239'	29 AUG 1937	South Side/Mazamas Old Chute
Mt. Washington	7,794'	06 SEP 1937	North ArLte
Mt. Hood	11,239'	19 DEC 1937	South Side/Mazamas Old Chute
Mt. Hood	11,239'	27 FEB 1938	South Side/Mazamas Old Chute
Mt. Hood	11,239'	20 MAY 1938	South Side/Mazamas Old Chute
Mt. Hood	11,239'	30 MAY 1938	South Side/Mazamas Old Chute
Mt. Hood	11,239'	14 SEP 1938	South Side/Mazamas Old Chute
Mt. Hood	11,239'	28 APR 1939	South Side/Mazamas Old Chute
Mt. Hood	11,239'	07 MAY 1939	South Side/Mazamas Old Chute

Mt. Hood	11,239'	14 MAY 1939	South Side/Mazamas Old Chute
Mt. Stuart		29 MAY 1939	South ArLte
Mt. Hood	11,239'	25 JUN 1939	South Side/Mazamas Old Chute
Mt. Hood	11,239'	02 JUL 1939	Steel Cliff (Modified Wy'East)
Mt. Hood	11,239'	09 JUL 1939	Leuthold Couloir
Mt. Hood (Second Ascent)	11,239'	23 JUL 1939	Pulpit Ridge
Mt. Hood	11,239'	30 JUL 1939	Cathedral Ridge
Mt. Hood	11,239'	06 AUG 1939	Sunshine (Eliot Glacier/Cathedral)
Mt. Hood	11,239'	13 AUG 1939	South Side (Inner Crater Wall)
Illumination Rock (Traverse)		20 AUG 1939	South Chamber Route
Mt. Hood	11,239'	17 SEP 1939	South Side (Inner Crater Wall)
Mt. Hood	11,239'	24 SEP 1939	South Side (Inner Crater Wall)
Mt. Hood	11,239'	22 OCT 1939	South Side/Mazamas Old Chute
Mt. Hood	11,239'	29 OCT 1939	South Side/Mazamas Old Chute
Mt. Hood	11,239'	19 MAY 1940	South Side/Mazamas Old Chute
Mt. Hood	11,239'	26 MAY 1940	South Side/Mazamas Old Chute
Mt. Hood	11,239'	16 JUN 1940	South Side (Inner Crater Wall)
Mt. Hood (Traverse)	11,239'	23 JUN 1940	Cooper Spur/Descent of Old Chute
Mt. Hood (First Ascent)	11,239'	30 JUN 1940	Eliot Glacier Cirque
Mt. Hood	11,239'	07 JUL 1940	Steel Cliff (Modified Wy'East)
Mt. Hood	11,239'	14 JUL 1940	South Side (Inner Crater Wall)
Mt. Hood	11,239'	21 JUL 1940	South Side/Mazamas Old Chute
Mt. Hood (50th Ascent)	11,239'	28 JUL 1940	South Side/Mazamas Old Chute
Mt. Hood	11,239'	04 AUG 1940	Sunshine (Eliot Glacier/Cathedral)
Mt. Hood	11,239'	11 AUG 1940	South Side/Mazamas Old Chute
Mt. Hood	11,239'	23 AUG 1940	South Side/Mazamas Old Chute
Mt. Hood	11,239'	15 DEC 1940	South Side/Mazamas Old Chute
Mt. Hood (New Year Laurel's)	11,239'	01 JAN 1941	South Side/Mazamas Old Chute
Mt. Hood	11,239'	25 MAY 1941	West Face
Mt. Hood	11,239'	15 JUN 1941	South Side/Mazamas Old Chute
Mt. Hood	11,239'	22 JUN 1941	Pulpit Ridge
Mt. Hood	11,239'	04 JUL 1941	Steel Cliff (Modified Wy'East)
Mount St. Helens	9,677'	06 JUL 1941	Dog's Head
Mt. Hood	11,239'	13 JUL 1941	South Side (Inner Crater Wall)
Mt. Jefferson	10,497'	20 JUL 1941	North Ridge
Mt. Rainier	14,410'	28 JUL 1941	Winthrop Glacier
Mt. Baker	10,778'	30 JUL 1941	Coleman Glacier
Mt. Shuksan		31 JUL 1941	Fisher Chimney
Mt. Hood	11,239'	17 AUG 1941	South Side/Mazamas Old Chute

CANADIAN ROCKY MOUNTAINS AND COLUMBIA ICEFIELD

Mt. Fairview	16 JUL 1942	South Face
Mount St. Piran	16 JUL 1942	South Side
Unnamed Peak	21 JUL 1942	North Face
Unnamed Peak	25 JUL 1942	Southeast ArLte
Unnamed Peak	25 JUL 1942	East ArLte
Unnamed Peak	25 JUL 1942	East ArLte
Snow Dome (South/North Traverse)	02 AUG 1942	South Side
Mt. Kitchener	02 AUG 1942	Southwest Side
Snow Dome (North/South Traverse)	02 AUG 1942	North Side
Unnamed Peak	14 AUG 1942	South Face
Unnamed Peak	15 AUG 1942	Northeast ArLte
Unnamed Peak	15 AUG 1942	East Ridge
Mt. Columbia	19 AUG 1942	East Face
Mt. Castleguard	10 OCT 1942	East Side
Mt. Castleguard	13 OCT 1942	East Side
Unnamed Peak	25 OCT 1942	West Ridge

COLORADO ROCKY MOUNTAINS

Homestake Peak	09 FEB 1943	Southeast Ridge
Mt. Sugarloaf	01 JUL 1943	West Side
Elk Mountain	03 JUL 1943	Northwest Ridge
Mt. Fletcher (North/South Traverse)	27 JUL 1943	Northwest Side
Mt. Wheeler	28 JUL 1943	Northwest Ridge
Quandary Peak	29 JUL 1943	West ArLte
Mount of the Holy Cross	08 AUG 1943	Northwest ArLte
Pyramid Peak	22 AUG 1943	West Face
Ptarmigan Peak	12 NOV 1943	Southwest Side
Ptarmigan Peak	22 NOV 1943	Southwest Side
Mt. Sugarloaf	22 NOV 1943	Northwest Ridge
Jacque Peak	22 NOV 1943	Northwest Ridge
Mt. Sugarloaf	23 NOV 1943	Northwest Ridge
Ptarmigan Peak	24 NOV 1943	Southwest Side
Ptarmigan Peak	29 NOV 1943	Southwest Side
Mt. Sugarloaf	03 DEC 1943	Northwest Ridge
Mt. Sugarloaf	06 DEC 1943	Northwest Ridge
Mt. Elbert	28 DEC 1943	East Side
Mt. Massive	30 DEC 1943	East Side
Mt. Bartlett	12 JAN 1944	Southeast Ridge
Traver Peak	12 JAN 1944	South Ridge
Mt. Sugarloaf	06 FEB 1944	Northwest Ridge

JULIAN ALPS

Mt. Cucla	11 JUN 1945	Southeast Side
Mt. Cucla	15 JUN 1945	Southwest Side
Mt. Rombon	15 JUN 1945	South Ridge
Mt. Mangart	16 JUN 1945	East Side

EASTERN ALPS-ZILLERTHAL MOUNTAINS

Klein Glockner	22 JUN 1945	Hofmann Glacier
Gross Glockner	22 JUN 1945	Hofmann Glacier

DOLOMITE ALPS

Mt. Marmolada (West/East Traverse)	10 JUL 1945	Marmolada Glcr./NE Cirque Wall
Mt. Marmolada (First Ascent)	13 JUL 1945	Marmolada Glcr./N. Cirque Wall

ITALY-PLAIN OF CAMPANIA

Mt. Vesuvius	31 JUL 1945	West Side

COLORADO ROCKY MOUNTAINS

Mt. Democrat	27 OCT 1945	East Side
Mt. Cameron	27 OCT 1945	West Ridge
Mt. Lincoln	27 OCT 1945	West Side
Mt. Bross	27 OCT 1945	North Side
Mt. Cameron	27 OCT 1945	South Side

VOLCANOES OF MEXICO

Popocatepetl	17,887'	12 MAY 1946	North Side
Zinantecatl	15,016'	13 MAY 1946	North Ridge
Pico de Orizaba	18,700'	16 MAY 1946	Southwest Ridge
Ixtaccihuatl	17,340'	19 MAY 1946	South Side

CASCADES

Mt. Hood	11,239'	02 JUN 1946	South Side/Mazamas Old Chute
Illumination Rock (Mt. Hood)		04 JUL 1946	South Ledge
Mount St. Helens	9,677'	14 JUL 1946	South Side
Mt. Hood	11,239'	28 JUL 1946	South Side/Mazamas Old Chute
Mt. Jefferson	10,497'	11 AUG 1946	Southeast ArLte
Mt. Washington	7,794'	15 SEP 1946	North ArLte

COLORADO ROCKY MOUNTAINS

Pikes Peak	07 DEC 1946	North Side
Pikes Peak	31 DEC 1946	North Pit Wall

ALASKA RANGE

Mt. Oastler (First Ascent)		10 APR 1947	West Side
Carlson Peak (First Ascent)		12 APR 1947	Northeast Side
Gunsight Mountain (First Ascent)		12 APR 1947	Northeast Ridge
McGonagall Peak		12 APR 1947	South Side
Denali (4th Ascent)	20,320'	06 JUN 1947	Muldrow Glacier
Denali/North Peak (2nd Ascent)	19,370'	07 JUN 1947	Muldrow Glacier

ARGENTINE ANDES

Cerro Banderita Nord	13 FEB 1949	Southwest Side
Cerro Banderita Sud	14 FEB 1949	Northeast Side
Cerro Aconcagua	19 FEB 1949	Northwest Side

EAST AFRICA

Kilimanjaro	10 FEB 1950	Southeast Side
Point Lenana	16 FEB 1950	Lewis Glacier
Mt. Kenya (First US Ascent)	17 FEB 1950	Southeast Ridge

CHUGACH RANGE, ALASKA

Unnamed Peak	22 OCT 1950	Southwest Ridge
Unnamed Peak	22 OCT 1950	Northwest Ridge
Unnamed Peak	22 OCT 1950	North Ridge
Unnamed Peak	29 OCT 1950	Northeast Side
Unnamed Peak	29 OCT 1950	Southeast Ridge
Unnamed Peak	05 NOV 1950	Southwest Ridge
Unnamed Peak	05 NOV 1950	South Side
Unnamed Peak	05 NOV 1950	South Side
Unnamed Peak	05 NOV 1950	East Ridge
Unnamed Peak	05 NOV 1950	Northeast Ridge
Unnamed Peak	05 NOV 1950	North Side
Unnamed Peak	16 JAN 1951	West Side

ALASKA RANGE

Mt. Capps (First Ascent)	24 JUN 1951	Northeast Ridge
Mt. Capps	25 JUN 1951	Southwest Ridge
Kahiltna Dome (First Ascent)	26 JUN 1951	Northeast Ridge
Kahiltna Dome	02 JUL 1951	Northeast Ridge
Mt. Capps	03 JUL 1951	Southwest Ridge
Denali (First Ascent)	10 JUL 1951	West Buttress

CHUGACH RANGE ALASKA

Unnamed Peak	23 SEP 1951	Southwest Ridge
Unnamed Peak	23 SEP 1951	South Side
Unnamed Peak	23 SEP 1951	South Side
Unnamed Peak	23 SEP 1951	East Ridge
Unnamed Peak	30 SEP 1951	Southeast Side
Unnamed Peak	30 SEP 1951	Southeast Ridge
Unnamed Peak	25 SEP 1952	Southeast Side

ALASKA RANGE

Denali (7th Ascent)	20,320'	12 JUL 1952	Muldrow Glacier

CHUGACH RANGE, ALASKA

Unnamed Peak	29 AUG 1952	Southeast Ridge
Unnamed Peak	29 AUG 1952	Southeast Ridge

COLORADO ROCKY MOUNTAINS

Torreys Peak	21 JUN 1953	North Ridge
Grays Peak	21 JUN 1953	Northwest Ridge
Mt. Sherman	28 JUN 1953	Southwest Ridge
Mt. Sheridan	28 JUN 1953	Northeast Side
Mt. Evans	04 JUL 1953	Northeast Side
Mt. Bierstadt	04 JUL 1953	North Side
Longs Peak	05 JUL 1953	North Side
Culebra Peak	12 JUL 1953	Northwest Ridge
San Luis Peak	19 JUL 1953	North Ridge
Mt. Tabeguache	09 AUG 1953	Northwest Ridge
Mt. Shavano	09 AUG 1953	North Ridge
Humboldt Peak	15 AUG 1953	Northwest Ridge
Crestone Needle	16 AUG 1953	Southeast Ridge
Crestone Peak	16 AUG 1953	Northeast Ridge
Mt. Belford	23 AUG 1953	Northwest Ridge
Mt. Oxford	23 AUG 1953	Southwest Ridge
Old Baldy Peak	29 AUG 1953	Northwest Ridge
Pikes Peak (New Year Laurels)	31 DEC 1953	Barr Trail

ALASKA RANGE

Denali (First Ascent)	20,320'	27 MAY 1954	Northwest Buttress (to North Peak)

COLORADO ROCKY MOUNTAINS

Snowmass Peak	03 JUL 1954	East Side
Capitol Peak	04 JUL 1954	South Side
North Maroon Peak	10 JUL 1954	East Ridge
Maroon Peak	10 JUL 1954	North Ridge
Castle Peak	11 JUL 1954	East Side
Ptarmigan Peak	12 JUL 1954	Southwest Side
La Plata Peak	17 JUL 1954	Northwest Ridge
Grizzly Peak	18 JUL 1954	West Side
Ptarmigan Peak	21 JUL 1954	Southwest Side
Mt. Harvard	24 JUL 1954	East Ridge
Mt. Columbia	24 JUL 1954	Northwest Ridge
Mt. Yale	25 JUL 1954	West Side
Mt. Princeton	15 AUG 1954	West Ridge
Mt. Antero	22 AUG 1954	West Ridge
Kit Carson Peak	29 AUG 1954	West Ridge

Sierra Blanca Peak	19 SEP 1954	South Ridge
Little Bear Peak	19 SEP 1954	South Ridge
Pikes Peak (New Year Laurels)	31 DEC 1954	Barr Trail
Ptarmigan Peak	08 FEB 1955	Southwest Side

JAPANESE ALPS

Fujiyama	12,388'	28 AUG 1955	Yoshida Trail

AUSTRALIAN ALPS

Gunartan	07 FEB 1956	Southwest Ridge
Dicky Cooper Bogong	07 FEB 1956	South Ridge
The Ghost	07 FEB 1956	North Ridge
Jagungal (The Big Bogong)	08 FEB 1956	Southwest Ridge
Grey Mare	08 FEB 1956	North Side
The Cup and Saucer Hill	09 FEB 1956	Southwest Ridge
Garruthers Peak	11 FEB 1956	South Side
Twynam	11 FEB 1956	West Side
Little Twynam	11 FEB 1956	Northwest Ridge
Caruthers Peak	11 FEB 1956	Northeast Side
Mt. Lee	11 FEB 1956	North Ridge
Mt. Northcote	11 FEB 1956	North Ridge
Kosciusko	11 FEB 1956	North Ridge
Etheridge Peak	11 FEB 1956	West Side
North Rams Head (Cathedral)	11 FEB 1956	North Side
Rams Head	11 FEB 1956	Northeast Side
Little Bogong (South Rams Head)	11 FEB 1956	Northeast Side
Mueller's Peak	12 FEB 1956	South Ridge
Mt. Alice Rawson	12 FEB 1956	South Ridge
Mt. Townsend	12 FEB 1956	East Side
Abbott Peak	12 FEB 1956	Northeast Side
Lower Abbott Peak	12 FEB 1956	Northeast Ridge
Kosciusko	12 FEB 1956	South Ridge
Mt. Clarke	13 FEB 1956	Southwest Side

SOUTH KOREA

Halla-San	21 AUG 1956	Northwest Ridge

FRENCH ALPS

Mont Blanc	30 SEP 1956	Aiguille du Gouter

SIERRA NEVADA MOUNTAINS

Mt. Whitney	14,494'	21 OCT 1956	East Side

ALASKA RANGE

Denali	02 JUL 1958	West Buttress

ST. ELIAS RANGE, CANADA

Mt. Logan/			
North Peak (First Ascent)		21 JUN 1959	King Trench Route
Mt. Logan (4th Ascent)	19,850'	23 JUN 1959	King Trench Route

BAVARIAN ALPS

Wallberg	28 FEB 1960	North Side
Wallberg	13 MAR 1960	North Side
Rechelkopf	27 MAR 1960	Northwest Side

Rechelkopf		03 APR 1960	Northwest Side
Luckenkopf		03 APR 1960	West Side
Blomberg		22 OCT 1960	North Side
Rechelkopf		06 NOV 1960	Northwest Side
Rechelkopf		26 MAR 1961	Northwest Side
Rechelkopf		08 APR 1961	Northwest Side
Rechelkopf		16 APR 1961	Northwest Side
Rechelkopf		10 JUN 1961	Northwest Side
Brauneck		17 JUN 1961	East Side
Latschenkopf		18 JUN 1961	Northeast Ridge
Benediktenwand		18 JUN 1961	East Ridge
Rechelkopf		07 JUL 1961	Northwest Side
Teufelskopf		14 JUL 1961	West Side
Seekarkreuz		22 JUL 1961	Southwest Ridge
Buchstein		23 JUL 1961	West Side
Rosstein		23 JUL 1961	East Ridge
Zugspitze		06 AUG 1961	East Side

KARAKORAM

K2 (Attempt)	28,250'	Summer, 1960	Abruzzi Ridge

ITALIAN ALPS

Matterhorn	14,870'	03 SEP 1961	Italian Ridge

BAVARIAN ALPS

Rechelkopf		18 MAR 1962	Northwest Side

FRENCH ALPS

Aiguille Rouge		23 JUN 1962	East Ridge

BAVARIAN ALPS

Zugspitze		02 SEP 1962	East Side

CASCADES

Mt. Hood	11,239'	17 AUG 1963	South Side/Pearly Gates
Mt. Hood	11,239'	08 SEP 1963	South Side/Pearly Gates

ST. ELIAS RANGE, CANADA

Mt. Newton (First Ascent)		28 JUN 1964	North Ridge

CASCADES

Mt. Hood	11,239'	14 MAR 1965	South Side/Pearly Gates
Mt. Hood	11,239'	30 JUN 1985	South Side/Pearly Gates

SENTINEL RANGE/ELLSWORTH MOUNTAINS, ANTARCTICA

Pyramid Peak (2nd Ascent)	10,000+	22 NOV 1985	North Ridge
Vinson Massif (Attempt)	16,067'	22 NOV 1985	Shinn-Vinson Saddle

CASCADES

Mt. Hood	11,239'	23 JIUL 1985	South Side/Pearly Gates

COLORADO ROCKY MOUNTAINS

Red Cloud	14,034'	21 SEP 1992	Northeast Ridge
Sunshine Peak	14,001'	21 SEP 1992	North Ridge

BIBLIOGRAPHY

PRIMARY SOURCES CONSULTED

-Beckey, Fred, *Challenge of the North Cascades*, The Mountaineers, Seattle, 1969.
 -Mount McKinley: Icy Crown of North America, The Mountaineers, 1993.
-Blanchard, Smoke, *Walking up and Down in the World: Memories of a Mountain Rambler*, Sierra Club Books, San Francisco, 1985.
-Browne, Belmore, *The Conquest of Mt. McKinley*, Houghton Mifflin Company, 1956.
-Conway, *Aconcagua and Tierra del Fuego: A Book of Climbing, Travel and Exploration*, Cassell and Company, London, 1902.
-Earle, Captain George F., *History of the 87th Mountain Infantry, Italy, 1945*, privately published, 1945.
-Fitzgerald, *The Highest Andes: A Record of the First Ascent of Aconcagua and Tupungato in Argentina, and the Exploration of the Surrounding Valleys*, Charles Scribner's Sons, New York, 1899.
-Herzog, Maurice, *Annapurna*, E.P Dutton, New York, 1953.
-Houston & Bates, *K2; The Savage Mountain*, McGraw-Hill, London, 1954.
-Meyer, *Across East African Glaciers*, George Philip & Son, Liverpool, 1891.
-Pearson, Grant, *My Life of High Adventure*, Prentice-Hall, Inc., 1962.
-Rebuffat, Gaston, *Men and the Matterhorn*, Nicholas Vane Publishers, London, 1967.
-Ridgeway, Rick, *The Last Step; The American Ascent of K2*, The Mountaineers, Seattle, 1980.
-Stuck, Hudson, *The Ascent of Denali,* Charles Scribner's Sons, 1925.
-Truffaut, *From Kenya to Kilimanjaro*, Robert Hale Limited, London, 1957.
-Washburn, Dr. Bradford and David Roberts, *Mount McKinley: The Conquest of Denali*, Abradale Press, New York, 1991.
-Wickersham, James, *Old Yukon-Tales, Trails and Trials*, Washington Law Book Company, Washington, 1938.
-Whymper, Edward, *Scrambles Amongst the Alps in the Years 1860-69*, John Murray, London, 1900

CLIMBING JOURNALS

The American Alpine Journal (AAJ)

-Beckey, Fred, *Mt. Deborah and Mt. Hunter: First Ascents.* Vol. IX, No. 2, 1955.
-Bohn, Dave, *K2-Giant of the Karakoram*, Vol. XII, No.2, 1961.
-Hackett, William D., *American Mount Logan Expedition.* Vol. XII, No. 1, 1960.
-McLean, Donald, H.O., *McKinley, Northwest Buttress.* Vol. IX, No. 2, 1955.
-N.K.A., *Aconcagua*, Vol. VII, No. 3, 1949.
-N.K.A., *Kilimanjaro and Kenya* (Hackett's ascents), Vol. VII, London, 1950.
-N.K.A., *Mexico*, Vol. VI, No. 3, 1947.
-Washburn, Bradford, *Mount McKinley from the North and West*, Vol. VI. No. 3, 1947.
 -Mount McKinley: The West Buttress, 1951, Vol. VIII, No. 2, 1952.

The Alpine Journals (AJ)

- N.K.A., *Ascent of Kilimanjaro* (report of the First Ascent), Vol. XIII, London, 1887.
- N.K.A., *Aconcagua*, Vol.. XXXVII, London, 1925.
- N.K.A., *Dr. Gussfeldt in South America*, Vol. XI, London, 1884.
- N.K.A., *Mountain Exploration in Africa*, Vol. VI, London, 1874.
- N.K.A., *Mountaineering in Central Africa, With an Attempt on Mount Kenya* (Dr. Gregory's Speech before The Alpine Club, February 6, 1894), Vol. XVII, London, 1894.
- N.K.A., *South African Notes*, Vol. XXXVIII, London, 1926.
- N.K.A., *The Ascent of Aconcagua*, Vol. XVIII, London, 1897.

Die Bergklub van Suid-Afrika

-Griffin, *Kilimanjaro-33 Years On, Die* Joernaal van die Bergklub van Suid-Afrika, Capetown, 1994.

Appalachian Mountain Club (AMC)

-Hall, Henry S., *Mount Logan*, Vol. XIX, No. 7, 1926.
-Wiessner, Fritz H., *The K2 Expedition of 1939*, Vol. XXII, No. 7, 1956.

The Mazama Club Journals (MCJ)

-Bohn, Dave, *The High Yukon*, Vol. XL, No. 14, 1959.
-Hackett, William D., *Aconcagua Expedition Equipment List*, 1949.
    -First U.S. Ascent of Aconcagua, 1949.
    -Mt. McKinley; 1947 Climbs of North and South Peaks, Vol. XXIX, No. 13, 1947.
    -Mt. McKinley from the West, Vol. XXXIII. No. 13, 1951.
-NKA, *Bill Hackett to Climb Mt. McKinley*, Vol. XXIX, No. 4, 1947.
-NKA, *Bill Hackett Scales Mt. McKinley*, Vol. XXIX, No. 7, 1947.
-NKA, *Hackett Made It*, Vol. XXXI, No. 3, 1949.
-NKA, *Hackett Tops Third Continent*, Vol. XXXII, No. 4, 1950.
-NKA, *Summit of Mt. McKinley*, Vol. XXIX, No.8, 1947.
-Scott, John D., *We Climb High: A Chronology of the Mazamas (1894-1964)*, Published by the Mazamas, Portland, 1969.
- Staender, Vivian, *First Ascent of Monkey Face*, MCJ, Vol. XLII, No. 13, 1960.

The Mountaineers (TMN)

-Craig, Robert, *Operation White Tower*, Volume XXXIX, No. 13, December 15, 1947.

The Mountain Club of East Africa (MCEA)

-Gillman, *Bibliography on Kilimanjaro* (Chronological List of Works and Papers Dealing with all expeditions from 1848 to 1928), The Ice-Cap, Vol. I, No. 1, 1932.
-Methner, *The Ascent of Mount Kilimanjaro-An Outline of its History*, The Ice Cap, Vol. I, No. 1, 1932.

-Reusch, *Mount Kilimanjaro and Its Ascent*, The Ice Cap, Vol. I, No. 1, 1932.
  -*The True Summit of Kilimanjaro*, The Ice Cap, Vol. I, No. 1, 1932.
-Shipton, *Note on an Ascent of Mawenzi (Kilimanjaro)*, The Ice Cap, Vol. I,
   No. 1, 1932.

NEWSPAPERS

-Church, *Famed Climber Places Flag Atop Mt. Logan; Conquers Second Largest
   Peak in North America*, The Pioneer, Anchorage, July 17, 1959.
-Lyhne, *Towering Yukon Peak Defeats Local Climbers*, Advance-Star (Second
   Section), Burlingame, California, July 19, 1959.
   -*Local Men Fail, but Friends Reach Summit*, Advance-Star (Second Section),
   ——-Burlingame, California, July 19, 1959.
-N.K.A, *For First Time a North American, Hackett, Reaches Highest Peak on
   Continent: Mottet Makes Ascent for Second Time*, Los Andes newspaper,
   Mendoza, February 23, 1949.
-N.K.A., *2 Oregon Mountain Climbers Gird For Assault on 28,500-Foot Peak*,
   The Oregonian, May 13, 1960.

MAGAZINES

La Montana
-Gonzalez, *Ascension al Aconcagua*, No. 190, Mexico, 1948. Translated by
   Maria Gamon.

National Geographic Magazine
-Lambart, H.F, *The Conquest of Mount Logan*, Vol. XLIX, No. 6, 1926.
-Washburn, Dr. Bradford, *The Conquest of Mount Logan, Canada's Loftiest Peak*,
   Vol. XLIX, No. 6, June, 1926.
   -*Over the Roof of our Continent*, Vol. LXXIV, No. 1, July, 1938.
   -*Mount McKinley Conquered by New Route*, Vol. CIV, No. 2, August, 1953.

Revista Andina
-*Expedition Chileno-Argentina Llega a la cima norte del Monte Aconcagua*:
   Humberto Escobar de Chile y Miguel Caffaro de Argentina se dieron un
   abrazo simbolico en la cumbre del coloso. Es la 26.a expedition que llega
   a esa cumbre, No. 56, Santiago, Chile, 1947. Translated by Maria Gamon.
-*Resumen de Ascensiones*, No. 50, Santiago, Chile, 1946. Translated by Maria
   Gamon.

Trail and Timberline (The Colorado Mountain Club)
-More, Jerry, *To The Top of McKinley*, No. 397, January 1952.

ADDITIONAL PRIMARY SOURCES

The William D. Hackett Papers (WDHP)
-The William D. Hackett Diaries, 1939-1966. (WDHD).
-Hackett, William D. & Grauer, Jack, *Hackett's Odyssey,* unpublished
 manuscript, Circa, 1992.

-Hackett, William D., *Mount Logan (1959),* unpublished article, WDHP.
-Hackett, William D., *Report on 1951 Mount McKinley Expedition,* sponsored by
 the Boston Museum of Science, University of Denver and the University
 of Alaska, Fort Richardson
 Headquarters, Alaska, October 31, 1951.
-Hackett, William D., *Individual Clothing En route to Skardu and Return, 1960
 American/German Karakoram Expedition to K2.*
-Hackett, William D., *Crate List, 1960 American/German Karakoram Expedition
 to K2,*
-Hackett, William D., *Food Procured From US Army, 1960 American/German
 Karakoram Expedition to K2.*
-Hackett, William D., *Porter Load List, 1960 American/German Karakoram
 Expedition to K2.*
-Correspondence between William D. Hackett and William E. 'Smoke'
 Blanchard, March 14, 1961.
-*Mountaineering Record of William D. Hackett,* WDHP0001.
-President Juan Perón's Address, Argentina, 1949.
-Special Release #323, Headquarters, U.S. Continental Army Command,
 Public Information Division, Fort Monroe, Virginia, 1956.
-Hackett, William D., *I Can't Stop Climbing,* Undated letter to Hal Burton of
 New York, Circa, 1949.
-Hackett, William D, Letter to the Colorado Mountain Club, August 18, 1992.
 WDHP.
-Hackett, William D, Letter to Allan Striker, August 30, 1992. WDHP.
-Hackett, William D, Letter to Dr. Rodman Wilson, August 5, 1998. WDHP.
-Hackett, William D, *Colorado Rocky Mountains Fourteen Thousanders,* WDHP.
-NKA, *National Association of the 10th Mountain Division, National Roster* (1994).

RECORDED STATEMENTS
The Conrad Collection (TCC)

-Anderson, Bob   R/S I., *Mount McKinley (1952)*

R/S II., *Mount McKinley (1952)*

-Hackett, June   R/S I., *K2 (1960)*, 01-16-2001.

R/S II., *K2 (1960)*, 01-16-2001

R/S III., *K2 (1960)*, 01-16-2001

-Kester, Randall   R/S II., *Mount Hood (1935-1955)*, 08-06-1999.

R/S III., *The Wy'East Climbers*, 10-01-1999.

R/S IV., *Mount Hood Ski Patrol*, 10-06-1999.

-Lewis, Hank   R/S II., *Mount Hood Personalities*, 09-23-1998.

R/S III., *Mount Hood*, 10-03-1998.

R/S IV., *Mount Hood*, 10-03-1998.

R/S V., *Mount Hood Ski Patrol*, 09-17-1999.

R/S VI., *The Wy'East Climbers*, 09-17-1999.

R/S VII., *The Wy'East Climbers*, 09-17-1999.

R/S VIII., 10th *Mountain Division*, 09-29-1999.

R/S IX., 10th *Mountain Division*, 09-29-1999.

R/S X., 10th *Mountain Division*, 09-29-1999.

-Loveland, Charles   R/S I., *Mount Hood (1919-1934)*, 03-18-1998.

R/S II., *Mount Hood Tragedies*, 03-23-1998.

R/S III., *Mount Hood*, 03-27-1998.

-McGown, Bob   R/S I., *K2 (1960)*, 11-07-2000.

-Molenaar, Dee   R/S II., *K2 (1960)*, 05-06-2000.

-Norene, Lu   R/S II., *The Wy'East Climbers*, 09-21-1999.

-Powers, Dick   R/S I., *The* 10th *Mountain Division*, 10-01-2001.

ORAL COMMUNICATIONS
The Conrad Collection (TCC)

-Anderson, Bob   OC, 12-27-2001. *McKinley (1952)*.

-Carter, John   OC, 12-03-2001. *Hackett's Early Climbing Days*.

-Hackett, June   OC, 10-05-1999. *Hackett and Gary Leech*.

OC, 01-18-2000. *Hackett on Kilimanjaro & Mt. Kenya*.

OC, 09-17-2001. *Boy scout Ascent of Mt. Hood (1933)*.

OC, 09-27-2001. *Hackett and Timberline Lodge*.

OC, 01-02-2002. *Mount Fuji*.

OC, 01-02-2002. *Kosciusko*.

OC, 01-04-2002. *Vinson Massif*.

-Morrow, Pat	OC, 01-04-2002. *Vinson Massif.*
	OC, 01-05-2002. *Climbing background.*
-Lewis, Hank	OC, 08-29-1999. *Hackett and the Wy'East Climbers.*
-Lockerby, Robert	OC, 11-27-2001. *Gary Leech and Early Mt. Hood.*
-Loveland, Charles	OC, 09-12-1997. *"A Good Night's Sleep."*
	OC, 08-02-1998. *Climbing Record of Gary Leech.*
-Powers, Dick	OC, 10-01-2001. *10th Mountain Division.*
-Stiker, Allan	OC, 01-14-2002. *Bill's Last Ascents.*
-Washburn, Bradford	OC, 12-12-2001. *Operation White Tower.*
	OC, 01-12-2002. *Operation White Tower.*

SECONDARY SOURCES CONSULTED

-Burton, Hal, *The Ski Troops: A History of the 10th Mountain Division, its battle record in World War II and the influence it has had on the development of skiing in the U.S.,* Simon and Schuster, New York, 1971.

-Casewit, Curtis W., *Mountain Troopers! The Story of the Tenth Mountain Division,* Thomas Y. Crowell Company, New York, 1972.

-Coombs, *Denali's West Buttress; A Climber's Guide to Mount McKinley's Classic Route,* The Mountaineers, Seattle, 1997. Includes Bradford Washburn's *A Brief History of the West Buttress Route's Origins & Photographs.*

-Harper, Frank, *Night Climb: The Story of the Skiing 10th,* Longmans, Green & Company, New York, 1946.

-Monge, Carlos, *Acclimatization in the Andes,* The John Hopkins Press, 1948.

-Ormes, Robert M., and the Colorado Mountain Club, *Guide to the Colorado Mountains* (9th Edition), Colorado Mountain Club, 1992.

-Thomas, Jeff, *Oregon High: A Climbing Guide,* Keep Climbing Press, Portland, 1991.

-Ullman, James Ramsey, *The White Tower,* J.B. Lippincott Company, New York, 1945.

ABOUT THE AUTHORS

June Hackett

June Hackett married Bill in 1989, and accompanied him on his travels through Africa, Europe, South America and Asia. She explored Mount McKinley's Kahiltna Glacier and accompanied Bill on his last ascent of Oregon's Mount Hood. A member of the Portland-based Mazamas mountaineering association, she volunteers her time working for their extensive archives. A retired interior decorator and sculptor, she has recently re-opened her West Hills studio.

Ric Conrad

Ric Conrad has trekked in the Andes of South America and climbed extensively throughout the Pacific Northwest and Tetons of Wyoming. A member of the Mazamas and American Alpine Club, he is currently editing the *William D. Hackett Papers*. He has recently completed, *Mount Hood: Adventures of the Wy'east Climbers* and is currently working on his next project, *In The Shadow of Chogo Ri*, the story of the first attempt on K2.